CONTRACTS OF EMPLOYMENT

CONTRACTS OF EMPLOYMENT

Vivien Shrubsall

LL.B., Senior Lecturer in Law, University of Nottingham
Member of Industrial Tribunals

BSP PROFESSIONAL BOOKS

OXFORD LONDON EDINBURGH

BOSTON MELBOURNE

First published 1989

British Library
Cataloguing in Publication Data

Shrubsall, Vivien
    Contracts of employment.
    1. Great Britain. Employment.
    Contracts. Law
    I. Title
    344.106'24

ISBN 0-632-02145-4

BSP Professional Books
A division of Blackwell Scientific
    Publications Ltd
Editorial Offices:
Osney Mead, Oxford OX2 0EL
    (Orders: Tel. 0865 240201) 01865-206206
8 John Street, London WC1N 2ES
23 Ainslie Place, Edinburgh EH3 6AJ
3 Cambridge Center, Suite 208, Cambridge,
    MA 02142, USA
107 Barry Street, Carlton, Victoria 3053,
    Australia

Set by DP Photosetting, Aylesbury, Bucks
Printed and bound in Great Britain by
Mackays of Chatham PLC, Kent

Contents

Introduction

Normal contract law principles apply to employment except in so far as they are modified by statute. A contract of employment is a legally enforceable agreement under which the employer's basic obligation is to pay wages or salary and the employee's basic obligation is to provide labour. The normal elements of a valid contract must be present, i.e. offer and acceptance, capacity to contract, intention to create legal relations and there must be no vitiating element of mistake, duress or undue influence. Just as for any type of contract, if the parties do not expressly agree all the terms of their arrangement, the law will try to make the agreement workable by implying supplementary terms. Normally, no formalities are necessary to create a contract of employment; an oral agreement is as valid as a written agreement but it will be easier to prove the terms of the latter.

Sources

Common law

Contract law principles have developed by judicial pronouncements and case law precedents over centuries. The judges' decisions which form a code of legal principles are known as 'the common law'. Common law will dictate the legal propriety of action in the absence of superseding legislation.

Statute

There is a wealth (or some may say an overwhelming burden!) of employment legislation. Statutory intervention in imposing rights and obligations on parties to employment contracts began in the mid-1960s, but mushroomed in the 1970s. The main statutory rules are as follows:

(a) The Employment Protection (Consolidation) Act 1978 (EP(C)A). This Act

(i) replaces the Contracts of Employment Act 1963 which was amended in 1972. The equivalent rules are now in Part I of the 1978 EP(C)A. Those rules oblige an employer to provide an employee with a written statement of the main contract terms and any variation of those terms. For details see Chapter 2.

(ii) replaces the Redundancy Payments Act 1965. The equivalent rules are in Part VI of the 1978 Act and oblige an employer to compensate an employee if he closes his business or reduces his business activity or reorganises his undertaking with the result that he needs fewer employees. The compensation depends on length of service and the employee's weekly earnings. For details see Chapters 9 and 10.

(iii) replaces the unfair dismissal provisions first contained in the Industrial Relations Act 1971 and then enacted in the Trade Union Labour and Relations Act 1974. Those provisions are now in Part V of the 1978 Act. For details see Chapter 9.

(iv) consolidates the miscellaneous employment protective measures introduced in 1975. They include maternity rights, guarantee pay rights, rules which protect trade union members against action short of dismissal and which allow time off for trade union participation. For details see Chapter 3.

(v) replaces the right to minimum notice of termination. The length of notice depends on length of service and varies from one week to twelve weeks. For details see Chapter 9 and Appendix C.

(b) The Equal Pay Act 1970 and the Sex Discrimination Act 1975. Both these Acts became operative at the end of 1975. Together they are intended to eliminate sex-based discrimination in employment pay rates, recruitment, training opportunities and promotion. For details see Chapter 7.

(c) The Race Discrimination Act 1976 is modelled on the SDA 1975 and combats race related discrimination. For details see Chapter 7.

(d) The Health and Safety at Work Act 1974 imposes general duties on employers and employees for the safety of others and incorporates legislation imposing specific duties for particular industries and undertakings. See Chapter 3.

(e) The Wages Act 1986 repeals 19th century legislation on 'trucking' i.e. payment of workers in goods (often overvalued) or vouchers (exchangeable only at the employers' shops). The old legislation was felt to be outmoded and unnecessary but several 1980s cases showed that certain unscrupulous deduction of wages practices still remained. The 1986 Act allows deduction from wages (e.g. to cover cash or stock shortfall) only where the employee agrees in writing and then subject to a maximum limit. See Chapter 3.

(f) The Employment Act 1980, 1982 and The Trade Union Act 1984 are mainly concerned with collective labour relations and the legal regulation of industrial action and trade union liability. Most of this legislation is outside the scope of a discussion based on the individual contract of employment.

Statutory provisions apply throughout the United Kingdom unless a particular Act contains a clause which restricts its application. The above employment protection statutes apply to Scotland but not to Northern Ireland. However, Northern Ireland usually has separate but equivalent provisions.

Litigation

If a dispute arises between an employer and employee which cannot be resolved without recourse to law, the appropriate court to hear the case will depend on the nature of the action. If the action is based on the common law of contract, e.g. a claim for withheld wages or a claim to force the employee to adhere to a covenant restricting him from competition, the appropriate court will be the normal civil court, i.e. the High Court, with appeal to the Court of Appeal. If the claim is founded on statute, usually jurisdiction is given by the statute to an industrial tribunal. Appeal lies to the Employment Appeal Tribunal (the EAT) and then to the Court of Appeal. The difference between the two is that the tribunal system is less formal, quicker and cheaper than a civil court action. There is lay representation from both sides of industry on the tribunal both at lower and appeal level and since legal aid is not available to finance legal representation at the tribunal hearing, the hope was that it would keep the lawyers out and resemble more closely an arbitration hearing rather than the usual adversarial combat!

Abbreviations used in the text

ACAS: The Advisory, Conciliation and Arbitration Service.
CAC: Central Arbitration Committee.
DHSS: Department of Health and Social Security.
EEC: European Economic Community.
EAT: Employment Appeal Tribunal.

EP(C)A: Employment Protection (Consolidation) Act 1978.
EqPA: Equal Pay Act 1970.
J: Justice (judge in the High Court).
LJ: Lord Justice (judge in the Court of Appeal).
MR: Master of the Rolls.
PAYE: Pay As You Earn (Scheme for deduction at source of Income Tax due from employees).
SDA: Sex Discrimination Act 1975.
SERPS: State Earnings – Related Pension Scheme.
SMP: Statutory Maternity Pay.
SSP: Statutory Sick Pay.

Chapter 1

The Employment Relationship

1.01 Introduction

The overwhelming irony of the law of employment is that an acceptable definition of 'employment' is so elusive. The term is used colloquially to describe any arrangement whereby labour is put at the disposal of another person but the law regards only *contracts for service* as creating the employment relationship. The law makes a crucial distinction between a contract of service and a *contract of services*, the former creating the relationship of employer/employee and the latter that of hirer/self-employed contractor or freelance worker. In both cases the arrangement is for the supply of labour but in the former case the labourer enters into a personal relationship of service, usually on a long-term basis. In the latter case the worker operates as an independent contractor carrying on a business on his own account but, as part of that business, agreeing to carry out a task for the hirer. The traditional role of the legislators and judges has been not to control the choice of the form of labour but to leave that decision to the parties and then to attach different consequences according to the choice made. It is for the parties to decide on the status of the worker. It follows that, irrespective of the job to be performed, the choice can be either for an 'employee' in the strict legal sense or for a freelancer or an independent contractor. Other choices follow. Should the person taken on be full-time or part-time, temporary or permanent, engaged on a regular or casual basis? Should he work from home or from the employer's premises, be paid a fixed salary or according to results achieved? Because there is no fixed definition of employment, those choices themselves may affect the law's view of the contract and its classification as one of service or for services.

1.02 Employed or self-employed?

The distinction between an employee and an independent contractor materially affects the legal obligations and rights of the parties. The main differences are as follows:

(i) The employer is obliged to deduct class 1 national insurance contributions from an employee and to pay the employer's own contribution in respect of each employee. An independent contractor pays his own class 2 contribution.

(ii) The employer deducts Schedule E income tax from an employee's wages or salary under the Pay As You Earn scheme on a current year basis and accounts for it to the Inland Revenue. An independent contractor pays his own tax under Schedule D, on a preceding year basis.

(iii) Only employees are covered by the unfair dismissal provisions in Part V EP(C)A 1978 and the redundancy payments provisions in Part VI of the same Act.

(iv) Only employees have the right to written particulars of the main terms of the contract and to itemised pay statements under Part I EP(C)A 1978.

(v) Only employees have priority over ordinary (unsecured) creditors on the insolvency of the employer.

(vi) The miscellaneous rights in Part II of the EP(C)A 1978 are limited to employees. They include the right to guarantee payments when no work is available, protection for trade union membership and participation in trade union activities, time off work for public duties, or to look for alternative employment or retraining in the case of a redundancy dismissal.

(vii) The scope of the duty of care for safety owed to an employee is more extensive than that owed to an independent contractor.

(viii) An employer is vicariously liable for the negligent acts of an employee committed in the course of employment, i.e. a third party who suffers damage or injury because of an employee's negligence can sue the employer for compensation provided the employee was carrying out his employment duties at the time of the incident.

1.03 How the law distinguishes

The status of the worker is a matter of choice of the parties. The law will only intervene in determining the status if the parties are in dispute or if some third party (for instance the DHSS, Inland Revenue or injured member of the public) challenges the claimed independence of the worker. The distinction is not easy to make and does not depend on whether the contract is oral or in writing nor on the nature and magnitude of the task nor whether the remuneration is 'salary' or 'wages' or 'commission'. So whereas in one case a labourer employed to clean drains at 5 shillings for the job was held to be employed, in another a plumber called in by a landlord to mend a leaky cistern was found to be an independent contractor. The irony is that the distinction between an employee and a self-employed worker is fundamental to the legal obligations for both, but that it is so difficult to make objectively. It is all a matter of construction of the particular contract to determine what the parties are taken to have intended.

1.04   *Control*

Originally, the test used for distinguishing between an employee and a self-employed contractor was one of *control*. This notion resulted from the common law conception of the employment relationship as one of 'master' and 'servant'. The master once had property rights in the service of his servant and could sue to enforce them and, until 1875, it was a criminal offence for a servant to withhold his labour. Modern law discards the old terminology of servitude but the notion of the employer's right to control remains. The degree of control which the hirer can exercise is a determining factor in distinguishing between an employee and a self-employed worker. The greater the control, the more likely that the worker is an employee. So if the hirer can dictate not only what is done, but the time, manner and place of performance, the worker will probably be regarded as an employee. So, in *Walker* v. *Crystal Palace Football Club* (1910) a professional football player sued for compensation for permanent incapacity resulting from an injury which he sustained during a football match. He was entitled to this compensation only if he was working under a contract of service. The Courts held that he was entitled to compensation. Lord Cozens-Hardy MR in the Court of Appeal emphasised the control which the club exercised over the player. He had agreed to play only for Crystal Palace, to keep himself temperate, sober and fit and to attend regularly for training. He undertook to observe the general regulations of the club and do all the club deemed necessary to fit himself as an efficient football player and to conform in all respects to the rules of the Football Association. It had been argued by the club that since it could not control the performance of the player and his exercise of skill during play, he could not be working under a contract of service. That argument was rejected. Even when playing and exercising his own skill and judgment, the player was subject to the instructions of the team captain and manager.

The degree of control was emphasised in *Gould* v. *Minister of National Insurance* (1951) when the issue was whether a music hall artiste should pay insurance contributions as an employee or self-employed person. He had agreed to appear at a particular theatre for one week on the standard form of contract used by music hall variety artistes. That contract obliged artistes to attend rehearsals, to abide by management rules, to obey rules regarding the use of improper words and gestures, to accept management instructions as to the taking of encores. It also gave management the power to veto any unsuitable part of an act and prohibited any variation from songs or dialogue previously approved. Whilst stating that the determining factor was the degree of control exercised, the judge in that case found that management had no control over the method of performance of the act. The conditions referred to were simply thcse necessary to the proper working of the theatre and to prevent offence to the audience; the performance of the act depended entirely on the skill, personality and artistry of the performer. The contract was therefore a contract for services only.

However, it was always acknowledged that factors besides control were relevant in making a distinction between employment and self-employment. In *Performing Rights Society Ltd* v. *Mitchell & Booker Ltd* (1924) the defendants were sued for breach of the plaintiffs' copyright by a jazz band which performed in the defendants' dance hall. The defendants were only liable if the band were their employees, which they were held to be. The judge said that the nature of the task undertaken, the freedom of action given, the magnitude of the contract amount, the manner in which it was to be paid, the powers of dismissal and the circumstances under which payment could be withheld all bear on the solution of the question of the worker's status. Other cases show that whether or not the worker agrees to serve the employer exclusively, or works at the employer's premises will help determine his status as employed or self-employed. But the final test and the one generally applied is the nature and degree of detailed control. Indeed, it could be said that the other matters referred to are all aspects of the employer's right to control.

1.05   Integration or organisation

It does not matter that the employer cannot control the actual skill and expertise of the worker, indeed he may not himself possess the means to control. So, a surgeon can still be employed by an area health authority although no-one on the governing board has the necessary knowledge, skill or experience to control the surgeon's operations. A company can employ an expert computer programmer though its managing director has never used a keyboard. The control looked for, then, is over the circumstances of performance i.e. the hours of work, the place of work, the rate of pay, exclusivity of service, subjection to a disciplinary procedure. This is sometimes referred to as the *integration or organisation test.*

In one case – *Stevenson, Jordan and Harrison* v. *Macdonald and Evans* (1952) – Lord Denning said:

'One feature which seems to run through the instances is that, under a contract of service, a man is employed as part of the business, and his work is done as an integral part of the business; whereas, under a contract for services, his work, although done for the business, is not integrated into it but is only accessory to it.'

Lord Denning gave a ship's master, a chauffeur and a reporter on the staff of a newspaper as examples of persons employed under contracts of service. But a ship's pilot, a taxi-man and a newspaper contributor were examples of persons working under contracts for services. The distinction was in the permanency of the post and its place within the organisation and business structure of the employing undertaking. So the court decided that the copyright in the manuals prepared in the course of advising a particular client belonged to the company of management consultants for which the accountant author worked. That assignment was part of the usual business of the company. But another part of the accountant's manuscript was based on lectures delivered to universities and professional societies. The company did not own the copyright in that part since the lectures were not given as part of a contract of service. They were accessory to the contract and though of benefit to the company since they advertised the company services and enhanced its reputation, they were not part of the accountant's service.

It may be that this so-called integration or organisation test is merely an application of the control test. If the employee is an integral part of the business, he is subject to the employer's organisational control. The employer engages the staff and has the ultimate sanction of dismissal. The trouble with the test is that it often begs the question to be answered or produces a circular result. If the power to hire and fire is at the heart of the organisation test, it will not be very helpful since that power is commonly found also in a contract for services.

1.06   A mixed test?

The more modern cases suggest that the courts make the distinction
by balancing those terms of the contract which are usually suggestive
of employment against those which are inconsistent with it. The
starting point is control and the greater the employer's power to
control the more likely that the worker will be an employee but certain
factors, for instance the right to delegate performance or the worker
bearing the risk of loss, will usually negate a construction of the
contract as one of service.

   This approach was adopted by Mr Justice Mackenna in *Ready Mixed
Concrete* v. *Minister of Pensions and National Insurance* (1968). The contract
between the parties was a detailed one and it described the worker as
an independent contractor. The MPNI (now the DHSS) alleged the
company was nevertheless liable for national insurance contributions
in respect of the worker since he was in fact an employee. He was
contracted to deliver the company's concrete for five years. He bought
his delivery lorry by entering into a hire-purchase scheme financed by
an associated company. He was paid according to loads delivered and
distance carried but there was a provision for minimum annual
earnings. There was considerable control given to the company: the
lorry had to be painted with the company insignia, the driver had to
wear company uniform and was obliged to carry out all reasonable
orders of the company servants 'as if he were an employee'. However,
he did not work set hours and had no fixed meal break. Order of
loading was in accordance with a rota system operating amongst nine
owner-drivers on similar terms nationally and the number engaged by
the whole group was up to 709. The driver had to fund the
maintenance of the lorry, to make it available at all times to the
company and he agreed not to use it except for the company's
purposes. The company was entitled to require him to drive the lorry
himself for the maximum hours permitted by law but he could, subject
to the company's satisfaction, employ competent substitute drivers. In
fact, the nine owner-drivers based at the same premises employed a
relief driver to cover for their sickness and holidays and each
contributed weekly towards his wages. In busy seasons the company
also used 'employee' drivers at different rates of pay. The court found
that the owner-driver was self-employed. Emphasis was placed on his
ownership of the vehicle, his chance of profit and risk of loss and
freedom in the manner of performance, maintenance of the vehicle
and power to substitute another driver. He was running a business on
his own account.

   The right to choose whether, and when, to work was regarded as crucial in *O'Kelly* v. *Trust House Forte plc* (1983). Regular casual waiting staff called in for special functions were found to be self-employed. The tribunal said that an obligation to work was essential for employment. In another case the EAT suggested that the worker should be asked. 'Are you your own boss?' If he could justifiably answer 'no' he was an employee.

1.07   Substance not form

What the parties call themselves in the contract will be relevant but not conclusive of the status of the worker. So, in *Davis* v. *New England College of Arundel* (1977) a lecturer who had previously worked on a freelance self-employed basis agreed to teach for the respondent college but wished to retain his self-employed status for tax and national insurance purposes. His contract was on the same terms as other teaching employees but the college agreed to pay his salary without deduction of tax or national insurance. The lecturer subsequently argued that he was an employee and within the protection of the statutory unfair dismissal provisions. And that was what he was held to be. The court said that the classification depends on the rights and obligations under the contract, not on the nomenclature. But terminology is not always ineffective: if the terms of the contract are finely balanced between one of service and one for services what the parties call themselves may well tip that balance.

However, where an objective interpretation of the terms shows clearly that the contract is one of service, that the parties call it one of self-employment will be irrelevant. A similar principle was expressed in *Ferguson* v. *J. Dawson & Partners (Contractors) Ltd* (1976) in which a labourer working 'on the lump' in the building trade claimed damages as an employee for injury suffered at work. No tax or national insurance was deducted and indeed the workman gave a false name to the site agents, presumably to evade tax. The Court of Appeal held the labourer to be an employee, irrespective of the label attached by the parties. However, there was a strong dissenting judgment from Lord Justice Lawton. He said that labour only lump-working was common practice in the building industry (so much so that Finance Acts subsequently contained payment procedures for gang leaders to stop tax evasion). Although the building site agent exercised control of the labourers by directing work, control was not necessarily inconsistent with a contract for services and its presence could not override the parties' clear objective to make a labour-only agreement. The parties' intention to avoid the relationship of employer and employee was the predominating and all-important factor and was the only expressly agreed term of the contract. Lord Justice Lawton was unwilling to allow a man to claim he was self-employed for the purpose of avoiding the incidence of taxation but employed so as to claim damages for injury at work. He was also unwilling to accept a public policy argument that lump working was socially undesirable and workers should be protected from their own folly in depriving themselves of statutory employment protection on the chance of fiscal advantages flowing from self-employment.

But the principle remained – what the parties label their relationship will not be conclusive and will be irrelevant where the terms of the agreement clearly show it is something else. However, where the contract is clearly aimed at self-employment, or it is ambiguous but the terminology shows that self-employment was the parties' intention, the worker should not be held to be employed. That was the result in *Massey* v. *Crown Life Insurance Co.* (1978). An insurance company's branch manager had been an employee and wished to change to self-employment. A new agreement was drawn up under which the manager's duties remained the same but his remuneration was paid without deduction of tax and national insurance. He was also repaid his previous contributions to the pension fund and he contracted with the company under a new registered business name. When he was dismissed, he claimed that irrespective of terminology and the method of tax payment he was actually an employee and entitled to unfair dismissal protection. None of the courts, up to and including the Court of Appeal would accept his claim. Lord Denning said that the manager had 'made his bed as being self-employed and must lie on it'.

1.08   Status for unfair dismissal

Since the mid-1970s, most of the cases turning on the distinction between employment and self-employment have been unfair dismissal cases. Only employees are within the protection against unfair dismissal. The commentary above has suggested that the distinction is very difficult to draw and some cases are so borderline that a tribunal might properly decide either way. That is exactly what happened in two cases which went to the Employment Appeal Tribunal together in 1984. On very similar facts, one salesman was found to be an employee, the other a self-employed agent. The EAT endorsed both decisions and congratulated the tribunals on their analyses!

In *Jose Piscardor (UK) Ltd* v. *Stanton* (1984), S was employed by J Ltd as a sales representative for 2½ years. In February 1982 he became a selling agent for an area under an agreement which bound him to supply his labour, skill and expertise selling company products and to assist with any request made in connection with the company's business. He was paid an annual sum of £7,500 and percentage commission on sales. He was supplied with a car and had specified holiday entitlement. He accepted a P45 showing his employment had ended and he registered himself as self-employed for VAT and national insurance purposes. One year later his agency was terminated. The question was whether the tribunal had jurisdiction to hear his unfair dismissal complaint. The tribunal found that he was an employee. They said that the working arrangements apart from tax and insurance continued as before and the applicant was not carrying on business on his own account; he was a sales executive working in the sort of way and with the degree of control which is the accepted norm in his occupation. The employer's appeal was dismissed. The EAT said that *although another tribunal might reasonably have taken a contrary view* they could see no basis for concluding the decision was unreasonable.

In the other case, *Davies* v. *Dennis Edwards & Co.*, D was dismissed by E & Co. after 11 months' employment as a salesman of household equipment. Immediately prior to that he had worked for three months on a commission only basis with self-employed treatment in respect of tax and national insurance. Could he add the periods together to give sufficient service for an unfair dismissal claim? The tribunal held he could not. They analysed the terms of engagement during the three month period and balanced those terms indicating independence with those more naturally associated with employee status (e.g. a requirement that D spend one day each week in the company salesroom). Their overall conclusion was that D was not employed for the first three months. The EAT dismissed the appeal. (The remarkable aspect was that the industrial tribunals had the same chairman for both cases!)

Mr Justice Waite in the EAT said the cases did not show uncertainty or inconsistency in the tribunal system. On the contrary, they demonstrated that the line of distinction separating a contract of employment (or service) from a contract of agency (or services) may often be no more than a hair's breadth, with the most seemingly insignificant factor being sufficient by its weight (feather-light though that may be) to tip the scale of decision.

This is a very unsatisfactory state of affairs particularly if the decision taken by the tribunal cannot be appealed. A party can only appeal against an industrial tribunal decision on a question of law. So if the status of the worker is a question of fact to be determined by the tribunal, no appeal will lie unless the facts as found by the tribunal are so unreasonable or perverse as to suggest an error of law. That might be shown where a tribunal took into account the wrong criteria or gave undue weight to one or more relevant factors (e.g. if the tribunal decides that the terminology used by the parties is conclusive and overrides clear terms showing a contrary status). The effect of such an approach would be to leave the distinction between employment and self-employment for determination by the tribunal. Any appeal from the decision would be useless if the tribunal could properly have reached a conclusion either way. However, the result of that approach would be gross uncertainty in the law. It would mean that two tribunals hearing cases involving exactly the same terms could reach different conclusions. One could hold the worker to be an employee, the other that he is self-employed. No appeal would lie against either decision.

So is the question of the worker's status one of fact or one of law? Two cases in the Court of Appeal in 1983 took the view that it was a question of fact for the tribunal. But in 1986 in *Davies* v. *Presbyterian Church of Wales* the House of Lords said the matter was one of law and therefore was subject to appeal. That decision does not make it any easier to differentiate between employment and self-employment but it does at least suggest there is only one objective and correct answer to the question.

1.09   *How to achieve the desired status*

Since the balancing process outlined above remains the basis of distinguishing between a contract of service and a contract for services, it cannot be guaranteed that any offered draft of either will produce the desired result. But one can be fairly certain how to tip the scales in favour of one or the other and the following guiding principles are offered. They apply also to part-time workers who may be engaged either as employees or as independent contractors.

Factors suggesting a contract of employment

- Obligation to render personal performance.
- Fixed hours and regular work.
- Remuneration by time.
- Permanent, periodic contract.
- No, or minor, investment in equipment.
- Exclusivity of service.
- Work performed at employer's premises.
- Disciplinary procedure, power of dismissal.

- Tax deducted and national insurance paid by employer.
- Terminology of employment used in contract.
- Presence of sick pay scheme.
- Eligibility for membership of pension scheme.
- Little or no discretion as to manner of performance.

Factors suggesting self-employment

- Power to delegate performance to another worker.
- Substantial investment in equipment, or business assets used in performance.
- Remuneration linked to completed task, payment by results.
- Presence of penalty clause.
- Casual work, no obligation to render service.
- Fixed period of service.
- Freedom to work for others.
- Freedom to determine work method, hours of work.
- Base of service away from 'employer's' premises.
- Own tax payments made and national insurance contributions made as self-employed.
- Differences from standard employment contracts used by that 'employer' for comparable class of worker.
- Terminology of self-employment used in contract.
- Custom and practice in the trade or industry for that category of work to be performed by labour only contractors.
- Irregular service, according to 'employer's' business demands.
- Running own small business with own business name, letterhead, etc.
- Registration for VAT.

Chapter 2

Taking Employees On

2.01 *Part-time or full-time?*

The last chapter discussed the status of the worker and the advantages or disadvantages of opting for an employment relationship. Once that option has been chosen, the employer must decide on the main employment terms. Where the work to be offered is part-time, a crucial decision is the number of normal weekly hours since these will determine whether or not the employee is entitled to the benefit of the protective provisions of employment legislation.

The basic rule is that only employees normally working sixteen or more hours weekly are within the legislation. Then the qualifying period varies according to the particular provision. For example, to be within the unfair dismissal or redundancy protection, an employee has to have two years' continuous service with the employer. However, part-time workers who normally work between eight and sixteen hours weekly qualify after five years' continuous service. For a fuller discussion of continuity of employment see Chapter 8 below.

Another crucial factor affecting part-timers' employment is the earnings' threshold for national insurance contributions. An employer must pay class 1 earnings-related contributions if an employee's earnings exceed the lower earnings limit. For 1988/89 that limit is £41 weekly, £178 monthly or £2133 yearly. The employer's contribution is tapered in respect of low earnings as follows:

Employee's weekly earnings	Employer's NI rate (on full earnings)
£41–£69.99	5%
£70–£104.99	7%
£105.00–£154.99	9%
£155 +	10.45%

PAYE thresholds for 1988/89 are £50 per week and £217 per month. Employers need not deduct tax for employees who earn less than those amounts since total earnings will not exceed the annual personal allowances.

2.02   Advertising, short-listing and interviewing

An employer's freedom to select whomsoever he chooses is curtailed by the Sex Discrimination Act 1975 and the Race Relations Act 1976. Both Acts make it unlawful to discriminate in the arrangements for the purpose of determining who should be offered employment, in the terms on which employment is offered or by failing to offer employment. Clearly those provisions apply to selection procedures and there are specific provisions in the Acts which make discriminatory advertisements unlawful. Use in an advertisement of a job discription with a sexual connotation (such as 'waiter' or 'salesgirl') should be avoided but where a neutral expression is awkward and the usual terminology suggests a particular sex (such as 'postman' or 'cook'), the advertisement should contain a clear statement that applications are invited from either sex.

Though it is not automatically unlawful discrimination to ask a woman questions at a selection interview which are not asked of a man (*Saunders* v. *Richmond Borough Council* (1977)) such sexually biased questions may well raise an inference of discrimination. Further, *Johnson* v. *Timber Tailors (Midlands) Ltd* (1978), shows that a cursory and superficial consideration of a black Jamaican's employment application raised an inference of race discrimination. The interviewer had not elicited appropriate information concerning the skill and qualificiations of the applicant and had been elusive and evasive when the applicant tried to follow through his application.

Note that an apparently neutral job qualification, such as an age criterion or a mobility requirement, may still infringe the Sex Discrimination Act if the qualification has a disproportionately adverse effect on women. For example, in *Price* v. *Civil Service Commission* (1977) a condition of eligibility for appointment as executive officer was that candidates should be within the age range 17–28. That condition was held to have a disproportionate effect on women since fewer women than men of that age were available for employment. The employer would then have to show by way of defence that his job qualification was justifiable irrespective of sex. Recent cases suggest that the test of justification is whether the qualification reflects a real need on the part of the undertaking and whether it is appropriate and necessary to achieve that objective (*Bilka Kaufhaus GmbH* v. *Weber von Hartz* (1986) and *Rainey* v. *Greater Glasgow Health Board* (1987)). In *Greater Glasgow Health Board* v. *Carey* (1987) 'administrative efficiency' was emphasised as justifying a requirement for five day cover in the health visitor service.

It is not unlawful to discriminate against job applicants on grounds of race or sex where there is a genuine occupational qualification that the worker be a member of a particular racial group or of a particular sex. This matter is considered in detail in Chapter 7.

There is no legal provision preventing an employer discriminating against a job applicant (as opposed to an employee) on the grounds of trade union membership or non-membership or because he has a record of active participation in trade union affairs.

2.03   *References*

Since the decision in the leading case of *Hedley Byrne & Co. Ltd* v. *Heller & Partners Ltd* (1964) it has been recognised that liability for negligent misstatement may exist even in the absence of a contractual or fiduciary relationship between the parties. The circumstances giving rise to a duty of care between the provider and receiver of information remained unclear but what seemed necessary was a special relationship or proximity between the parties making it reasonable to allow the recipient of information to rely on its accuracy. Recent case law has recognised the existence of a duty of care as between the provider and recipient of a character reference for a job applicant. In *Technovision Ltd* v. *Reed* (1964) the plaintiffs engaged an accountant in reliance on a reference, apparently from the defendant, his former employer, which praised his integrity and ability. The accountant subsequently stole money from the plaintiffs. A settlement was reached whereby the defendant acknowledged his carelessness in respect of the reference. More recently, in *Lawton* v. *BOC Transhield Ltd* (1987) Mr Justice Tudor Evans held that a duty of care is owed to the subject of the reference himself to ensure that the opinions contained in the reference are based on accurate facts. The test is whether a reasonably prudent employer would have expressed such opinions. On the particular facts of the case, however, there was ample evidence to support the defendant's opinions contained in the reference and since it was honest, accurate and not negligently written the plaintiff's action failed.

These cases suggest that an employer who suffers loss by engaging a person on the basis of a false reference might have a claim in damages against the provider of the reference where the referee has fallen short of a reasonable standard of care. Where, for example, he has singled out the subject's time-keeping or attendance record for praise or has emphasised the subject's honesty in circumstances that a reasonable employer would have qualified his statement or known the statement to be misleading, a damages action may succeed. Care should be taken in formulating a reference request to identify those qualities which are important in relation to the employment to be performed. The more specific the reference request, the higher the standard of care owed by the referee in expressing his opinions.

2.04   *The job offer*

An employment contract, like any other contract, is an agreement made by acceptance of an offer. The offer can be oral or written and most commonly is made by letter from the employer to the individual employee. It is usual for the offer letter to set out the main terms and conditions of the contract or to refer to documents containing those terms. The offer letter may even be the contract, once it is accepted. The minimum legal requirement is that a written statement of main contract terms should be given within thirteen weeks of the commencement of the employment. (see [2.07]) However, the clearer and more specific the offer letter the less likely that there will be any later dispute about the terms of the agreement between the parties. The terms of any advertisement are not likely to form part of the employment offer. A job advertisement is often couched in general terms or suggests the most attractive terms in order to encourage interest. It is the usual expectation that at interview and during selection procedures negotiations between the parties will vary the advertised terms.

   Where there is a conflict between a job advertisement and a job offer it is likely that the latter will prevail. See, for example, *Deeley* v. *British Rail Engineering* (1980). D answered an advertisement for a 'Sales Engineer (Export)'. His letter of application was headed 'Sales Engineer (Export)' and so was the employer's acknowledgement. However the actual offer of employment was headed 'Sales Engineer' and enclosed terms of appointment headed 'Sales Engineer'. D's acceptance of the offer was also headed 'Sales Engineer'. After a few months D was promoted to Senior Sales Engineer, a position dealing with exports. Some two years later D developed a medical condition which made it undesirable that he should visit hot climates. That meant he was unable to continue his business dealings in the Middle East, an important part of the export trade. The issue between the parties was whether the employers could transfer D to a comparable post dealing entirely with domestic sales or whether they were obliged to continue to allow him to work in the export trade, excluding the Middle East. The Court of Appeal confirmed the tribunal decision that the employers did have the right to transfer D to duties relating to the home market. The employers' offer of appointment and D's acceptance expressly referred to the position as 'Sales Engineer'. The word 'export' was omitted. Further, there was no basis for implying a term into the contract that D was only to be engaged on export duties. Since the contract made a clear, express provision in unrestricted language it was impossible to imply a term which would restrict the agreement.

However, if there is no clear evidence of the contract terms, a tribunal or court may refer to the job advertisement as an aid in determining the terms.

Where an offer letter is subject to a condition, for example that a medical check-up should be satisfactorily completed, the contract will not be binding until the condition is met. That is so even where the employee has accepted the job offer. However, the employer should make it clear in his offer that the appointment is subject to the condition. In *Stubbes* v. *Trower, Still & Keeling* (1987) a firm of solicitors failed to make an offer of articles of clerkship conditional on the applicant's success in professional examinations. All the offer letter said was that starting salary would be £x if the final examinations were passed, but slightly lower if the applicant began his articles before the examination results were known. The Court of Appeal held that the employers were bound to employ the applicant even though he failed resoundingly in the professional examinations and indicated that he had no definite plans to resit them. The Court of Appeal reversed the High Court decision that a term should be implied that a solicitor's articled clerk must have passed the Law Society examinations. The obligation was on the employers to use a express condition. They were not entitled to repair the omission to do so by claiming the implication of a term into a contract which made perfect sense without it. The applicant was awarded damages of some £14,000 for the employers' failure to honour their employment offer.

If the employer does make the job offer clearly subject to a condition, he is not bound to proceed with employment if the condition is not met. However, if the person to whom the offer is made was induced to give up existing employment, he may have a remedy for breach of a collateral contract. In *Gill* v. *Cape Contracts Ltd* (1985) the plaintiffs gave up jobs in Belfast after being offered by the defendants six months work in the Shetlands at much higher rates of pay, subject to satisfactory medical examinations. Before the plaintiffs left for the Shetlands the offer of work was withdrawn because of threatened industrial action by the union if workers from outside the region were brought in. The High Court of Northern Ireland found that the defendants' representation of six months' available work formed a contract collateral to the employment contract. The assurance was intended to be acted upon and was in fact acted upon. Each plaintiff received £2500 damages for breach of the collateral contract.

An offer of employment can be withdrawn at any time before acceptance. If a letter of withdrawal crosses in the post with a letter of acceptance, a valid contract is made since acceptance is effective on posting but an offer withdrawal is effective only on receipt. Acceptance must be on the same terms as the offer letter, otherwise it constitutes a counter-offer and no contract is concluded until the employer accepts the counter-offer. An employer should take care to reject specifically any terms of the counter-offer which he regards as unacceptable since if he allows the employee to work under the assumption that his counter-offer terms govern the agreement, he may well be taken to have impliedly accepted those terms.

2.05 The employment contract

The agreement reached by the employee's acceptance of the employer's offer becomes a legally enforceable contract provided that there is consideration moving both ways and the parties intend to enter a legally binding relationship.

The consideration in an employment contract is the payment of wages or salary in return for the performance of duties. An agreement to perform voluntary work without payment is not an enforceable contract therefore since no consideration moves back from the employer to the employee. It is probable that also missing from such an agreement is the intention to create legal relations. So, in one case, auxiliary coastguards were held not to be subject to employment contracts. They were local residents who volunteered for auxiliary watch duties. They were paid 'allowances' when they were called out. An industrial tribunal found that there was no legally enforceable obligation at all. The applicants were still volunteers, though they were paid, and there was no intention on either side to create a relationship of master and servant or of employer and independent contractor. In another case an applicant for appointment as a trainee voluntary counsellor in a branch of the Citizens' Advice Bureau was held ineligible to complain to an industrial tribunal of unlawful race discrimination. The tribunal's jurisdiction was limited to access to employment or a contract personally to execute any work or labour. Since there was no contract between the Citizens' Advice Bureau and its volunteer workers, the discrimination provision did not apply.

2.06   Contract terms

As outlined above, it is desirable for an employer to stipulate the main terms and conditions of the employment in the offer letter or in accompanying documents. That reduces the risk of any later dispute about the agreed, or express, terms. The best evidence of express terms is documentary evidence, but orally agreed terms unsupported by writing still form part of the express terms. For instance, statements made at interview may form express terms of the contract. In *Redbridge London Borough Council* v. *Fishman* (1978) an employee was interviewed on the basis that her main duties were to be performed in the resources centre of a large comprehensive school and she was to encourage pupil use of video tapes, film, cassettes and other modern teaching aids. A tribunal found that it became an express term of her engagement that her main function was to direct the use of the resources centre and the local authority was not entitled to insist that she be transferred principally to traditional teaching duties.

As in other contracts, where there is a gap in the express terms of an employment contract, or it is silent on a particular issue, terms may be implied to supplement the express terms:

(a) where it is necessary to give business efficacy to the agreement;
(b) where the implied terms are so obvious as not to require express agreement (usually called the 'officious bystander' test);
(c) where custom and practice shows that such a term was intended; or
(d) where the conduct of the parties to date suggests that such a term must have been intended.

Examples of situations in which terms have been implied into employment contracts are:

Sagar v. *Ridehalgh* (1931) in which the defendant employers deducted sums from the plaintiff weaver's wages because defects in his cloth reduced its value. There was no express term justifying the deduction but the defendants gave evidence that that had been the practice at their mill for many years and it was common practice in Lancashire mills generally to deduct for bad workmanship. The Court of Appeal accepted that a term authorising the deduction should be implied.

O'Grady v. *Saper* (1940) in which the plaintiff commissionaire claimed wages for periods during which he was absent because of illness. There was no express term on whether wages continued to be payable during sickness. The court drew an inference from the parties' past conduct that it was an implied term that the plaintiff should not be paid during sickness absences. The evidence was that on at least three prior occasions when the plaintiff had been away sick he was not paid wages and he had acquiesced in that position. He did not expect to be paid until he read a piece in a newspaper about another employee's success in claiming wages during sickness absence. But the terms of an agreement have to be judged at the time of the agreement (unless there is a subsequent mutually acceptable variation). At that time the parties did not intend wages to be payable during a sickness absence.

Shirlaw v. *Southern Foundries Ltd* (1940). The defendant company appointed S managing director for a term of 10 years. There was no express provision enabling the defendant company to remove S during that 10-year term. The company was taken over by another company and its articles of association were changed so that S could be removed from his office as managing director. When S was removed he successfully sought damages for breach of contract. The courts held that there was an implied term that S could not be removed during the 10-year term and that the company would not alter its articles to create a power of removal. Lord Justice Mackinnon said:

'That which in any contract is left to be implied and need not be expressed is something so obvious that it goes without saying; so that, if while the parties were making their bargain, an officious bystander were to suggest some express provision for it in their agreement, they would testily suppress him with a common, "Oh, of course!"'

Courts will not imply a term into a contract merely because its inclusion would be reasonable. It must be justified on the basis that if the parties had thought of the matter at the time of reaching their agreement, such a term would have been included. It follows that if the parties have reached an express agreement on the matter, there is no room for the implication of an inconsistent term. That was clearly spelled out by Lord Justice Roskill in *Nelson* v. *BBC* (1977). He said, 'it is a basic principle of contract law that if a contract makes express provision in almost unrestricted language, it is impossible in the same breath to imply into that contract a restriction'.

Certain terms are implied automatically into contracts of employment. Employers have implied duties to pay wages, to provide a safe system of work and a safe working environment, to maintain mutual trust and confidence. Employees have implied duties of loyalty, obedience and good faith, and to exercise reasonable care. Those implied terms are considered in detail in Chapters 3 and 4 respectively.

2.07   *The written statement of contract terms*

The law requires that written particulars of main contract terms should be given to an employee not later than thirteen weeks after the commencement of employment. (A specimen form of written statement is contained in Appendix A.) The requirement has existed since the Contracts of Employment Act 1963 but the statutory provisions are now contained in the EP(C)A 1978.

(1) The statement must:

   (a) identify the parties;
   (b) specify the date when the employment began;
   (c) specify the date from which the employee's period of continuous employment began (that puts the employee on notice that his continuity runs from previous employment or has been broken by a change of employer).

(2) The statement must also give the following particulars as at a specified date and not more than one week before the statement is given:

   (a) the scale or rate of remuneration or the method of calculating remuneration;
   (b) the intervals at which remuneration is paid (weekly, monthly, quarterly etc.);
   (c) terms relating to hours of work (i.e. pattern of normal working hours or shift system);
   (d) terms relating to holidays and holiday pay, giving sufficient information to enable an employee to calculate accrued holiday on termination (e.g. $1\frac{1}{2}$ days' holiday for each calendar month worked in the holiday year from 1st January to 31 December);
   (e) terms relating to sickness or injury including provisions for sick pay (if any);
   (f) terms relating to pensions and pension schemes;
   (g) the job title;
   (h) the length of notice to which the employee is entitled and which

he is obliged to give. The parties can agree a longer period of notice if they wish but the Act specifies the minimum periods of notice to which the employee is entitled as follows:

— one week for any employee who has been employed for less than two years;
— one week for each year of service for any employee who has been employed for more than two but less than twelve years;
— twelve weeks for any employee who has been employed twelve years or more.

If the contract is for a fixed term, the date of expiry of the contract must be stated.

(3) The statement must also include specification of any disciplinary rules applicable to the employee and designation of a person to whom the employee can present a grievance and the procedure consequent upon such presentation. There must also be included reference to an appeal mechanism following disciplinary action. It must also state whether or not the employment is contracted-out of the state earnings-related pension scheme (SERPS).

It is worthy of note that the Act does not specifically require the place of work to be mentioned in the written statement. Nor, although the job title must be stated, need there be any discription of the duties of the job. However, since 'job' is defined in the Act in terms of the nature of the work, the capacity and place in which the employee is employed, it may be that these matters should be included under (2)(g). Since the right of the employer to transfer workers is often the cause of dispute and since the place of employment is crucial in determining whether or not the employee is redundant, an employer anyway is well advised to include reference to place of work and to insert a mobility clause where it is foreseeable that transfer may be required. Whether it is desirable to include a description of the duties will depend on whether they can be expressed in sufficiently general terms to give the employer reasonable flexibility. The more precisely the duties are expressed, the less room for subsequent dispute but it will require the employee's agreement if he is to be asked later to perform duties which are clearly outside the terms of the description.

2.08 *Entitlement to written statement*

Any individual working under a contract of employment is entitled to the written statement except the following:

(i) Dock workers are excluded by section 145 EP(C)A 1978.

(ii) Merchant seamen are excluded by section 144 EP(C)A 1978.

(iii) Part-time employees do not qualify unless they work sixteen hours a week or more or they have been employed for at least five years and work between eight and sixteen hours weekly.

(iv) An employee who has received a written contract containing express terms on the matters included in (2) and (3) above (i.e. if the employer has included in his offer letter written particulars of the main terms of the contract he does not have to repeat them in a subsequent written statement).

(v) If an employee begins employment with the same employer within six months after termination and the new employment is on the same terms as the old employment no new written statement need be given.

It is significant that an employer is taken to have complied with the obligation to issue a written statement if he refers the employee to a reasonably accessible document which contains the required particulars. So, it is not uncommon for an employer to include in a written statement the personal details of the contract but to refer to other documents for information of a general applicability, e.g. sickness schemes or pension schemes. Such documents may be posted on notice boards in staff canteens or rest-rooms or made available from the personnel office on request.

It used to be a criminal offence for an employer to fail to meet his obligation to issue a written statement in accordance with the legislation. Now the remedy is a civil action only: the employee can present a complaint to an industrial tribunal. The tribunal has no power to award damages but can amend and substitute particulars if the written statement omits any term which should have been included. The decision in *Construction Industry Training Board* v. *Leighton* (1978) shows how limited is the jurisdiction of the industrial tribunal in relation to the written statement. In that case L was in dispute with his employers over whether the salary stated in his letter of appointment included a cost of living supplement to which he was entitled. They claimed it did, L claimed it did not. An industrial tribunal amended the statement of salary by the addition of the supplement. The EAT allowed the appeal holding that the tribunal's powers were limited to requesting the inclusion of any term required by statute which had been omitted from the employer's statement. The tribunal had no power to rectify an error if a term was included. Here the salary was set out in the contract. All that was unclear was whether the supplement was already included in the expressed figure. The tribunal had no right to exercise the contractual jurisdiction of the ordinary civil courts.

The result of the case is to require an employee to proceed with an ordinary breach of contract action in the County Court or High Court where he claims there is an error in the written statement of contract terms. Industrial tribunals have no general contractual jurisdiction. Section 131 EP(C)A 1978 gives the Lord Chancellor the power to confer general contractual jurisdiction on industrial tribunals but that power has never been exercised.

2.09   *The effect of the written statement*

There has been some debate over the status of the written statement issued under the legislation. Strictly, the written statement is not the contract of employment itself but the employer's version of the main contract terms. However, it is often taken as evidence of the contract. In *Gascol Conversions Ltd* v. *Mercer* (1974) the Court of Appeal held that the written statement, which the applicant received as the contract itself, was conclusive evidence of the contract terms. However, in *System Floors (UK) Ltd* v. *Daniel* (1981) the earlier case was distinguished. In the later case the issue between the parties was the date on which employment began. That date was crucial in order for D to satisfy the qualifying period of employment to allow him to bring an unfair dismissal claim. D had worked at the company premises at the direction of an employment agency but then became directly employed by the company. The question was whether the date of employment specified in the written statement was the true date from which the contract began. The EAT took the view that a statement issued under the EP(C)A 1978 does not constitute a written contract between the parties but is merely a unilateral document stating the employer's understanding of the contract terms. It provides very strong *prima facie* evidence of what the contract terms are and, since it is issued by the employer, he has a very heavy burden of proof to show that the actual terms were different to those contained in the statement. However, the EAT thought that the written statement was not conclusive and distinguished *Gascol Conversions Ltd* v. *Mercer* on the grounds that there the employee had signed an acceptance of the written statement as the contract terms. In the absence of any such acknowledgment the written statement is *prima facie* evidence of the contract but not the contract itself.

Trusthouse Forte (Catering) Ltd v. *Adonis* (1984) shows a common tribunal approach to the status of the written statement. A was dismissed from his job as head waiter for smoking in a non-smoking area. Six months before the incident a notice had been posted by management stating that anyone caught smoking in a non-smoking area would be dismissed. However, ten days after the notice was posted, the employers issued new written statements of contract terms which referred to that offence as one for which a warning would be given. The issue was whether A had been unfairly dismissed. The industrial tribunal and the EAT found dismissal was unfair as being in breach of the contract as set out in the written statement. That was the later version and it had been issued by the employers. The written statement was taken as containing the true terms of the contract instead of the earlier, inconsistent notice.

It is interesting to speculate on what would have been the decision if the notice had been posted *after* the issue of the written statement. The statement would still have been regarded as *prima facie* evidence of the contract terms but whether the notice would have displaced the statement would depend on whether the employee could be taken to have accepted the variation.

2.10   Variation of contract terms

If there is a change in any of the terms covered by the written statement, the EP(C)A 1978 requires the employer to issue an amending statement not more than one month after the change. Again, the statement of variation will be treated as evidence of the contract terms but, in the absence of acceptance by the employee as the new contract terms, it will be only the employer's version and may be treated as a unilateral variation which is not binding on the employee. So, in *Hawker Siddeley Power Engineering Ltd* v. *Rump* (1979) a verbal term of the contract that R would not be moved away from the south of England was held not to be effectively changed by a written variation some five years later that he could be transferred anywhere within the UK. And in *Jones* v. *Associated Tunnelling Co. Ltd* (1981) the EAT held that the fact that an employee works on without objecting to the variation in the written statement will not always make the variation binding on him as having been impliedly accepted. It depends on the nature of the variation and its immediate practical application. If, for example, the written variation changes the rate of pay and the employee works on without objection, he may well be taken to have agreed to the variation. But, according to Mr Justice Browne-Wilkinson in that case, it is asking too much of an ordinary employee to require him to object to an erroneous statement of terms having no immediate practical impact. It would be unrealistic of the law to require an ordinary employee to risk a confrontation with his employer on such a matter. It should be otherwise if the employer takes pains to explain the effect of the variation and gives every opportunity for comment, negotiation and objection. (For further discussion see Chapter 6, 'How to Manage Change'.)

Chapter 3

Obligations of the Employer – Terms Implied by Common Law and Duties Imposed by Statute

3.01 *Terms implied by law*

The last chapter referred to the terms of the contract and advised that the agreement be spelled out as fully and clearly as practicable to avoid any later dispute over what the employee understood and what he agreed to. However, in the absence of any express agreement on the matter, certain terms are implied into the employment relationship to supplement even the most outline contract. Also, certain duties are imposed on the employer and employee by statute. Chapter 4 discusses the implied obligations of the employee. This chapter deals with the employer's obligations under the following heads:

(1) Wages.
(2) The provision of work.
(3) The duty of care for the health and safety of employees.
(4) The duty to preserve mutual trust and confidence.
(5) The obligation to allow time off for trade union duties and activities and for public duties.
(6) Disclosure of computerised records under the Data Protection Act 1984.

3.02 *Wages*

The employer's duty to remunerate lies at the heart of the contract of employment. Reduced to fundamentals, the contract of employment obliges the employee to work and the employer to pay for the work. Failure to pay agreed wages will be breach of contract. Since the employee will be enforcing a term of the contract, the ordinary civil courts have jurisdiction. The industrial tribunals have jurisdiction over statutory employment protection rights, not over actions based on the contract. So, an employee who is not paid agreed wages can sue to recover them in the County Court, where the claim is below £5,000, or the High Court where it is above that figure. It may be that failure to pay wages entitles the employee to leave and claim constructive dismissal, or that the employer is entitled to deduct a sum from wages to reflect the employee's own breach of contract. As to these matters, see below. Statutory provisions in respect of wages are included in this section.

3.03   *Agreeing wage rates*

The amount of remuneration payable depends on the agreement between the particular employer and employee. Often, individual negotiation of wage rates is inappropriate since the rate is determined by joint negotiating machinery and the resultant collective agreement is incorporated into the individual contract. Also, there have been a number of statutory measures to help the low-paid and protect employers against others who undercut wage rates and thereby produce at more competitive prices. The statutory 'props' establish a floor of minimum wage rates which are legally enforceable. The Wages Councils are the oldest of them and, although their effect is greatly diminished by the Wages Act 1986, they are all that remain in 1988. If there is no collective agreement and no statutory regulation of wage rates, remuneration must be fixed by individual agreement. If there has been no agreement, the law will probably imply a term that the employee is entitled to a reasonable sum.

The way in which collective agreements are incorporated into individual contracts is explained in Chapter 5. This section deals with Wages Councils and express and implied pay terms.

3.04   *Wages Councils*

Originally called trades boards, Wages Councils were established in 1909, with consolidating legislation in 1945, 1959 and 1979. They are tripartite bodies having equal representation from workers and management of the relevant industry plus independent members, one of whom is chairman. Their purpose is to agree minimum wage and holiday pay rates, though their jurisdiction was extended in 1975 to cover other terms and conditions of employment contracts. Wages Councils operate in trades and industries in which the work force is scattered into small and disparate units such that voluntary representation and collective bargaining is difficult and impractical.

In 1986 there remained 26 Wages Councils covering some 2.7 million workers in a wide range of industries including catering, hairdressing, laundry, retailing and clothing manufacture. Copies of orders made by Wages Councils can be obtained from the Secretary, Office of Wages Councils, 12 St James Square, London SW1Y 4LL.

Wages Councils cover 'workers'. The term includes anyone working under a contract of service, or of apprenticeship, or a contract personally to execute any work or services but not a person who is employed casually or otherwise than for the purposes of the employer's business. The definition has been held not to apply to an outworker in the Sheffield cutlery trade but the current definition expressly includes home-workers.

The terms of Wages Council orders become part of the individual worker's contract and he can sue to enforce them. As well, it is an offence for an employer to fail to observe the minimum terms fixed by the order. If a prosecution ensues, as well as imposing a fine, the court can order the employer to make good deficits against the statutory minimum payments for up to two years preceding the particular offence. Enforcement is the responsibility of the Wages Inspectorate. Machinery for the enforcement has been described as manifestly inadequate: in 1978 there were 150 inspectors, 32,000 inspections, 16 prosecutions and 16 civil actions. In 1984 there were 120 inspectors and 27,000 inspections covering only 184,000 workers. Underpayments were £2.4 million.

Wages Councils after the Wages Act 1986

In 1984/5 the Government proposed the abolition of Wages Councils. The minimum rates for young workers were said to be too high and discouraged the employment of school leavers. It was also argued that the employer's obligation under the 1979 Act was too burdensome and 'the labour market should be free from any unnecessary and artificial restraints which may affect business performance, competitiveness and jobs' (Consultative Paper on Wages Councils, Department of Employment, February 1985).

In fact, the 1986 Act does not completely abolish Wages Councils. It restricts their area of operation, removes workers under the age of 21 from the scope of orders and removes the procedure for the creation of any new wages council, whilst simplifying the mechanism for abolition.

The 26 Wages Councils in existence at the commencement of the 1986 Act (i.e. 25 July 1986) continue and existing wages orders continued to have effect for a transitional period pending the issue of new-style wages orders. A specific duty is imposed on Wages Councils, before making any new-style order, to have regard to the effect the proposed minimum rate will have on employment levels, particularly in areas where pay rates are generally less than the national average.

New-style wages orders may fix *only*:

(i)   a single minimum hourly rate for any time worked in any week;
(ii) a single minimum basic hourly rate and a single minimum hourly overtime rate;
(iii) a maximum rate to be deducted from wages or paid by the worker for living accommodation provided by the employer.

These are the only matters which can be included in new-style wages orders. Wages Councils can no longer prescribe holiday entitlement, holiday pay nor special overtime rates for Sunday or Bank Holiday work. Note also that a *single* minimum rate can be fixed so there can no longer be a scale of minimum rates to be applied to different grades of staff, nor different minimum rates according to the place of employment (i.e. no London weighting provision). Further, the single rate must apply to *all* time workers covered by the Wages Council so the minimum rate fixed can be the part-time rate. There are rules for applying wages orders to piece-workers; piece rates are set by employers, not the Wages Councils but they must be set so as to produce comparable pay to that of a time-worker, i.e. the piece rate must be such as to enable an ordinary worker (without any disability) to achieve the same pay in any given time as that paid to a time worker receiving the minimum Wages Council rate. That provision will be of particular importance to those employing home-workers who are usually paid piece rates.

The effect and enforcement procedure for the new-style wages orders are the same as under the 1979 Act, except that it seems the individual worker can now apply to an industrial tribunal as well as the County Court for payment of the minimum rate. This seems to be the effect of a provision in the Act which treats any amount less than that 'properly payable' as a 'deduction' and jurisdiction over unauthorised deduction from wages is given to industrial tribunals (see [3.08]). Also, as well as posting the terms of a wages order on his premises, an employer is obliged to notify home-workers of its terms. When it introduced the Wages Bill, the Government expected to be able to reduce the complement of wages inspectors from 120 to 71 because of the greater simplicity of new-style wages orders. Existing wages orders ceased to apply to workers under 21 on 25 July 1986, subject only to accrued holiday and holiday pay rights. About a half million young workers were removed from the scope of wages orders.

3.05   *Other statutory regulation of wage rates*

In 1959 the Terms and Conditions of Employment Act provided a scheme to prevent employers undercutting recognised pay rates. That scheme was replaced with effect from 1 January 1977 by Schedule II Employment Protection Act 1975. The Schedule enabled complaint to be made to ACAS that one or more employers were failing to observe recognised terms and conditions or the general level of terms and conditions. If it was shown that the employer complained about (and the complainant could be another employer facing unfair competition as a result of the undercutting practice) was paying less favourable rates, an award could be made which became incorporated into the individual contracts of his workers (i.e. he was then contractually obliged to pay the agreed rates). It was alleged that the Schedule II machinery was inflationary and that it was used by white-collar unions to evade Government incomes policy. It was repealed in 1980 and not replaced.

The other main prop to minimum wages was the Fair Wages Resolution passed in the House of Commons in 1891, amended subsequently, with the last version approved in 1946. Its purpose was to oblige contractors tendering for and receiving Government and local authority contracts to observe not less favourable pay rates than those established for the relevant trade or industry in the particular district. The sanction was commercial: the loss of competence to tender and the loss of future contracts. The Fair Wages Resolution was rescinded with effect from September 1983.

3.06   *Express and implied agreement on wages*

Even if only a skeleton agreement exists between an employer and employee, such an agreement is likely to include wages payable. It is an unusual employee who does not want to know from the outset what he is to be paid. Exceptionally, where there is no clear agreement on wages, the law will imply a term that reasonable remuneration is payable. A case in 1954 established that this implied term for reasonable remuneration to be payable also extended to an additional bonus, which had been agreed in principle but not in amount. Some older cases held that agreements which gave the employer the right to fix payment, gave him the right to fix *no* payment but those are unlikely to be followed in modern circumstances unless the contract is clear and the parties clearly intended to reach such an agreement.

Indeed, the EP(C)A 1978 requires the written statement of terms which the employer is obliged to issue (see Chapter 2) to contain details of the scale or rate of remuneration or the method of calculation (for example, piece rates) and the intervals at which it is paid. As well, the employer is obliged to issue an itemised pay statement with wages or salary detailing:

- the gross amount payable;
- the amounts of any fixed and variable deductions and their purpose (e.g. pension contributions, PAYE income tax,
national insurance contributions, union deductions);
- the net amount payable;
- the amount and method of payment of each part where parts of the sum due are paid differently (e.g. some cash, some by way of cheque or direct credit transfer).

The employee can bring no action for payment of wages until they become due. That depends on the contract and in theory it is possible for the contract to provide that no payment is due until performance by the worker is complete. Such an agreement would preclude an implied term for reasonable payment for performance short of completion. So, in the old case of *Cutter* v. *Powell* (1795) a second mate engaged for a ship's voyage from Jamaica to Liverpool died three weeks before the end of a two month journey. A court held that his widow was unable to recover a proportion of the agreed pay since the whole sum was payable only at the end of the voyage. Actually that rule is modified by the Apportionment Act 1970 which treats wages and salaries as accruing on a day-to-day basis and, where the performance is prevented by an extraneous event outside the control of the parties the employee can claim a just amount under the Law Reform (Frustrated Contracts) Act 1943.

3.07   *Manner of Payment – The Truck Acts*

Early legislation protected workers against the abuses of 'truck' and 'Tommy shops', i.e. payment other than in cash (in kind), and payment by the issue of vouchers which were exchangeable only at shops controlled by the employer. The Truck Acts, from 1831 onwards, required payment of wages in current coin of the realm only and made void any stipulation as to the place or manner in which any part of the wages were to be spent. The Acts also restricted fines and deductions from wages for bad work backed by criminal sanctions. The Acts continued right up to 1986, though they were increasingly felt to be anachronistic, piecemeal and absurd. The definition of workers covered by the legislation was outmoded with its reference to 'manual labour' except 'domestic and menial servants' and unjustifiable distinctions were made. So a bus driver was within the Truck Acts but a tram driver was not; a seamstress was, but a hairdresser was not. White-collar workers and retail sales people were not included. Increasingly the distinction between manual and non-manual labour became unrealistic and supplementary legislation became an unnecessary historial legacy. So, the Payment of Wages in Public Houses Prohibition Act 1883 remained on the statute book. Also, the main statutory prohibition on cashless pay became commercially unrealistic. Although the Payment of Wages Act 1960 enabled payment of wages and salary by cheque, it depended on the employee's agreement in writing and required him to waive his right under the Truck Acts to payment in cash.

Ironically, just as proposals to repeal the truck legislation were made in 1985, several cases concerning deductions made from wages to cover cash and stock shortages of shop assistants and petrol forecourt attendants hit the headlines. These cases suggested that some form of protection was still required. Changes were made by the Wages Act 1986 but a measure of protection is still afforded under that Act.

3.08   The Wages Act 1986

Part I of the Wages Act 1986, which came into effect on 1 January 1987, implements the following changes:

(1) The Truck Acts and supplementary legislation, including the Payment of Wages Act 1960, are repealed. Workers no longer have a statutory right to payment in cash. This will allow employers to insist on cashless pay for new employees but people already in employment on 1 January 1987 who were then paid in cash have a contractual right which continues. An employer who tries to force cashless pay will be acting in breach of contract, but in practice it is unlikely that an employee would sue to recover cash wages. Also, if an employee resigned over the issue and claimed constructive dismissal, the recent management reorganisation cases suggest that a tribunal would not find it an unfair dismissal. To avoid the possibility and, anyway, in the interests of harmony and good industrial relations practice, an employer might buy out payment in cash or introduce cashless pay as part of a normal wage increase or a new contract caused by promotion or transfer.

(2) New rules restricting deduction from wages and salaries are introduced. Apart from statutory deductions (i.e. income tax and national insurance contributions), any deduction must be authorised by the contract and the worker must sign his agreement in advance. A copy must be supplied to the employee or its existence and effect must be notified to him in writing. The provision covers *all* employees and any self-employed person providing personal services provided he is not a professional man or genuinely running his own business (this is a wage protection provision and is not meant to affect commercial rights or set-off in a contract of sale). The provision does not apply to the following deductions:

- in respect of overpayment of wages or expenses;
- in consequence of disciplinary proceedings held under a statutory provision, e.g. regulations applying to the police and fire service;
- to attachment of earnings orders imposed by a court;
- to agreed trade union check-off procedures;
- in respect of strike or other industrial action (see separate discussion below).

(3) There are new restrictions on deductions from wages of workers in retail employment on account of cash shortages or stock deficiencies. Such deductions still have to be authorised as under (2) above but even if authorised are limited to 10 per cent of the gross wages payable. The provisions apply to demands for payment from the worker too because otherwise it would be possible to avoid the effect of the Act by making continued employment depend on the employee making good the loss, rather than deducting from wages. The expression 'workers in retail employment' will include shop assistants, cashiers, ticket clerks, fare collectors, catalogue sales people, car park attendants – indeed anyone receiving payment in a retail transaction which includes the supply of services, as well as goods, including financial services (so an insurance agent is included).

The 10 per cent limit applies in respect of any one pay day. But there is nothing to stop the employer spreading the recoupment forward if his loss is greater than 10 per cent of gross wages, provided the total deduction is authorised and the 10 per cent limit for any one pay day is not exceeded. He cannot recoup by way of deduction after 12 months from the day the deficit was discovered, or should have been discovered. There is no statutory requirement that the deductions should be fair and reasonable as there was under the Truck Act of 1896 and when the employment comes to an end there is no limit to the amount that can be deducted from the final instalment of wages. Any sum paid in lieu of notice is included as part of the final instalment of wages. Legal proceedings can be instituted by the employer to recover any balance due provided a demand for payment is presented within 12 months from discovery of the deficit.

(4) The enforcement of the new rules is by the individual worker before an industrial tribunal. There are no criminal sanctions in respect of unauthorised deductions. Complaint lies to an industrial tribunal within three months of the unauthorised deduction and that is the only remedy available; the worker cannot bring an ordinary civil action for recovery of unpaid wages representing the deduction. If the tribunal finds the complaint to be well-founded it can order the employer to reimburse the worker.

Any contractual provision which purports to limit or exclude the restrictions on deductions are void. It is not possible to contract out of these provisions of the Wages Act 1986.

It has been argued that these replacement provisions which sweep away the truck legislation are an illusory protection. In so far as the written 'consent' of the worker is required, unless the employee is in a strong bargaining position he will have little alternative but to accept a standard authorisation of deductions. It may be that when hearing unfair dismissal claims, tribunals will apply the standards set out in the Wages Act 1986 in respect of deductions as yardsticks for determining fairness.

3.09   Deduction from wages for strike or other industrial action

If an employee refuses to work for the whole or part of a week, is the employer entitled without terminating the contract, to withhold the whole or a proportionate part of the week's salary? Yes, according to the House of Lords in *Miles* v. *Wakefield Metropolitan District Council* (1987). In that case Lord Templeman said:

> 'A worker who is on strike ... does not usually line up for his pay packet on pay day during a strike. The worker thus recognises and accepts that ... he is not entitled to be paid if he declines to work. ...
> In a contract of employment wages and work go together. The employer pays for work and the worker works for his wages. If the employer declines to pay, the worker need not work. If the worker declines to work, the employer need not pay.'

And in *Cresswell* v. *Board of Inland Revenue* (1984) Mr Justice Walton referred to 'no work, no pay' as an obvious principle.

It is more difficult to answer the related question: if an employee refuses to work properly, where for example, he 'goes slow' or refuses to carry out part of his duties, is the employer entitled to deduct an appropriate proportion of his pay? Some cases suggest that he is. In *Royle* v. *Trafford Borough Council* (1984) a primary school teacher refused, from January to July 1980, to take five extra pupils into his class of 31. That was in accordance with his union's objection to the reduction of teachers by the local education committee. Throughout the period the teacher continued to take his usual 31 pupils for normal classes. The Council refused to pay him anything. In an action for recovery of salary, the High Court held the teacher was entitled to his salary *less* $5/36$ths which represented the services which he had not performed. And in *Sim* v. *Rotherham Metropolitan Borough Council* (1986) in the course of the long-running teachers' dispute, certain teachers refused to cover for absent colleagues. The local authority was held entitled to deduct from salaries sums representing the value of the lost services. The plaintiff teachers were unable to recover sums between £2 and £3.37 which had been deducted from their monthly salaries.

The right to reduce wages to reflect only partial performance of the employment contract was the central issue in *Miles* v. *Wakefield Metropolitan District Council*. The plaintiff was a superintendent registrar of births, deaths and marriages. His normal weekly working hours were 37, including three on Saturday mornings, the most popular time for civil weddings. In the course of a trade dispute, the plaintiff obeyed his union's instructions to refuse to perform wedding ceremonies on Saturday mornings. He attended for work on Saturdays but would not conduct civil weddings. The Council made it clear by letter that whilst the plaintiff was not willing to carry out his full duties on Saturdays, he was not required to attend on those days and he would not be paid. The plaintiff continued to attend his office to do other work on Saturdays. The Council deducted $3/37$ths of the plaintiff's salary throughout the duration of the dispute, which was a total deduction of £744. The plaintiff sought to recover this sum. Ultimately, the House of Lords held that the plaintiff could not recover. The reasons behind their Lordships' judgments are not easy to state plainly. The most convincing analysis is that of Lord Oliver. He treats the case as one in which the plaintiff is not performing at all, i.e. the equivalent of strike action. It follows from that that the employer can deduct from wages to reflect the non-performance for certain working hours. However, if an employee is 'going-slow' rather than striking, Lord Oliver thinks that the employer cannot deduct from remuneration self-assessed damages. That would be to impose unilaterally a variation on the contract terms. The employer's choices in that case are to accept the partial performance and pay the full remuneration or to dismiss the employee and pay nothing.

Lords Bridge and Brandon were also very cautious about the imposition of a 'quasi-contract' where the employee was 'going-slow'. That would presuppose that the contract of employment had been superseded by some new agreement between the employer and employee which was contrary to the realities of the situation.

Lords Templeman and Brightman thought, however, that an employer can make a deduction from wages where an employee is 'going-slow'. The employee is only entitled then to so much pay as represents the value of the work done. He cannot claim the full amount, because he has not performed the full duties. But he has provided some service and should recover a proportionate part of his pay.

The difficulty with this last approach is seeing the reduced payment as made under any contract. Where does it come from and what happened to the original contract? It may seem a neat solution at first sight: the employee's performance is only partial so he is entitled to only partial payment. But how is the deduction to be calculated? There is a big difference between a half-day's strike (where it is possible to calculate the deduction reasonably fairly and objectively) and a half-day's work to rule or go-slow where the evaluation of the service lost is likely to be subjective and uncertain.

The issue was considered again in *Wiluszynski* v. *London Borough of Tower Hamlets* (1988). The plaintiff was an estates officer in the council's Housing Directorate. During a dispute between the plaintiff's union, NALGO, and the council, the plaintiff followed union instructions to boycott inquiries from council members. Employees, including the plaintiff, were told that if they attended for work but refused to work normally the work would be regarded as unauthorised and voluntary and they would not be paid. The plaintiff worked throughout the five-week dispute and carried out his normal duties except replying to council members' inquiries. When the dispute ended it took the plaintiff two to three hours to reply to the member's inquiries which had built up during the boycott. The council refused to pay any of the plaintiff's salary for the five-week period. The High Court held that the plaintiff was entitled to his *full* salary for the duration of the dispute. The plaintiff's breach of contract was minimal and did not justify withholding the whole of his pay. The employers did nothing to show that they were treating the breach as terminating the contract. On the contrary, they took the benefit of the substantial performance. The judge did suggest, however, that the employers might have been entitled to deduct two to three hours' pay from the five weeks' salary due.

Conclusions

(1) An employer is entitled to refuse to pay wages or salary during a period of strike action even though the contract of employment continues.

(2) If an employee attends work and offers partial performance which is unacceptable to the employer, the employer should make it clear that he regards the service as inadequate and unacceptable. The employee might then be considered as on strike and so not entitled to any payment.

(3) An employer is not entitled to accept substantial performance and refuse all payment.

(4) If failure to perform is not so serious as to constitute the equivalent of strike action, authorities are divided as to whether the employer can deduct from wages. If he can link any deduction to damage sustained (e.g. the cost of replacement labour) he probably can deduct.

(5) The employer always has the option of accepting the employee's breach of contract in refusing to perform properly and terminating the contract. Provided he does not discriminate by dismissing only some of the strikers, no one of them can claim unfair dismissal.

Note that the Wages Act 1986, which restricts deductions from wages, does not apply where the worker has taken part in a strike or other industrial action.

3.10 Statutory sick pay

With effect from 6th April 1986 an employer is obliged to pay statutory sick pay (SSP) if his employee is away sick for four or more qualifying days. A qualifying day is a day on which the employee would normally be available for work.

There is no statutory sick pay entitlement for the first three qualifying days' absence. There are two rates of SSP which depend on the employee's level of earnings. The rates for 1988–89 are: £49.20 per week (or £9.84 daily assuming a five-day working week) where the employee's normal earnings are not less than £79.50. The rate is £34.25 per week (or £6.85 daily) if earnings are less than £79.50 but more than £41 per week.

The employee has a maximum entitlement to SSP for 28 weeks of a period of sickness. Any two periods of sickness which are separated by eight weeks or less are treated as the same period of sickness. Regulations require the giving of notice by the employee to the employer (usually on the seventh day after the sickness absence commences) which must be supported by a medical certificate in the prescribed form. That certificate can state that the employee will be unfit for work for up to six months. SSP is treated as contractual remuneration and is subject to PAYE income tax and national insurance contributions. Employers are required to maintain records for three years after the end of each tax year in respect of each employee of periods of absence of four or more days in that tax year. Employers recover the cost of SSP payments generally by making deductions from their subsequent national insurance contributions although in certain circumstances the DHSS make refunds.

If an employer's occupational sick pay scheme provides greater benefits than the statutory scheme the extent of the latter can still be deducted from subsequent national insurance contributions, e.g. if the employer pays full wages during a period of sickness the amount of SSP from day four onwards can be deducted. The employer therefore bears the cost only of the excess of his contract benefits over the statutory benefits.

3.11   Statutory maternity pay

Statutory maternity pay (SMP) is payable by the employer at either of two rates. The higher rate of $9/10$th of the normal weekly earnings is payable for the first six weeks maternity absence to an employee who has at least two years' service. The lower rate of £34.25 weekly (from April 1988) is payable for up to 12 weeks after the entitlement to the higher rate is exhausted or for up to 18 weeks if the employee has between six months' and two years' service and so never qualified for the higher rate. Anyone with less than six months' service does not qualify for SMP but maternity allowance may be payable by the DHSS based on national insurance contributions through previous employment.

The cost of SMP is recoverable in the same way as statutory sick pay. An employer may have a maternity leave scheme which provides for greater maternity pay entitlement. If he does, he bears the cost of any excess provision.

3.12   Guarantee payment

The statutory obligation to pay guarantee pay was first contained in the EPA 1975 and is now in Sections 12-18 EP(C)A 1978. Guarantee or 'lay-off' pay may be payable under express agreement between the parties or under an employer/union agreement which has become a term of the individual contract. In the absence of any such agreement the statutory scheme will apply but *only* where there is a right to lay-off without pay in the first place. The statutory scheme does not entitle an employer to argue that he has no available work and is therefore entitled to lay-off workers and pay only the statutory payment. An employer who anticipates fluctuating work levels should insert an express clause entitling him to lay-off without pay in slack periods. That provision will trigger the statutory rules. It is not possible for the employer to restrict the statutory entitlement or contract out of the minimum guarantee pay provisions except where an exemption order has been made by the Secretary of State. Note that the statutory provisions are the minimum and the contract may provide for the full amount of earnings lost to be payable. Also note that only *employees* are entitled to guarantee pay to compensate for earnings lost on a normal day of work. The scheme was not intended to protect casual irregular workers.

The statutory scheme gives any employee with one month's service who loses a day's work a right to guarantee pay of normal daily earnings up to a maximum of £11.30. His entitlement to guarantee pay is for a maximum of (usually) five days in any period of three months. The number of days' entitlement is the same as the usual number of days or shifts worked in any week. So, if an employee has his weekly hours spread over four shifts of ten hours each, his maximum entitlement to guarantee pay in any three month period will be for four lost shifts, or 4 × £11.30 if his normal earnings for each shift exceed £11.30. If an employee normally works five days, his maximum entitlement is for five days in any three month period or 5 × £11.30 if his normal daily earnings exceed £11.30.

The lost day must be a normal working day under the employment contract. If the employer anticipates a continuing reduction of workload and varies the contract by reducing the usual days at work from five to four the employees affected have no entitlement to guarantee pay since the fifth day is no longer a day on which the employee is required to work under the contract. However, the employer who does act in that way risks an action being brought against him for breach of contract or constructive unfair dismissal (see Chapter 6, 'How to Manage Change').

Before any employee has an entitlement to statutory guarantee pay it must be shown that the lost day's work is caused by a diminution in the employer's business requirements for employees or some other occurrence affecting the normal working of the employer's business.

The first cause is worded similarly to the redundancy definition and will apply where there is a falling off of orders and consequently a reduction in production requirements. It will also apply where introduction of new processes or reorganisation mean that the employer's need for so many full-time workers has decreased. If that diminution is likely to be permanent the employer should declare redundancies. If it is temporary, then lay-off, subject to guarantee payments being made may be the appropriate management reaction. The 'some other occurrence' cause of lay-off will apply to disruption caused, for example, by weather or plant breakdown or failure of power supply or other essential service.

There is no entitlement to guarantee payment if the lack of work occurs in consequence of strike, lock-out or other industrial action involving any employee of the same or an associated employer. So, if one section of the undertaking is taking industrial action which stops or diminishes the flow of work to another section, any workers laid off in consequence are not entitled to guarantee pay. The exclusion does not apply to industrial action involving a supplier or customer of the employer if they are not associated employers. However, if his own employees become involved in the strike, for example by refusing to cross picket lines, and that action causes workers to be laid off the exclusion applies (see *Garvey* v. *S. & J. Maybank (Oldham) Ltd* (1979)).

There are two more exclusions from guarantee pay entitlement: if the employee does not comply with reasonable requirements to ensure his services are available he is not entitled nor if he unreasonably refuses suitable alternative work. Again, the second exclusion contains wording similar to that in the redundancy provisions. The application of judicial interpretation of those provisions suggests that the work offered would have to be appropriate in terms of the status, skill and experience of the employee and reasonableness of the refusal depends on the personal situation of the employee, e.g. if the work offered is at a different location which involves considerable extra travelling time refusal might be reasonable, or if the hours are different and would substantially interfere with the employee's domestic commitments a tribunal might regard refusal as not unreasonable. The reference to compliance with reasonable requirements to ensure services are available means that the employer could require the employee to report at the commencement of each shift or be available for telephone contact in case circumstances change. In *Meadows* v. *Faithful Overalls Ltd* (1977) that exclusion applied. The heating system had stopped and the temperature was below the statutory minimum. The employees refused to wait in the canteen, where hot drinks were provided, whilst a delivery of oil was arranged. They were not entitled to guarantee pay for the lost day's work since the tribunal found they had failed to comply with the employer's reasonable requirements to ensure their services were available.

The guarantee payment entitlement is enforced through the industrial tribunals. Complaint must be presented within three months of the workless day.

3.13   *The provision of work*

The traditional view was that normally, in the absence of any express agreement, the employer was not under any duty to provide work so long as he continued to pay wages or salary. The employer's obligation was to pay, but it was a matter for him if, having paid, he chose not to avail himself of the worker's services. This principle was encapsulated in a famous dictum of Lord Asquith in *Collier* v. *Sunday Referee Publishing Co. Ltd* (1940): 'Provided I pay my cook her wages regularly she cannot complain if I choose to take all my meals out'.

However, it was always recognised that there were exceptions to this principle. An obligation to provide work does exist if work and wages go together and the denial of work means forfeit of wages, i.e. where the employee is working on piece rates. In *Devonald* v. *Rosser* (1906) workmen who were paid piece rates were given one month's notice of termination but no work to do during that period. The court held that they were entitled to be given work to enable them to earn wages during the notice period. Damages were awarded equivalent to average monthly earnings. Similarly, in *Bauman* v. *Hulton Press Ltd* (1952) a journalist/photographer who was paid only his nominal retainer during the notice period was held entitled to be provided with sufficient work to enable him to earn a reasonable level of remuneration. But even if the lack of work means no remuneration, the employer is not in breach of contract if he cannot provide work because of circumstances beyond his control. In those circumstances, guarantee pay will be due to employees under EP(C)A 1978 (see above).

Also, there is and always has been, an obligation to provide work if that can be implied as part of the consideration for the contract, e.g. if the opportunity for publicity is part of the agreement. In *Clayton* v. *Oliver* (1930) an artiste was engaged to play the lead in a musical theatrical performance. In fact, he was not cast in the lead but the producers paid him the full contract price. The artiste's action for damages succeeded – he had lost the opportunity of appearing in public and enhancing his theatrical reputation. That principle was extended in *Collier* v. *Sunday Referee Publishing Co. Ltd* (1940) to a chief sub-editor of a newspaper. The employers had sold the newspaper which put it out of their power to continue to provide the plaintiff with work although his salary was paid in full. He was held entitled to damages to compensate him for lack of work since failure to employ him affected his reputation and future employment prospects. The same argument could be deployed in respect of any professional or skilled worker whose expertise and/or reputation would be diminished by lack of work. Indeed, in *Langston* v. *AUEW* (1974) Lord Denning in the Court of Appeal suggested that a car worker had the right to work as well as a right to wages. In fact the case proceeded on a different basis and the other judges did not take nearly so emphatic a view as Lord Denning.

It is probably more realistic to regard the 'right to work' argument as part of an unfair dismissal claim than a cause of action for damages for breach of contract. Certainly that must be true in respect of the average employee who is unlikely to be awarded damages for breach of contract in an ordinary court when he continues to receive full wages. However, it may be that an employee who is not provided with work can convince a tribunal that the failure to give him work justifies his resigning and claiming constructive dismissal. In *Breach* v. *Epsylon Industries Ltd* (1976) a chief engineer whose work almost entirely dried up argued that his inactivity meant he would lose his expertise and become out of touch with industrial developments. The EAT accepted his argument in principle and remitted the case to the tribunal. In *Bosworth* v. *Angus Jowett & Co. Ltd* (1977) a tribunal applied the same approach to a sales director and suggested that the higher a man is in the management structure, the more important it is for him to be given work and the greater the damage to his reputation if it became known that work was being withheld from him. However, in *Hemmings* v. *International Computer Ltd* (1976) a planning engineer who was under-employed for a considerable time was held not to have been constructively dismissed. There was no suggestion in that case that work was being deliberately withheld from the employee; it simply was not available. The tribunal took the view that whilst the lack of work must have been worrying and frustrating to the employee, the employer was not in breach of contract.

The cases suggest then that apart from circumstances in which the employer can be seen as 'starving-out' the employee there remains no obligation to provide work as well as pay wages except where the provision of work is part of the contract consideration.

3.14   *The employer's duty of care for the health and safety of employees*

It is an implied term of the contract of employment that an employer will exercise reasonable care in respect of the health and safety of his employees. At common law that duty of care has four aspects:

(i) Safe staff. The employer is obliged to provide competent workers and safe fellow employees and to discipline and/or dismiss any worker who is a potential hazard to employees, e.g. a practical joker who persistently trips up fellow workers (*Hudson* v. *Ridge Manufacturing Co. Ltd* (1957)). Provided dismissal is carried out after a fair procedure the employer should have a good defence to any unfair dismissal claim.

(ii) Safe plant and equipment. The employer must ensure that tools and equipment provided for the employee's use are as safe as is reasonable in the circumstances. See, for example, *Taylor* v. *Rover Co. Ltd* (1966) where the employer was in breach of his duty of care in continuing with the use of a chisel after a defect appeared.

(iii) Safe premises. The employer must take reasonable care in respect of the premises in which the employee works, e.g. by providing suitable ventilation, hand-rails for steep steps, lighting in dark passages, guards and barriers to block access to dangerous sites. (See, for example, *McQuilter* v. *Goulandris Bros Ltd* (1951) – a ship-repairer tripped over a ring-bolt on an unlighted deck and fell into an uncovered hatchway.)

(iv) Safe system of work. The employer must organise and implement a safe working system. (See, for example, *Wilsons & Clyde Coal Co.* v. *English* (1938) where the employers were held in breach of their duty in allowing haulage plant to be in operation whilst miners were moving along haulage roads.)

An employee has an action for damages where the employer acts in breach of that duty to take reasonable care and the employee is injured as a result. Note that the emphasis is on that which is reasonable in the circumstances and the level of duty owed will depend on such factors as the degree of expertise claimed by the employee, what precautions were reasonably practicable and whether the cause of the injury was reasonably foreseeable. Note also that the employer's duty to take reasonable care for the health and safety of his employees is personal and it is no defence for the employer to argue that he delegated that duty to a person he reasonably believed to be competent to perform it. The employer remains liable for breach of the duty. (See, for example, *McDermid* v. *Nash Dredging and Reclamation Co. Ltd* (1987). The employee, a deckhand, was working on a tug engaged on a dredging contract which was being directed by a captain who was an employee of the employer's parent company. The captain was negligent in directing the manner of work with the result that the deckhand was seriously injured. Although there was no employment link between the captain and the deckhand's employer, his employer was held liable in damages for failing to provide a safe system of work.)

Many of the elements of the common law duty of care are supplemented by statutory provisions. For example, the Employers' Liability (Defective Equipment) Act 1969 makes the employer liable where the employee sustains personal injury in the course of his employment as a result of defective equipment and the defect is attributable to the fault of a third party, e.g. the manufacturer of the equipment. See, for example, *Yuille* v. *Daks Simpson Ltd* (1984) where the employers were held liable when ventilation ducts gave way because of defective supports supplied by heating engineers. (Note that under the Consumer Protection Act 1987 the manufacturer's own product liability is strict and does not depend on proof of fault. However,there is a 'state of the art' defence available, i.e. the state of scientific or technical knowledge at the time was not such that the manufacturer might have been expected to discover the defect.) Common law liability for defective premises is supplemented by the Occupiers' Liability Act 1957, by Construction Regulations made under the Factories Act for the protection of building workers and by regulations under the Public Health Acts. The Factories Act 1961, the Health and Safety at Work Act 1974 and regulations and codes of practice made under them superimpose on the common law a plethora of statutory obligations. Reference should be made to specialist works for detailed discussions of those obligations but an outline of the principal statutory provisions is given below.

The Health and Safety at Work Act 1974

Section 2 of the Act makes it the duty of every employer to ensure, so far as is reasonably practicable, the health, safety and welfare at work of all his employees. In particular, the duty includes

(a) the provision and maintenance of plant and systems of work that are so far as is reasonably practicable, safe and without risks to health;

(b) arrangements for ensuring, so far as is reasonably practicable, safety and absence of risks to health in connection with the use, handling, storage and transport of articles and substances;

(c) the provision of such information, instruction, training and supervision as is necessary to ensure, so far as is reasonably practicable, the health and safety at work of his employees;

(d) so far as is reasonably practicable as regards any place of work under the employer's control, the maintenance of it in a condition that is safe and without risks to health and the provision and maintenance of means of access to and egress from it that are safe and without such risks;

(e) the provision and maintenance of a working environment for his employees that is, so far as is reasonably practicable, safe, without risks to health, and adequate as regards facilities and arrangements for their welfare at work.

These general safety duties are modelled on the common law. They do not give rise to civil liability but to criminal prosecution and the burden is on the defence to show that it was not 'reasonably practicable' to do more than was in fact done. Failure to comply with Health and Safety Commission codes of practice will raise a presumption of breach of duty.

Also, every employer has a duty to prepare and periodically revise a written statement of his general health and safety policy and the organisation and arrangements in force for carrying out that policy. Regulations enable recognised trade unions to appoint safety representatives and the employer is obliged to consult those representatives over health and safety measures. The representatives appointed can require the employer to establish a statutory safety committee to review health and safety measures. The employer is obliged to allow the safety representatives time off with pay to perform their functions and undergo reasonable training. Guidance on what constitutes reasonable training is given by a Health and Safety Commission Code of Practice of 1978.

Health and safety regulations provide the real teeth of the Act and create specific duties breach of which usually gives rise to civil liability. Schedule 3 of the Act sets out the subject matter in respect of which regulations may be made.

Under the Health and Safety at Work Act 1974 the employee owes safety duties as well. Every employee has a duty while at work to take reasonable care for the health and safety of himself and other persons who may be affected by his acts or omissions and to co-operate with the employer to enable statutory safety provisions to be complied with. Subject to adherence to fair procedures, it will usually be a fair dismissal if an employee's contract is terminated for misuse or neglect of safety equipment or procedures. (See, for example, *Martin* v. *Yorkshire Imperial Metals Ltd* (1978) in which the employee was held fairly dismissed for deliberately jamming a safety guard which rendered his automatic lathe inoperable unless both hands were used by the operator.)

The Factories Act 1961

The 1961 Act provisions take effect under the Health and Safety at Work Act as relevant statutory provisions. A factory is any place where manual labour is used in the manufacture of goods or certain analogous processes for trade or profit and certain premises are specifically included. Usually it is the occupier of the premises who is responsible for compliance with the Act. The safety rules are imposed primarily for the benefit of employees but other persons working at the premises (e.g. contractors) have been held to be within the protection. The specific obligations include sound construction and proper maintenance of the premises themselves and lifting tackle, the fencing of dangerous machinery and vats of dangerous substances, practicable precautions in the use of explosive and inflammable substances and steam or compressed air apparatus. Regulations supplement the Act's general duties. There are, for example, specific regulations prescribing the use of woodworking machines, milling machines, power presses and abrasive wheels.

3.15   *The employer's vicarious liability*

If an employee acts negligently in the course of his employment and injures another employee or a third party, the employer is vicariously liable. The crucial issue is whether the negligent employee acted 'in the course of employment'. That phrase includes any act which is within the employer's express or implied authorisation even though the act which caused the injury may have been an improper and unauthorised method of performing the authorised task. But if the negligent act is separate from the employer's business activity so that it must be regarded as the independent act of the employee, there is no vicarious liability attributable to the employer.

There is no single test for determining whether an act is performed in the course of employment and it seems that the question is one of fact according to the circumstances of the case. Extreme circumstances can be categorised with certainty, as for example where a delivery driver negligently injures a road user whilst on his round; the employer would be vicariously liable. Or, at the other extreme, the driver may be off duty and driving his own vehicle for his own purposes, say to a football match, when the negligent act occurs. Now there would be no vicarious liability. But, if there are elements of authorisation *and* independence of action it is difficult to determine the scope of vicarious liability. (See, for example, *Rose* v. *Plenty* (1976). A milk roundsman was expressly prohibited from giving lifts on milk floats and from employing children to help with the round. Contrary to these instructions, the roundsman did invite a child to help with the delivery for payment. The child was injured by the roundsman's negligent driving and the Court of Appeal held the employer vicariously liable. According to the court, the milkman was acting in the course of his employment when he caused the injury. The prohibitions affected the manner of performance of his duties but not the duties themselves. The milkman was still acting for the purpose of the employer's business when he committed the negligent act.)

For a more recent illustration see *Smith* v. *Stages and Darlington Insulation Co. Ltd* (1988). The plaintiff was seriously injured as a result of negligent driving caused by the fatigue of another employee. Both men had been working long hours away from home and although the employers paid rest time, they travelled home during that time. Again, the Court of Appeal held that the employers were vicariously liable. They had authorised the negligent employee to drive himself and the plaintiff but had failed to direct them not to travel on the rest day. For a recent finding that the negligent act was *not* performed in the course of employment see *Aldred* v. *Nacanco* (1987). The plaintiff suffered a back injury when she moved awkwardly after another employee negligently pushed an unsteady wash-basin towards her. The incident happened in the washroom at the end of the day when the employees were preparing to leave work. The Court of Appeal held the employers were not vicariously liable. The judges adopted the following state-ment of principle from *Salmond on Torts*:

'If a servant does negligently that which he was authorised to do carefully, or if he does fraudulently that which he was authorised to do honestly, or if he does mistakenly that which he was authorised to do correctly, his master will answer for that negligence, fraud or mistake. On the other hand, if the unauthorised and wrongful act of the servant is not so connected with the authorised act as to be a mode of doing it, but is an independent act, the master is not responsible; for in such a case the servant is not acting in the course of employment but has gone outside it.'

In the case before it the Court of Appeal held that the act of the fellow employee which caused the plaintiff's injuries was a deliberate act which had nothing whatsoever to do with anything that she was employed to do. It was not an improper way of doing her job: it was something wholly outside her job.

If the employee who acts negligently is seconded temporarily to another employer, it becomes even more difficult to determine liability. Is the original employer responsible or has liability passed to the second employer? In *Mersey Docks & Harbour Board* v. *Coggins & Griffiths Ltd* (1947) the House of Lords held that the original employer remains liable unless he can show that control over the act which caused the injury passed to the temporary employer. The harbour authority hired out a mobile crane together with an operator to a firm of stevedores. The hire agreement provided that the operator should become the stevedore firm's employee. The operator drove the crane negligently and injured a third person. The House of Lords held that responsibility for the employee's negligence could not be determined by the hire agreement (although that might create a right to indemnity) but, as a matter of law, responsibility rested with the original employers who remained in control of the skill of the employee in the manner of the operation of the crane. Although the stevedores were directing the loading operation, the manipulation of the crane was not under their control. Where a complicated piece of machinery and a skilled operator are lent or hired it is difficult to show that control over the operation has passed. Where, however, it is unskilled, manual labour which is lent it will be easier to show vicarious liability has passed.

3.16   *The duty to maintain mutual trust and confidence*

Whilst some older cases suggest the proper relationship between parties to an employment contract is analogous to that of Czar and serf, there has been a tendency recently to require *mutual* respect and *mutual* trust and confidence. Neither party should act in a way calculated to undermine that trust and confidence. So, in *Wilson* v. *Racher* (1974), Lord Edmund Davies said that a contract of service imposes upon the parties a duty of mutual respect and the employer was in breach of that duty in adopting a provocative and unseemly manner to his head gardener. He goaded the employee, showered him with questions implying that he was shirking and was aggressive but then sacked him when he responded by using offensive language. The employee's action in wrongful dismissal succeeded.

The implied duty to maintain respect has received endorsement in recent unfair dismissal cases. It has featured as part of the employee's justification for resignation and his subsequent claim of constructive dismissal, i.e. the employer has acted in breach of contract in failing to treat him with respect and the employee is justified in resigning and claiming unfair dismissal. *Western Excavating Ltd* v. *Sharp* (1978) emphasises the continuing contractual basis of the employment relationship and requires a repudiatory or serious breach from the employer before the employee can resign and complain of constructive dismissal.

The decision of the EAT in *Woods* v. *W.M. Car Services (Peterborough) Ltd* (1981) shows the modern attitude to this implied term. The EAT held that an employer who persistently attempts to vary an employee's conditions of service with a view to getting rid of the employee or continually varies the terms of service acts in a manner calculated or likely to destroy the relationship of confidence and trust. In that case the employer tried to reduce the employee's wages, to increase the hours of work, to change the job title and job content and to impose a job description which was more than could be managed. Each time the employee protested the employer withdrew but then made a different change. The EAT said they would have held that this conduct was in breach of the implied term but the industrial tribunal had not so concluded and they would not interfere with the decision. However, the EAT declared that as a matter of principle where an employer stops short of any major breach of contract but attempts to make the employee's life so uncomfortable that he resigns or accepts inferior terms, he acts in a totally unreasonable manner and in breach of the implied term of mutual respect.

The Court of Appeal affirmed that approach in *Lewis* v. *Motor-World Garages Ltd* (1985). The employee, an after-sales manager was demoted to service manager which meant the loss of his office, a smaller car and a change in salary structure. Also, he was denied a salary increase which was given to other employees. Some months later when his performance was criticised by senior management he resigned and claimed constructive dismissal. The Court of Appeal held that the cumulative behaviour of the employer could amount to a breach of the implied term of mutual trust and confidence even though no single action amounted to repudiatory breach of contract.

3.17 The obligation to allow time off for trade union duties and activities and for public duties

By section 27 of the Employment Protection (Consolidation) Act 1978 an employer is obliged to allow officials of recognised independent trade unions who are employed by him reasonable time off *with pay*.

The time off must be for the official's *duties* which are concerned with industrial relations with the employer or any associated employer or to undergo relevant training for carrying out such duties. A trade union 'official' is any person elected or appointed under the rules to represent members at section, branch or higher level and will include shop-stewards, branch secretaries, treasurers, chairmen, etc. The obligation is incurred only in respect of recognised, independent trade unions. Since the repeal of the relevant provisions of an Act of 1975, there is no longer any procedure under which an employer can be required to recognise a trade union. However, there does not have to be a formal recognition agreement in order to trigger the time off obligations if practice justifies an implication of recognition.

An ACAS Code of Practice of 1977 supplements the section and provides guidance as to what are union duties for which time off with pay should be allowed. It includes the following:

(a) collective bargaining with the appropriate level of management;
(b) informing constituents about negotiations or consultations with management;
(c) meetings with other lay officials or with full-time union officers on matters which are concerned with industrial relations between his or her employer and any associated employer and their employees;
(d) interviews with and on behalf of constituents on grievance and discipline matters concerning them and their employer;
(e) appearing on behalf of constituents before an outside body, such as an industrial tribunal, which is dealing with an industrial relations matter concerning the employer; and
(f) explanations to new employees whom he or she will represent of the role of the union in the workplace industrial relations structure.

The Code does not indicate what number of days or hours off might be regarded as reasonable, preferring to leave that to agreement between the parties according to the circumstances.

An employer is also obliged to allow any employee who is a member of a recognised trade union reasonable time off during working hours to take part in trade union *activities*. This time, time off is without pay. The ACAS Code of Practice envisages that members be allowed reasonable time off to vote in union elections, to attend union meetings where attendance during normal working hours would not adversely affect production or services, to attend policy-making executive or annual meetings and to represent the union on external bodies. In fact, employers commonly give time off without loss of pay to encourage all employees who are members to attend appropriate union meetings.

It is common practice for employers to run those two obligations together and fix a maximum number of days off annually for duties (with pay) and activities (without pay) for designated trade union representatives.

Complaint of breach of section 27 or 28 lies to the industrial tribunals and the cases emphasise the distinction between trade union duties and trade union activities. In *Vine* v. *DRG (UK) Ltd* (1978) a union branch committee member was held not entitled to time off with pay to attend a course on the trade union movement. The tribunal held that the employer had not acted unreasonably in allowing the claimant time off, but without pay. Since the employers had no industrial relations dealings with the branch committee, none of the claimant's functions as a committee member constituted trade union duties, as opposed to activities.

In other cases trade union officials have been refused paid time off to attend a union 'exchange of information' meeting and a union course on 'job security'.

A very recent case has required the purpose of the time off to relate not to industrial relations generally but to industrial relations between the employer and the employees represented by the claimant. In *British Bakeries (Northern) Ltd* v. *Adlington* (1988) four union branch officials claimed time off with pay to attend a union meeting on opposition to the proposed repeal of an Act regulating hours of work in the baking industry. The employers agreed to allow time off but without pay. The EAT overruled a tribunal decision that the four were entitled to be paid for the time off. The EAT held that the proposed meeting had no direct relevance to industrial relations between the employer and his employees and was not within the meaning of the claimants' trade union 'duties'.

3.18 Time off for public duties

An employer is obliged by section 29 of the EP(C)A 1978 to allow an employee reasonable time off to perform duties as:

- a justice of the peace;
- a member of a local authority;
- a member of a statutory tribunal;
- a member of a health authority;

- a member of the managing or governing body of a state-maintained educational establishment;
- a member of a water authority.

Time off for jury service is not specifically included within section 29 but electors are obliged to attend for jury service when summoned and any employer who dismissed because of absence on jury service would be held to have acted unreasonably and even be in contempt of court. Loss of earnings by the juror are recoverable from public funds.

Time off is without pay and what is reasonable depends on how much time off is required for the performance of the particular public duty, how much the employee has already been permitted for trade union duties or activities or other public duties and the effect of the employee's absence on the running of the employer's business. In *Emmerson* v. *I.R.C.* (1977) the employee had regularly been allowed 18 days' unpaid leave each year to carry out his duties as a member of a local council. When he was elected leader of the opposition party on the council he asked for additional time off. A tribunal held that he should be allowed 30 days' leave each year. He would need even more than that to fulfill his duties properly but the remainder could be discharged during part of his annual holiday entitlement.

Another tribunal thought 38 half-days unpaid leave appropriate for a local councillor and 21 days leave was thought reasonable by the EAT for a justice of the peace.

An employer should not expect an employee who is allowed time off for public duties to perform his full employment duties in the reduced time at work.

3.19   *Disclosure of computerised employment records – The Data Protection Act 1984*

The Data Protection Act 1984 has been fully operative since November 1987. From that time individuals have rights of access to computerised data held concerning them and civil remedies in respect of inaccurate data. A system of registration is imposed for holders and users of computerised personal data and it is a criminal offence to hold unregistered data. Personal data is computerised information which can identify a living individual, including any expression of opinion about the individual. Employers who use computerised personnel and payroll systems should register under the Act. A data user does not have to process data himself to be covered by the Act. The emphasis is on control and use and an employer must register even if the processing is done by an agency on his behalf (but see below for payroll exemption). Registration is effected through the enforcement officer appointed under the Act, the Data Protection Registrar. An advisory booklet on registration is available from the Registrar. The forms for application for registration require a description of the data held, the purposes for which it is used, the sources from which it is obtained and the persons to whom it may be disclosed. The standard 'Personnel/ Employee Administration' purpose envisaged covers 'administration of prospective, current and past employees, including where applicable, self-employed or contract personnel, secondees, temporary staff or voluntary workers'. The activities included within this standard personnel purpose are: 'recruitment; recording or working time; administration and payment of wages, salaries, pensions and other benefits with deductions, employee assessment and training; negotation or communication with employees; manpower and career planning; compliance with company policy and/or legislation in relation to health, safety and other employment matters; analysis for management purposes and statutory returns'.

There is a separate standard purpose (for which a separate registration must be made) for 'Work Planning and Management' which includes 'job or task scheduling; roster administration; progress or piecework monitoring; identification of relevant resources; monitoring the delocation, use or performance of plant, equipment, vehicles. or services; analysis for management purposes and statutory returns'.

There are exemptions from the Act and registration is not required in respect of certain types of personal data. Neither do the disclosure or other provisions of the Act apply. The most relevant exemption for employers is that for payrolls and accounts. The exemption applies to data held for the purpose of calculating amounts payable by way of remuneration or pensions in respect of employment or for making payments or deductions from such remuneration or pensions. That must be the *only* purpose for holding the data; exemption is lost if the payroll system is used in any way to monitor employee performance (e.g. a link with bonus or incentive payments) or as a means of cost analysis or if the payroll data is used as an address bank to send material other than payment information. The payroll data can only be disclosed:

- to a person who actually makes payment, e.g. a bank;
- to obtain actuarial advice;
- to provide information for medical research into occupational health or injuries at work;
- if the individuals consents.

The data protection principles set out in Schedule 1 of the Act are as follows:

(i)   information contained in personal data must be obtained and processed fairly and lawfully;

(ii)   personal data may be held only for registered purposes;

(iii)   personal data must not be used or disclosed in any manner incompatible with the registered purposes;

(iv)   personal data held must be 'adequate, relevant and not excessive' in relation to the registered purposes;

(v)   personal data must be accurate and kept up to date;

(vi)   personal data must not be kept for longer than is necessary for the registered purposes;

(vii)   an individual is entitled at reasonable intervals and without undue delay or expense to be informed as to whether personal data about him is held, to have access to such data and, where appropriate, to have it erased or corrected;

(viii) appropriate security measures must be taken against unauthorised access to, alteration and disclosure of personal data.

It will be the principle of disclosure of computerised personnel records which will be of practical concern to the employer, i.e. principle (vii) above. The individual employee is entitled to a copy of personal data held about him and where any information is expressed in unintelligible terms it must be accompanied by an explanation. So if an employer used an evaluation or other code it must be explained, e.g. HAR (High Absence Rate), A1 (Excellent worker), XX (Union Member), SWW (Second Written Warning Issued).

The employer is not obliged to supply information unless he receives a written request and he can require a fee which may not be more than £10.

A key distinction in the Act is that between an expression of opinion about an individual (which is personal data subject to disclosure) and an indication of the intentions of the data user in respect of the individual (which is not personal data and so is not subject to disclosure). So if there were an entry against Mr X which described him as 'promotable' or 'executive material' or 'idle and incompetent' or 'a union troublemaker' those statements would have to be disclosed as statements of opinion. But if the entry stated an intention to promote, demote or dismiss at the earliest opportunity, does the information become protected against disclosure? The guidance from the Registrar says it is impossible to prescribe any general rule in making the distinction but it is suggested that it cannot be possible so easily to avoid the operation of the Act by turning what are matters of opinion in substance into statements of intention in form. A statement of intention to dismiss contains within it an implication of opinion and it is within the spirit of principle (vii) that disclosure can be required. However, it is common management practice to plan changes of staff at senior level well in advance and such plans are intentions and subject to amendment according to circumstances which might or might not unfold. Provided the plans are clearly expressed as intentions they should be outside the scope of the Act's disclosure provisions. In case of uncertainty the Registrar could be approached for clarification or the data could be transferred to manual files, which are outside the scope of the Act.

Disclosure of personal data should not include data from which a third party can be identified unless the disclosing employer is satisfied that the third party has consented. In such a case the personal data should be disclosed with the omission of names or other identifying particulars of third parties. However, if an employer has registered an intention to disclose complete personnel files, he can disclose regardless of third party consent in accordance with that registration.

Generally, a data user must comply with a request for disclosure of personal data within 40 days of receiving it. The data disclosed must be that held at the time of the request except that any amendment or deletion which would have been made regardless of the request can be made between the date of request and that of supply, i.e. employers must not delete sensitive information from the data disclosed but can include any routine updating or amendment. Enforcement is through the Data Protection Registrar or through the courts.

It is a defence to a complaint of inaccurate data being held or used that the employer took reasonable care to ensure the accuracy of the data at the material time or that the data accurately records information received from a third party, e.g. the employee's doctor or referee or from the employee himself.

Chapter 4

Obligations of the Employee

4.01 Terms implied by law

The law will imply certain terms into the contract of employment to which any employee is subject. These terms can be modified or extended by express agreement but in the absence of any reference to these matters the law imposes minimum obligations. They are discussed under the following heads:

(1) a duty to work;
(2) a duty of fidelity;
(3) a duty of obedience to reasonable instructions;
(4) a duty to take reasonable care.

It should be noted that although these obligations are based on terms implied into the contract, it is unusual for an employer to enforce them through breach of contract actions. Except in respect of breach of the fidelity obligation (e.g. by unlawful competition or misuse of confidential information where damages or an injunction might be the appropriate remedy) the usual employer's reaction to failure to comply with these obligations will be dismissal. The more serious the failure to comply the more likely that a tribunal will hold a dismissal fair, subject to adherence to a fair procedure. The obligations of the employee are discussed below against the background of the law of unfair dismissal.

4.02 The employee's duty to work

Reduced to its barest essentials the employment contract is an arrangement for work in return for payment. The fundamental obligation of the employee is to work. He cannot delegate performance to another person and if he fails to work reasonably diligently he can be fairly dismissed, provided proper procedures are complied with.

What is the effect on the individual contract of employment of a disruption of work caused by concerted industrial action? Discussed below are the effects of strike action and the usual forms of industrial action short of a strike, i.e. an overtime ban, a work-to-rule, a go-slow and the withdrawal of goodwill or co-operation.

4.03 Strike action

Much of the traditional argument over the effect of strike action on the individual contract was centred on whether or not the strike was preceded by 'due strike notice', i.e. notice of sufficient length as that which would be required from the employee to terminate his contract. If the strike took place without such notice it was said to be a breach of contract. (See Lord Loreburn in *Denaby & Cadeby Main Collieries* v. *Yorkshire Miners' Association* (1906): 'In as much as the men were all working under contracts which could not be terminated except after fourteen days' notice, it is manifest that the abrupt cessation of work ... involved a breach of contract and was unlawful'.) However, if due strike notice was given some judges regarded the subsequent strike as a suspension of the contract, though not a breach. (See Lord Denning in *Morgan* v. *Fry* (1968): 'Each side is content to accept a strike notice of proper length as lawful. It is an implication read into the contract by the modern law as to trade disputes. If a strike takes place, the contract of employment is not terminated. It is suspended during the strike: and revives again when the strike is over.')

These cases are concerned with whether or not the strike is unlawful for the purposes of establishing tortious liability of the strike organisers but the latter view received endorsement and application to breach of contract actions in section 147 of the Industrial Relations Act 1971. That section declared that a strike after due strike notice could not be regarded as a breach of contract for the purposes of any proceedings in contract brought against the employee. So, whilst that Act was current an employer could not sue a striking employee for damages provided due strike notice had been given. The section fell along with the repeal of the 1971 Industrial Relations Act itself and there is no corresponding provision presently on the statute book so the position must still be regulated by the common law of contract. It seems that a strike which is *not* preceded by due strike notice is a breach but it is arguable whether or not it remains a breach if strike notice is given. Whilst such action may not be unlawful for the purposes of establishing tortious liability, it probably is still a breach of the individual contract. Certainly Mr Justice Phillips in *Simmons* v. *Hoover Ltd*

(1977) was not prepared to hold that *Morgan* v. *Fry* had changed the common law position and he regarded strike action as gross misconduct which disentitled the applicant employee to redundancy compensation. However, the debate is probably academic since it is unlikely that an employer caught up in a strike will choose to bring damages action against individual employees. The realistic aim of most employers in that situation is the resolution of the dispute and the resumption of normal working rather than the exacerbation of the dispute that such litigation would entail. Anyway, a litigious employer would, after the Employment Act 1982, sue the union rather than individual employees and if he did sue employees the measure of damages would not be easy to establish (see Chapter 9 for a discussion of damages). One case in which the employer did sue a striking employee was *National Coal Board* v. *Galley* (1958) where a strike by pit deputies in breach of contract caused a stoppage of production. The defendant was held liable in damages for the cost of a substitute worker. The case has achieved a certain standing precisely because it is a very rare example of a striker being sued by his employer. Case law in the 1980s continues to show that employers who resort to litigation at all in an industrial dispute do so in order to stop industrial action and proceed with normal business rather than to recover loss sustained during the dispute.

What is the legal position if the employer dismisses the striking employees? There has been a change of emphasis during the currency of unfair dismissal provisions but essentially it has always been the case that no striker can succeed in an action for unfair dismissal unless there is evidence of 'picking and choosing' or victimisation, i.e. some but not all the strikers are dismissed or they are all dismissed but only some are re-engaged after resolution of the dispute.

When the unfair dismissal provisions were first enacted it was declared fair to dismiss a striker, subject to the no picking and choosing rule. The present provision, section 62 EP(C)A 1978, does not say that such a dismissal is fair but removes tribunal jurisdiction over strike dismissal unless there has been unequal treatment of relevant employees. The basic principal is that if the employer dismisses all those on strike no one of them can proceed in unfair dismissal. Further, if he dismisses all the strikers he can selectively re-engage after three months without having to defend unfair dismissal actions. The three month rule was introduced by the Employment Act 1982.

The blanket exclusion of jurisdiction still applies even if employees argue that there was no dismissal but that the employer was in serious breach of contract and the strike action was reaction to the employer's breach. In *Wilkins* v. *Cantrell & Cochrane (GB) Ltd* 1978 the EAT held that the contracts still terminated by the employer's dismissal of the strikers, not by the strikers withdrawing their labour as an acceptance of the employer's own breach.

Some recent cases show that it is not always easy to identify who are the relevant employees for the purpose of the no picking and choosing rule. If an employee is on holiday or off sick whilst the strike is on, presumably he is not striking and is not included in the pool of relevant employees. However, in *Bolton Roadways Ltd* v. *Edwards* (1987) the EAT held that such an employee *is* capable of being included if he associates himself with the strike, attends the picket line or takes part in other activities of the strikers with a view to furthering their aims. The difficulty for the employer is that if he does not dismiss every employee taking part in the strike the immunity from unfair dismissal proceedings brought by any one of them is lost. However, the employer may not know if an employee, purportedly on sick leave, is actually aiding the strike. The EAT says it does not depend on the employer's knowledge but is a matter of fact for the tribunal to determine. But if the reason for the loss of immunity is because the employer has selectively dismissed the strikers it should matter whether or not the employer knew that a particular employee was participating when he decides not to dismiss him. And how can the employer cover himself in those circumstances? Perhaps the best advice would be to contact every employee to ascertain his position but there is still the risk that an employee who claims to be sick is actually supporting the strike. The uncertainty encourages employers to dismiss whoever might be in doubt.

4.04 *Industrial action short of a strike*

Section 62 EP(C)A 1978, which prevents unfair dismissal actions being brought by dismissed strikers, also applies where the dismissed employee was taking part in 'other industrial action'. In *Power Packing Casemakers* v. *Faust* (1983) the Court of Appeal held that the section applied where employees were dismissed for refusing to work non-contractual overtime. It followed that in the absence of selective dismissals, no employee could complain of unfair dismissal. There was evidence of a wage dispute between the employees and the employer and the EAT held that the refusal to work overtime was to put pressure on the employer as part of that dispute. Against that background the Court of Appeal agreed that the employees were taking industrial action and could not complain when they were dismissed.

The decision is surprising since it means that an employee has no protection against dismissal for refusing to do something which he is not obliged to do under the contract anyway, i.e. industrial action does not have to be a breach of contract. The predecessor to section 62 referred to 'irregular industrial action short of a strike' and 'irregular industrial action' was interpreted as meaning action in breach of contract. It is also surprising from the common law view of the contract: if a striker cannot complain of unfair dismissal because in withdrawing his labour he has acted in repudiatory breach, the same justification should apply only to other industrial action which is also in repudiatory breach. This case suggests that any concerted course of action by employees to put pressure on the employer may be 'other industrial action' for the purposes of section 62.

It will be easier to claim the application of section 62 to action which does constitute a breach of contract. If the overtime is obligatory under the contract, refusal to work the stipulated hours will be a breach. It is not uncommon for contracts to impose an obligation to work 'such overtime as the employer might reasonably require' in which case evidence will be needed as to what has been accepted as reasonable in the past and refusal to continue at that level will be breach of contract.

Although it sounds a contradiction in terms, a work to rule might amount to a breach of the employment contract. In *Secretary of State for Employment* v. *ASLEF (No. 2)* (1972) a work to rule by railway workers was held by the Court of Appeal to be action in breach of contract. If the work to rule is designed to cause disruption by an unreasonable interpretation and application of the letter of the contract or rule-book, that is breach of the implied term to serve the employer faithfully and diligently. Rules must be construed reasonably and fitted in sensibly with one another. So if a rule requires an engine driver to satisfy himself that the engine is in proper order a reasonable interpretation would mean periodic routine checks and reaction to any apparent malfunction. An unreasonable interpretation would be the repeated and detailed checking of the whole engine at every stop or station. Similarly, a go-slow might give the same result. If performance is not to a reasonable level or standard and circumstances suggest that failure to perform is wilful, the action will be in breach of contract.

There is some support for the view that the withdrawal of goodwill or voluntary services might constitute a breach of contract. During the lengthy teachers' dispute of 1984/5, some teachers refused to attend out of hours meetings or to supervise lunch-time or after hours sports and society activities. In *Metropolitan Borough of Solihull* v. *NUT* (1985) the High Court held that those duties might well have become contractual by performance and acceptance over a period of time. The case was brought to force the NUT to ballot their members in accordance with the Trade Union Act 1984. Under that Act a ballot is required for any industrial action in breach of contract. If no ballot is held the organising union loses its protection in tort even in respect of primary industrial action. In fact, the NUT did not appeal on the issue of whether the action *was* in breach of contract preferring instead to demonstrate the support of its members by duly conducting the ballot. However, the case is consistent with *Power Packing Casemakers* v. *Faust* and suggests that an employee dismissed for such action will be without remedy.

4.05   The employee's duty of fidelity – competition and confidential information

The cornerstone of the employment relationship is said to be mutual trust and confidence. From the employee's side this means that he is subject to an implied duty of loyalty or good faith: he must work in the best interest of his employer's trade or business, he must not divulge trade secrets or confidential information and he must not compete with his employer. This duty will be implied into the contract whilst the employment continues and may be spelled out by an express term. Such an express term may seek to protect the employer's business or commercial interests even after the particular employment ends by restricting the employee's competitive activities. However, such clauses have to be carefully drafted since any clause which unduly restricts the employee from selling his labour, skill or experience will be unenforceable as being in unlawful restraint of trade. The onus of proving that a restrictive clause is reasonable is on the party seeking to enforce it.

4.06   Competition

Normally, an employee who agrees to work a fixed number of hours is not prevented from taking other employment or working for himself in his spare time. So a machine operator who works 39 hours a week during the day for X Co. cannot be prevented from working for Y Co. as a barman during the evenings. (But if his performance during the day is adversely affected, e.g. because of tiredness, that may be a matter for discipline.) Provided his performance for X Co. is undiminished he is free to supplement his earnings during his spare time.

However, he cannot work for himself or for a competitor on highly sensitive duties. That is shown by *Hivac Ltd* v. *Park Royal Scientific Instruments Ltd* (1946). Even though no evidence was given that the employees had actually divulged confidential information an injunction was granted to restrain spare time employment with a competitor. It is significant that the work was highly skilled and highly sensitive; if it had been ordinary, mundane work the decision would have been otherwise since no harm would have been caused to the employer's business. In recent unfair dismissal cases this distinction has been re-affirmed. In one case (*Novo Plastics Ltd* v. *Froggatt* (1982)) the dismissal of an odd-job man for working for a rival concern during his spare time was held to be unfair. The EAT confirmed the tribunal view that the nature of the work done by the employee for the rival company was not something which was contributing very seriously to any competition and so the employee was not in breach of his duty of good faith. The more important the work done by an employee and the higher up the company hierarchy, the more likely that work for a competitor will be seen as in breach of the implied term.

It may be appropriate to eradicate any uncertainty by inserting an express exclusivity of service clause into the contract. (See Appendix A Part II for a sample clause.) Provided the clause is only such as is reasonably necessary to protect the employer's legitimate business interests it will be enforceable. See, for example, *Thomas Marshall (Exports) Ltd* v. *Guinle* (1978) where the defendant managing director was subject to a clause restraining him from being directly or indirectly engaged, concerned or interested in any business save that of his employing company during the running of his ten-year service agreement. The company discovered that whilst ostensibly engaged on its business, the defendant had been arranging purchases on his own behalf preparatory to setting up his own business. An injunction against the defendant was granted. Compare *Schroeder* v. *Macaulay* (1974) in which an exclusive service clause between a young, unknown songwriter and a music publishing company was held to be unreasonable and unenforceable. The company was under no obligation to publish the plaintiff's work and yet his earning potential was sterilised for five years if the company chose not to publish. The company could terminate by one month's notice, the plaintiff could not. Remuneration was by meagre advance against royalties on published work only and, if the plaintiff's work was successful he would be bound by the agreement for a further five years. The House of Lords held the exclusive service agreement to be too one-sided, oppressive and unenforceable.

After the end of the contract an employer cannot generally stop an ex-employee from competing but provided an express clause restricting subsequent activities was written into the contract and provided that clause is reasonable in terms of duration, geographical extent and the nature of the activities restrained, competition can be limited. For example, sales representatives or marketing executives can be restricted from soliciting orders from the employer's existing customers or from canvassing among the employer's business contacts in a particular area for a limited time. (See, for example, *T. Lucas & Co* v. *Mitchell* (1972) and Appendix A Part II for sample clauses.) The cases suggest that a restrictive clause would be reasonable if the intended duration is from six months to two years after termination of the contract. But the clause must not sterilise the ex-employee's earning capacity: it should restrict against soliciting existing customers, it should be confined to the smallest area necessary to protect the employer's business and should only relate to the ex-employee's previous employment duties. Thus, if the ex-employee were selling a particular product the restriction should prevent him from selling rival products to existing customers: it would not be enforceable if it purported to stop him from selling altogether.

If the restrictive clause is written into a contract for the sale and purchase of a business it seems that the goodwill of the business will be protected by a more liberal attitude to the enforceability of such a clause. For example, in *Allied Dunbar (Frank Weisinger) Ltd* v. *Weisinger* (1988), the defendant sold his financial services practice to the plaintiffs for a large sum which included goodwill and the benefit of the defendant's business contacts. The defendant was to be kept on as a consultant but the contract included a wide clause which restricted the defendant from competing for two years after the termination of his consultancy. In effect, the clause meant that the defendant would have to retire from the financial services industry for the period of the agreement. The High Court held the clause to be enforceable. A non-solicitation clause would not have been adequate to protect the plaintiff's business interests. A clause preventing non-dealing with existing customers would also have been inadequate: it would have depended on the honesty and co-operation of the defendant and would have been difficult to police. Mr Justice Mullett thought that when the purchaser had paid some £386,000 for a business and its goodwill he was entitled to the protection of a clause which did not depend on the vendor's co-operation for its effectiveness. The clause was no greater than was necessary to protect the plaintiff's legitimate business interests in the circumstances.

4.07   *Confidential information*

During the running of the contract of employment the implied duty of fidelity obliges the employee not to misuse or divulge confidential information belonging to the employer. This obligation continues after the termination of the contract and may be spelled out by an express clause. One of the leading cases on the employee's use and misuse of confidential information and the type of knowledge which falls within the protection is *Faccenda Chicken Ltd* v. *Fowler* (1986). In that case the Court of Appeal had to consider whether sales information (including the names and addresses of customers, their usual requirements, their usual delivery days, the most convenient delivery routes and prices charged) was protected against use by certain ex-employees who were engaged in a rival business. There were no express clauses in the contracts. The Court held:

(1) There is no general restriction on an ex-employee canvassing or doing business with customers of his former employer. Any such restriction has to be expressly agreed and must be reasonable (see Appendix A Part II for a draft clause).

(2) Whilst the employee remains in employment he must not disclose information concerning his employer's business which is other than trivial or within the public domain. That principle will prevent the disclosure of information about the identity and requirements of his employer's customers or the services offered by his suppliers. Also, if the employee copies or memorises a list of customers or suppliers, intending to use that information afterwards for a rival business he acts in breach of his obligation of good faith.

(3) The obligations of an ex-employee are more restricted and he is only prevented from using or disclosing information which is truly confidential, i.e. trade secrets or their equivalent. An ex-employee cannot be restrained from using general skill, know-how and knowledge which he has acquired in the course of his employment. An express clause may be useful in identifying what is confidential information in the circumstances of the particular employment. In the absence of any such clause the nature of the employment and the information will determine confidentiality. Technical information about the employer's secret manufacturing processes or unpublished data from continuing research and development will be within the protection. (It remains confidential information even if the employee carries it away in his head: it does not thereby become part of his general skill and knowledge – see *Johnson & Bloy Holdings Ltd* v. *Wolstenholme Rink plc & Fallon* (1987).) Also relevant will be whether

confidentiality in relation to particular information was stressed by the employer and whether it is severable from the package of knowledge and experience which the employee is free to disclose and use.

Applying those principles to the facts of the case the Court of Appeal held that the sales information was not confidential and its use could not be restrained. The non-price information was within the ex-employee's skill and experience as recollections from employment and though it was of value to a competitor it was not a trade secret nor sensitive. Neither was it information access to which was restricted to senior management or confidential staff. It was generally known to employees at a comparatively junior level. The price information was not severable from the rest and there were no instructions about its confidentiality. Note that the Court of Appeal recognised that price information may well constitute confidential information in other circumstances. Where it is a crucial part of a tender document or where product competition is especially vigorous, prices may be business secrets. (See, for example, *Dyer* v. *Inverclyde Taxis Ltd* (1988) where the dismissal of a woman whose husband worked for a rival taxi firm was held fair since she had access to charges rates which was highly sensitive information for the purposes of competitive tendering. The tribunal held the employers had reasonable grounds for believing that the confidentiality of the information was at risk.)

4.08 *Inventions and research – patents and copyright*

At common law it was part of the implied term of faithful service that inventions produced or made by the employee in the course of his employment belonged to the employer. Whether the invention was made in the course of employment depended on the status of the employee, his duties, whether he used the employer's equipment and premises or the employer's time. The courts had little difficulty in finding that research, development and design workers made their discoveries in the course of employment and in *Sterling Engineering Co. Ltd* v. *Patchett* (1955) a production engineer who designed a paragun with an automatic trigger mechanism was held to have done so in the course of his employment so that the employer had patent rights.

Instead of relying on the uncertain extent of the implied term, it was common practice for employers to insert an express clause which vested ownership of employee's inventions in the employer, whether or not such inventions would have been treated as having been achieved in the course of employment. Such terms were generally regarded as enforceable. The common law was replaced by the Patents

Act 1977 but the position remains basically the same. Section 39 of the 1977 Act provides that an invention made by an employee shall belong to the employer if

(a) it was made in the course of the employee's normal duties or duties specifically assigned to him from which an invention might reasonably be expected to result, or
(b) it was made in the course of his duties, the particular responsibilities of which gave him a special obligation to further the interests of the employer's undertaking.

Any other invention belongs to the employee.

Design engineers, research and development workers would fall within (a), and (b) would probably cover employees having no special research function but who are sufficiently senior as to owe a high duty to the employer which extends the obligations of fidelity. One case which might be decided differently under section 39 1977 Patents Act is *Re Seltz Ltd's Application* (1953). The finding there was that a general manager of a lampshade manufacturer could patent in his own name an idea for adapting spray-plastic packing. He first saw this packaging whilst visiting an exhibition on the employer's behalf but he was not employed on research and development. Such a member of senior management might in those circumstances be taken under the Act to have particular responsibilities giving him a special obligation to further the employer's interests. The debates during the Act's progress through parliament suggest that that was what was intended. Indeed, in *Reiss Engineering Co. Ltd* v. *Harris* (1985) the judge said that whether an employee had a 'special obligation' depended on his status. There the employee, a sales manager, sold valves and provided an after-sales service. It was never part of his normal duties to apply his mind to defects and problems arising from the design of the valves. Whilst under notice of redundancy the employee invented a new type of valve which eliminated many of the operational problems of those sold by the employers. The High Court held that the patent belonged to the employee. He did not have a special obligation to further the employer's interests. The judge said that the duties of a managing director would extend across the whole spectrum of the employing company's activities but those of a sales manager such as the respondent did not.

Although section 39 of the Patents Act 1977 will determine ownership of an invention, section 40 enables the employee to apply for compensation from the employer where the patent is of 'outstanding benefit' to the employer. The compensation awarded should give the employee 'a fair share' of the benefit of the patent, having regard to his duties and remuneration and the effort and skill which he devoted to the invention. Section 42 of the Act prevents any express clause of a contract between the employer and employee from diminishing the employee's statutory rights.

Copyright confers a right to restrain infringement for 50 years. Under the Copyright Act 1956, the employer is the first owner of copyright in an original literary, dramatic or musical work if the maker produced the work in the course of his employment. Again, the issue is whether the creation of the work was in the course of employment and it will depend on the nature of the employee's duties. In *Beloff* v. *Pressdram Ltd* (1973) copyright in a memorandum written by the plaintiff political and lobby correspondent of *The Observer* newspaper was held to belong to the employers, the newspaper proprietors. In *Stevenson, Jordan & Harrison Ltd* v. *Macdonald & Evans* (1952) copyright in part of a book by an employed management consultant was held to belong to the employing firm. The employers owned copyright in that part of the book which was based on a particular assignment carried out by the employee on behalf of the firm. The part not covered by employer's copyright was made up of lectures given by the employee in his spare time or derived from his general skill and expertise.

The Copyright Act 1956 will be repealed when assent is given to the 1988 Copyright, Designs and Patents Bill. That Bill includes artistic works (graphics, photographs, sculptures, architectural models, etc.) and restates the presumption that where a literary, dramatic, musical or artistic work is made by an employee in the course of his employment, his employer is the first owner of copyright subject to any agreement to the contrary. However, the Bill gives the author the moral right to be identified whenever the work is published commercially, broadcast or performed or exhibited in public provided he has asserted that right by signed written document. The moral right does not apply to computer programs or computer-generated work nor where copyright would not be infringed. The employed author also has a moral right not to have copyright works falsely attributed to him in public. Infringement of these moral rights is actionable as a breach of statutory duty.

4.09 *Obedience to reasonable instructions*

The implied term of obedience to the employer's reasonable instructions is illustrated by some of the older wrongful dismissal cases. For example, in one case in 1845 a domestic servant was held to be lawfully dismissed for taking time off to visit her dying mother when the employer had refused permission. But what was reasonable in 1845 is not necessarily reasonable in 1988 and it is unlikely that a court or tribunal would regard dismissal in those circumstances now as lawful or fair. Indeed, in a case in 1959 the Court of Appeal doubted the scope of the earlier decision and said that a single act of disobedience could justify dismissal only if it showed that the employee was repudiating the contract by an act of wilful disobedience.

These days any issue of disobedience is likely to be part of an employer's defence to an action in unfair dismissal. To make out that defence the employer would have to show that the performance required was properly required under the employee's contract. There may be a dispute between the parties over where the employee could be required to work for example. If the employer is not entitled to require performance in the locality to which the employee was directed dismissal will be unfair. Or if the instruction is not reasonable in terms of the employee's status, dismissal will be unfair. Even if the instruction is legitimately given, the employer's action in dismissing will be judged against the standard of reasonableness in section 57(3) EP(C)A 1978. An employer should ensure that a fair dismissal procedure is complied with (see Chapter 9).

4.10   Reasonable care

As with the implied duty of obedience, the duty of the employee to take reasonable care over the performance of his contractual duties will commonly be measured in terms of the lawfulness of the employer's dismissal. So in wrongful dismissal actions, gross negligence or deliberate disregard of business standards by the employee led to findings of lawful dismissal. Similar gross breach would result in a finding of fair dismissal from an industrial tribunal. However, it is more commonly the case that the employee's conduct is not gross or deliberate but nevertheless his performance fails to measure up to the employer's required standard. In such a case a system of warnings and a careful monitoring of performance will be expected by a tribunal before a defence to an unfair dismissal is likely to succeed. If new procedures have been introduced or higher standards of performance are expected by, for example, a newly appointed manager, it may be appropriate for a period of instruction or training to be given to the employee. Again, the fairness of dismissal will depend on the statutory test of section 57(3) EP(C)A 1978 (see Chapter 9).

Note that an employee has a statutory duty under the Health and Safety At Work Act 1974 to take reasonable care for the safety of himself and other persons who may be affected by his acts or omissions at work. He is also under a duty to co-operate with the employer to enable the employer to comply with his statutory obligations. Any employee who intentionally or recklessly interferes with or misuses any safety measure or equipment is likely to be found fairly dismissed. So also is an employee who deliberately disobeys reasonable instructions to use safety equipment.

Chapter 5

The Contract of Employment, Collective Agreements and Employers' Rule Books

5.01 Collective agreements

Although British law still regards the relationship between employer and employee as regulated by the individual contract of employment, in reality the collective agreement is the most important source of terms and conditions of employment. Although trade union membership has fallen in the mid to late 1980s, collective bargaining still directly affects three-quarters of the working population. The enforceability of the collective agreements as between the parties to it, i.e. the employer or employers' organisation and the trade union or unions is separate from the enforceability as between the employer and the individual employee. The law of contract has a 'privity' rule, i.e. no-one other than a party to the contract can sue or be sued on that contract. It follows that the employee, a member of the union, is neither bound nor benefited by anything in a collective agreement unless he can be regarded as having become a party to it under agency principles or because the agreement has become incorporated into his individual contract with the employer.

5.02 The union as agent

If the union were acting as agent for the individual members employed by a particular employer or group of employers, those members would be taken to have given their authority to allow the union to reach agreement on their behalf and they would be bound by the agreement as principals. However, there are many difficulties in applying agency rules to collective bargaining. How are non-member employees affected? Can individual members terminate the authority to represent them? What is the extent of the authority and where is it to be found? British law does not normally regard a union as acting as agent for its members during collective bargaining unless there is a specific agency agreement between the individual member and the union. See for example *The Burton Group Ltd* v. *Smith* (1977), in which the issue between the parties was whether S's contract of employment was terminated by dismissal for redundancy or by his death. S's union had reached agreement with his employers that voluntary redundancies would be effective in December. S was absent from work because of sickness and his application for voluntary redundancy had been accepted but no effective date of termination had been agreed. He died in October. It was argued on his behalf that the agreement between the union and his employer fixed his termination date in December and he was therefore dismissed for redundancy and his widow was entitled to redundancy compensation. The EAT rejected that argument and concluded that the union representatives did not act as S's agents in agreeing a termination date. An agency relationship between union and member does not stem from membership alone. The EAT said that it must be supported in the particular case by the creation of some specific agency which can arise only if the evidence supports the conclusion that there was such an agency. That might arise where the union representative is negotiating on behalf of a specified member. On the facts of the present case there was no evidence of the existence of such an agency. It followed that S's contract was terminated by death, not by dismissal for redundancy.

The case admits of the possibility that the union representatives could have acted as S's agents in agreeing termination of S's contract. If S had given the representatives authority to reach that agreement and the employers had negotiated with them on that basis then they, and S, would have been bound and benefited by the agreement. Likewise, if a member gives union representatives specific authority to negotiate on his behalf in relation to, for example, disciplinary matters there may be a specific agency relationship. But usually the union representatives have no collective agency functions in negotiating collective terms and conditions. See for a further example *Ellis* v. *Brighton Co-operative Society Ltd* (1976) where the EAT refused to hold that E was contractually bound to comply with a reorganisation of duties and hours simply because his union had agreed the reorganisation with management. The union did not act as E's agent. (Note, however, that E was still found to have been fairly dismissed under the 'some other substantial reason' head of dismissal.)

5.03 *Incorporation of collective agreements*

The usual way in which collective agreements effect the individual employee's terms and conditions of service is by their incorporation into the individual's contract of employment. Indeed the whole point of collective bargaining is that contracts of employment will be subject to collective agreements and there is often an express clause of incorporation in the individual's contract or written statement of main contract terms. So in *National Coal Board* v. *Galley* (1958), mining deputies' contracts stated that they were subject to 'national agreements for the time being in force' between the NCB and NACODS, the deputies' union. The NCB were able to sue NACODS members for breach of contract in failing to comply with the collective agreement.

The written statement of main contract terms which employers are required to issue within 13 weeks of the beginning of employment is a very useful mechanism for express incorporation of collective agreements. Employers do not have to hand copies of the collective agreement to every employee but need only refer to collective agreements from specified bargaining units. If the statement provides that the terms of employment in any sphere shall be in accordance with the agreements 'reached from time to time' or 'for the time being in force' or 'as varied from time to time', then amendments will be binding on the individual employees without the need for individual documentation of variation. The collective agreement in its current form must be reasonably accessible for the employees affected by it and they must be given reasonable opportunities of reading it. It is often the case that all employees' contracts expressly incorporate collective agreements so as to make the employees bound by the terms of those agreements whether or not they are members of the union which is party to the collective agreement.

For examples of express incorporation of collective agreements see *Murray* v. *Robert Rome & Son (Rutherglen) Ltd* (1969) and *Lister* v. *Fram Gerrard Ltd* (1973). Both cases were concerned with whether the employer was entitled to transfer the employee to a different place of work. If not, the employees were redundant and entitled to compensation. In the *Murray* case the contract expressly incorporated the rules of the Scottish National Joint Council for the Plumbing Industry. Those rules contained no limitation on place of work but provided for travelling expenses and lodging allowances. The Scottish Court of Session held that the employer did have the right to transfer. In the *Lister* case the contract stated that the Working Rule Agreement of the Civil Engineering Construction Conciliation Board for Great Britain was incorporated. The Working Rule Agreement envisaged transfer of employees to any site not more than two hours' travelling distance from their homes. Again, the employee was bound by that right of transfer.

5.04   Implied incorporation

If there is no clause of express incorporation it is possible that terms of collective agreements can be *impliedly* incorporated into the individual contract. As has been noted before (see section 2.06) it is not possible to imply anything which is inconsistent with an express term so if the individual contract has a clause specifically providing for wages of £*x* per week it cannot be easily argued that a relevant collective agreement which fixes wages at £*x* + *y* weekly impliedly governs the situation. But, subject to that qualification, the courts have been willing to allow the principle of implied incorporation for a long time. In *Hill* v. *Levy* (1858) there was a dispute between compositors and master printers about the payment rates due to compositors for printing advertisements on magazine wrappers. The judge referred to the disputants' practice over fifty years as accepting agreements from representative committees as regulating their business relations. Those agreements had been treated and acted upon as binding and were taken to be imported into every engagement between master printer and compositor.

The basis of implied incorporation depends on custom and practice or knowledge and acquiescence of the parties which supports the implication that there was an intention to accept the terms of the collective agreement. A similar justification was used to support implied incorporation in *Joel* v. *Camel Laird (Ship-Repairers) Ltd* (1969). The employee refused to comply with his employers' instructions to move from repair work to shipbuilding work. A collective agreement between the employers and the employee's union which granted substantial wage increases also provided that employees could be interchanged between repair work and shipbuilding work. An industrial tribunal held that the employee knew of the collective agreement, he had accepted benefits under it and he had seen other employees transferred under it. In those circumstances he was taken to be bound by the transfer clause.

That case must be contrasted with *Young* v. *Canadian Northern Railway* (1931). Y was employed as a machinist at the 'going rate' of wages and was dismissed on the ground of reduction of staff numbers. He claimed that the dismissal was wrongful since it was in breach of a current wages agreement with the union which embodied the 'last in, first out' principle. The employers had not dismissed men with less service than Y. The Privy Council held that the wages agreement was not part of Y's contract in spite of the fact that the employers had paid Y in accordance with it. According to the Privy Council, the employers may have applied it to Y, not because they intended to be contractually bound but because as a matter of policy it was expedient to apply it to all employees. Further, the agreement was not apt for incorporation into individual contracts; it was a document of some 188 'rules' governing the relationship between the employers and the union. The tribunal in the *Joel* case were evidently concerned about the precedent in *Young* but distinguished that decision on the facts of the case and preferred to treat it as no more than support for the proposition that collective agreements are not *necessarily* incorporated into individual contracts. A better distinction may be that in *Young*, Y was not a member of the union and it was difficult to see how any consideration had moved from him to justify entitlement under the collective agreement. In *Joel* the tribunal were impressed by the fact that the employee was very conscious of his trade union activities and consideration did move both ways. Also, in *Young* the action supporting incorporation was by the party to the collective agreement. That was not real evidence of any intention to change contractual terms in relation to a third party. In *Joel* the action which justified incorporation was that of the third party, i.e. the employee, and he could not approve and disapprove at the same time.

More recently, in *British Leyland Ltd* v. *McQuilken* (1978) the EAT treated the *Young* case as supporting the contention that collective agreements are not necessarily incorporated into individual contracts of employment. In *McQuilken*, the EAT found that a collective agreement under which employees were to be given the choice of retraining or redundancy was not part of M's contract even though he was a member of the union which had concluded the agreement. The EAT held that the collective agreement was a long-term plan dealing with policy rather than the rights of individual employees so M did not have the right to insist on redundancy and compensation rather than retraining and transfer.

5.05   Binding in honour only – effect

It was generally understood that irrespective of whether or not a collective agreement was enforceable as between the parties to it, if it had become expressly or impliedly incorporated into individual contracts of employment it was binding as between employer and employee. In *Marley* v. *Forward Trust Group Ltd* (1986) the EAT held that a collective agreement which contained a clause stating that it was binding in honour only was not capable of creating legal obligations even when it was incorporated into the individual contract of employment. According to the EAT, it was the whole agreement which was incorporated including the 'binding in honour only' clause. If that decision had stood it would have had considerable consequences for the law and practice of labour relations since wage rates are commonly derived from collective agreements which are traditionally binding in honour only. The EAT seemed to overlook the fact that the 'binding in honour only' clauses were written into collective agreements during the currency of the 1971 Industrial Relations Act when there was a statutory presumption in the absence of evidence to the contrary that collective agreements *were* intended to be legally binding. Binding in honour clauses were inserted as standard practice to prevent the operation of that statutory presumption. The 1971 provision was repealed in 1974 but the binding in honour only clauses were sometimes left in collective agreements, not to achieve anything but more because of inertia. They simply were not taken out. Fortunately, the Court of Appeal reversed the EAT decision and held that even though a collective agreement which is binding in honour only may be unenforceable between the parties to it, it is binding as part of the individual employer's contract when it is incorporated.

Remaining problems with the incorporation of collective terms are the effect on the employment contract if the collective agreement is terminated, resolution of conflicting collective agreements and whether procedural collective agreements are apt for incorporation.

5.06 Termination of the collective agreement

If either party to the collective agreement or collective bargaining machinery pulls out of the arrangement, does the incorporation of any current collective agreement cease? Normally it does not since the relationship between the employer and the employee is determined by the contract of employment and any collective agreement which is incorporated into it will be binding until a mutual agreement between the employer and employee provides otherwise. The employer cannot unilaterally withdraw from incorporated agreements derived from bargaining between unions and an employers' association merely because he leaves the association or because the union withdraws from the agreement. See, for example, *Gibbons* v. *Associated British Ports* (1985) where the High Court held that employers were not entitled to reduce dock workers' guaranteed minimum weekly payment which had been incorporated into contracts because the collective agreement itself broke down. Termination of the collective agreement could not affect the existing terms of remuneration incorporated into the individual dock worker's contract. That term could only be varied with the employee's agreement, whether express or implied as in the case of a new rate negotiated on his behalf. The employees were entitled to stand on their existing rights under the contract.

A similar result was reached by the Court of Appeal in *Robertson & Jackson* v. *British Gas Corporation* (1983). Two meter readers/collectors successfuly claimed damages after their employer unilaterally gave notice to terminate incentive bonus payments. The contracts stated that an incentive bonus scheme would apply and the conditions were as determined under a collective agreement. The collective agreement modified the scheme's operation and payment levels from time to time but also enabled parties to terminate the arrangement. The Court of Appeal held that the employer's termination of the collectively agreed scheme did not affect the individual's entitlement to bonus payments under the contract of employment.

However, if an express clause of incorporation provides that incorporation should continue only so long as the employer remains party to the collective agreement or collective bargaining machinery it is difficult to see how, on normal contract principles, a court or tribunal could regard incorporation as continuing to bind employer and employee where the employer terminates his membership of the collective unit. Nevertheless, the Court of Session approached that result in *Burroughs Machines Ltd* v. *Timmoney* (1977). The employers had been members of the Engineering Employers Federation (EEF) which was party to a collective agreement providing for a guaranteed week. That guarantee was suspended under the agreement if production was disrupted due to an industrial dispute in a 'federated establishment'. The agreement was incorporated into employees' contracts. The employers left the EEF and thereby ceased to be a 'federated establishment' for the purposes of the suspension rule. However, the Court of Session held that the guaranteed week entitlement incorporated into the employee's contract continued on the basis that entitlement was suspended during industrial action at the employer's premises. The Court of Session refused to apply a literal reading to the incorporated term and said that common sense dictated that the guaranteed week provisions had to be interdependent terms. That must have been what the parties intended.

Instead of relying on a commonsense interpretation from the courts, which may or may not be forthcoming, where an employer wants to be sure to be subject to minimum pay or other obligations only so long as he obtains the benefit of collectivity, his clauses of incorporation in individual contracts should be very carefully worded and leave no room for uncertainty or argument. A suggested draft is as follows:

> 'Provisions fixing [minimum weekly pay rates] shall be those
> determined from time to time by agreement between the ...
> [employer's association] and the ... [union]. These provisions shall
> be incorporated into this contract and shall have effect for so long as
> the employer remains a member of the ... [employer's association].'

5.07 Resolution of conflicting collective agreements

It may be that collective agreements differ at varying levels of
bargaining, so that a local agreement is inconsistent with a national
agreement. In well-ordered circumstances correct drafting of incorporation clauses should provide resolution of any such inconsistency.
Certainly, no clear principle of resolution emerges from the cases. In
Loman & Henderson v. *Merseyside Transport Services* (1968) the issue between
employees and employer was the normal working week. A national
collective agreement said it was 41 hours, a local agreement said it was
68 hours. The tribunal awarded redundancy compensation on the
basis of a 41 hour week, saying that the local agreement had no binding
force. But as has been pointed out above, the enforceability of the
collective agreement by the parties to it should not determine the
enforceability of any term derived from it and incorporated into the
agreement between employer and employee. In *Gascol Conversions Ltd* v.
Mercer (1974) a 1970 national agreement provided for a 40 hour week
but a 1971 local agreement made it 54 hours. A written statement of
contract terms issued in 1972 followed the national agreement and the
employee signed a receipt confirming the 'new contract of employment'. The Court of Appeal held redundancy compensation was to be
calculated on the basis of a 40 hour working week but reached that
decision largely because of the employee's acceptance of the written
statement as embodying the contract terms. Lord Denning did say in
the course of his judgment that he did not think the local agreement
should be regarded as varying the national agreement and in any event
the national agreement contained a clause stating it should take
precedence over local agreements. But that could have been interpreted as applying only to existing local agreements and if circumstances showed that the employer incorporated a later local agreement into
his contractual dealings with his employees that should take
precedence.

So, the usual unsatisfactory answer to resolution of conflicting
collective agreements must be that it depends on the circumstances

and what the parties can be taken to have agreed. Again, a careful employer will have a clear corporation clause which brooks no debate, such as the following:

'The normal weekly hours of work [or other matter] shall be those determined from time to time by agreement between ... [the employer or employers' association] and ... [the unions]. Where any conflict or ambiguity exists between agreements concluded at local and national (or regional area, etc.) level the national agreement shall take precedence unless a later local agreement contains a provision to the contrary.'

5. 08   *Procedural collective agreements*

Where the procedural collective agreement contains procedures intended to affect the individual's relationship with the employer, incorporation is appropriate. That will be so where, for example, disciplinary and grievance procedures are collectively determined. But certain collective agreements are not apt for incorporation into individual contracts because they are intended to regulate the collective relationship between employer(s) and union(s) only. For example, arbitration and conciliation agreements for resolution of a collective dispute may not appropriately be incorporated into the contract. A usual view is that 'peace clauses' create collective not individual obligations. See, for example, *National Coal Board* v. *National Union of Mineworkers* (1986) where the NUM, trying to force the NCB to continue with a collective conciliation agreement which gave it exclusive recognition and negotiation rights and shut out the nascent UDM, argued that the agreement was incorporated into individual members' contracts with the NCB. The High Court held a clause of incorporation under which miners' wages and conditions of service were regulated by and subject to national agreements for the time being in force referred only to those national agreements which contained substantive provisions regarding wages or conditions of service. The procedural provisions were not apt for contractual enforcement by individual employees. The High Court regarded it as 'almost inconceivable' that a collective agreement providing machinery for collective bargaining and for resolving industrial disputes could have been intended to become legally enforceable by an individual worker. No part was played by any individual worker in the procedures laid down by the collective agreement: the machinery was designed to be invoked and operated either by the NCB or NUM.

Statute endorses that attitude towards procedural collective agreements at least so far as no-strike procedures are concerned. Clearly such procedural agreements do require the individual employee to play a part. Section 18(4) of the Trade Union and Labour Relations Act 1974 requires unambiguous and detailed steps to be taken before an individual employee is bound by a no-strike arrangement in a collective agreement. The collective agreement itself must be written, it must contain a provision expressly providing for incorporation into employees' contracts, it must be reasonably accessible to the employees at the workplace and available for them to consult during working hours. Every trade union which is a party to it must be an independent trade union and the individual contract must expressly or impliedly incorporate the agreement.

5.09 Employers' rule books

It is not uncommon for employers to issue workers with a book of works rules or to attach the rules to the written statement of contract terms or to display them at the workplace. It may be that these rule books are negotiated with employees' representatives in which case the effect on the individual contract will be as for collective agreements generally. If the rule book is not collectively agreed but is the employer's formulation of what he expects to happen then whether the individual employee is in fact bound by its terms depends on usual principles of contract law. If the contract expressly incorporates the rule book, the employee works subject to it. If the rule book accompanies the written statement of contract terms then its effect is commensurate with that of the written statement (see Chapter 2). The rule book may be regarded as impliedly accepted if the evidence shows that the employees knew of it, accepted it and worked under it. However, the employer would have a stronger case if he could adduce evidence of acceptance of the particular term relied on rather than acceptance of a different part of the rule book than that which he wishes to enforce. It would be preferable to insert an express clause of incorporation rather than to rely subsequently on the vagaries of implied incorporation. Even then, an employer should be careful to ensure that when actual practice does not accord with the rule book he periodically re-asserts his entitlement to rely on the rule book. Otherwise he may be regarded as having accepted variation by his conduct.

The following cases illustrate the application of some of the above principles.

Sutcliffe v. *Hawker Siddeley Ltd* (1973)

A written contract of employment provided that an attached document entitled 'Points for Guidance' was deemed to be incorporated into the contract and binding on both parties. The Points for Guidance provided that outworkers should be prepared to travel to outworking stations anywhere in the United Kingdom. The employee was held bound by that provision.

Pearson v. *William Jones Ltd* (1967)

A written statement of contract terms provided that normal working hours were in accordance with the works rules. The works rules stated that these were forty hours. The employee claimed that notwithstanding the works rules he regularly worked substantial overtime and his redundancy entitlement should have been calculated on the higher weekly hours. The High Court held that the works rule fixing normal weekly hours at 40 did apply. The employee was not obliged to work overtime and neither was the employer obliged to provide it.

Chapter 6

How to Manage Change

6.01 Is a change in practice a change in law?

An employer cannot unilaterally impose a change in the terms and conditions of employment on an employee. The relationship is based on agreement and any variation of the terms of that agreement must be by mutual consent. If the employer does attempt to impose a change without seeking agreement he acts in breach of contract and, depending on the seriousness of the breach, he may be liable in damages or the employee may resign and claim that he has been constructively dismissed.

However, not all changes in employment practices will be variation of the contract terms. If express terms are widely drafted to give the employer flexibility over, e.g. place of work or the nature of the duties, the employer acts in accordance with those terms, not in breach of them, if he modifies the pre-existing practice. Also, case law has established that, provided the essential function of the job remains the same, an employee is expected to adapt himself to new methods and technology.

In *Cresswell* v. *Board of Inland Revenue* (1984) members of the Inland Revenue Staff Federation who were all involved in the administration of the Pay As You Earn tax scheme, objected to the computerisation of the scheme because the Inland Revenue would give no guarantee that there would be no compulsory redundancies in consequence of computerisation. Members of the Federation refused to operate the computerised system but went on with the old manual system. They sought a declaration from the High Court that they were not bound under their contracts of employment to change the manner of performance of their duties and were entitled to refuse to operate the computerised system. They asked the High Court to declare that the employers were acting in breach of contract in insisting on the utilisation of the new technology or suspending (with or without pay) members for refusing to operate it. The High Court dismissed the action. The judge said that an employee is expected to adapt himself to

81

new methods and techniques introduced in the course of his employment, subject to the employer providing any necessary training. He said:

> 'It can hardly be considered that to ask an employee to acquire basic skills as to retrieving information from a computer or feeding such information into a computer is something in the slightest esoteric or unusual.'

On the facts of the case, the essential nature of the jobs had not changed by computerisation and although modern methods of performance had been introduced, no job had been altered sufficiently to fall outside the original job discription.

It follows from the *Cresswell* case that an accounts clerk, previously engaged on the compilation of manual figures and records can be asked to work instead with computer-produced information. A typist engaged to work with a manual or electronic typewriter can be asked to operate a word processor. A library assistant used to a card index system of cataloguing can be asked to change to microfiche or computer-based data. In such cases the employer would be obliged to provide reasonable instruction on the new methods.

6.02   Variation of contract

If the employer changes the nature of the duties, the starting point remains a consideration of whether the change is or is not a variation of the contract. That depends on what the employee could have been called upon to do under the contract, rather than that which he was actually engaged upon at the time of the change. In *O'Neill* v. *Merseyside Plumbing Co. Ltd* (1973) the employee had worked with the employers as a gas fitter for nearly 25 years. Then the employers directed him to work at a hospital site as a general plumber. He claimed he was not employed as a plumber, the work offered was different in nature and his job as a gas fitter was redundant. The issue was whether, though he had actually worked as a gas fitter for 25 years, the employers were entitled to employ him on other forms of plumbing work. That was a matter for interpretation by the tribunal, to whom the case was remitted.

The Court of Appeal held likewise in *Haden Ltd* v. *Cowen* (1982) and *Nelson* v. *BBC* (1977) that it is what the employer was entitled to require under the contract rather than what was in fact being required in practice which determines legality of the employer's action. It is, of course, possible that a wider express term will be seen as having been modified by long usage into a restricted term. So if an employer has a widely drafted flexibility clause in the contract but has never relied on it in many years or has led the employee to believe that it never will be relied upon, a tribunal may conclude that that term has been modified by implied agreement where practice differs from entitlement. An employer should take all reasonable steps to bring to the employee's attention his wider contractual entitlement.

6.03 *Agreeing variation of contracts*

If it is clear that the change proposed by the employer would be a variation of contract he should try to negotiate the agreement of the employee(s). Most employers in these circumstances wish to achieve a smooth, effective change in working practices without causing loss of co-operation, resignations or dismissals. It may be that where the need for the change is explained and justified to the employee(s), it is accepted. Or, negotiation may lead to payment of compensation for loss of a beneficial term or a 'buying-out' of the pre-existing practice. It may be appropriate to time the change of terms to make it coincide with a pay review and then link the acceptance of the change with a wage/salary award. Many employers used that device to change from cash to non-cash wages after the enactment of the Wages Act 1986. Or, if an employee is being promoted the change can be incorporated into the new contract terms. Where a variation has been agreed by the employee(s) affected and it relates to one of the particulars which must be included in the written statement (see Chapter 2), the employer should issue an amended written statement within one month of the change. The obligation is met by the employer referring the employee(s) to a reasonably accessible document setting out the varied term.

Employers should be careful to note that agreement to the variation by the union can not necessarily to taken to bind the individual employees represented by that union. Unions are not usually regarded as the agents of their members in respect of collective bargaining (see paragraph [5.02] above and *Ellis* v. *Brighton Co-operative Society Ltd* (1976)).

6.04 *Effect of imposed change*

If the employer does not obtain the agreement of the employee(s) to a variation of contract terms but nevertheless imposes the change unilaterally, he acts in breach of contract. If the variation is substantial, that action may result in the employee claiming constructive unfair dismissal, constructive redundancy dismissal or damages for breach of contract. The following recent case illustrates quite clearly how *not* to manage change.

In *Rigby* v. *Ferodo Ltd* (1987), as a result of a severe financial crisis, the employers tried to agree a wage reduction with the unions representing their employees. The plaintiff, a lathe operator, was a member of the only union which stood out against the wage decrease. Nevertheless the employers promulgated and acted on the new wage rates which had the effect of cutting the plaintiff's pay by some £30 per week. The plaintiff objected to the variation but continued working and claimed damages. It was significant that the employers had *not* terminated the old contracts and offered employment at the new wage rates. The courts held that the old contract continued and the plaintiff was entitled to damages representing the difference between the old contract wages to which he was entitled and the new wage rates which he received for the *complete* period between the imposed change and the date of the hearing, some three and a half years later. The courts held that there was no effective variation in the absence of agreement and rejected the employers' contention that since they could have dismissed lawfully by giving 12 weeks' notice, damages should be limited to that 12-week period. The employers also argued that if they had acted in repudiatory breach of contract in unilaterally imposing a wage cut, that repudiatory breach brought the contract to an end automatically without the need of any acceptance by the employee. If that was the situation, the plaintiff must be taken to have been working under the new terms in the meantime. The courts also rejected that argument. The House of Lords dismissed the employers' appeal. The employers had never given notice of termination and even if it were possible for conduct to amount to implied notice of termination that contention was not borne out by the facts of the case. Indeed, the employers had implemented a policy designed to keep the whole workforce in employment. Nor could it be accepted that the plaintiff had impliedly accepted the wage reduction by working on. He had clearly and repeatedly made his objection to the wage cut plain. He had not acquiesced in the change or waived his remedy for breach of contract.

A similar result was reached in *Miller* v. *Hamworth Engineering Ltd* (1986). The employers introduced a three-day short time working week, which resulted in the plaintiff suffering a shortfall in his weekly wage. He had not agreed to the change and the Court of Appeal held he was entitled to damages representing his net loss of wages.

These cases serve as a salutary warning to an employer that, wherever an agreement to a substantial variation cannot be secured, he should dismiss and offer new contracts on the changed terms to the dissidents. Then the maximum period for which damages could be awarded by the ordinary courts would be limited to the contractual notice period.

6.05   *Variation of contract terms and unfair dismissal*

The discussion above shows that an employer wishing to impose changed terms and conditions of employment on dissident employees is best advised to dismiss and offer new employment on the changed terms. That would limit the maximum period for which damages for breach of contract could be granted to the duration of the notice period. Breach of contract actions are heard by the ordinary courts, i.e. the County Court or High Court, depending on the amount of damages claimed. However, if the employer does dismiss, the employees affected may bring actions in unfair dismissal, provided they have the necessary two years' qualifying service at the date of dismissal. The action in unfair dismissal is heard by an industrial tribunal. The substantive provisions on unfair dismissal are contained in Part V of the Employment Protection (Consolidation) Act 1978 (EP(C)A). There is ample authority to show that in such a situation the reason for dismissal would be a 'substantial reason of a kind as to justify dismissal' within the meaning of section 57(1)(b) of the EP(C)A 1978. Then the fairness or otherwise of the dismissal would be judged by the tribunal against the test in section 57(3), i.e. whether in the circumstances, including the size and administrative resources of the employer's undertaking, he acted reasonably or unreasonably in dismissing the employee. Reasonableness is determined in accordance with equity and the substantial merits of the case.

One of the leading cases on business changes and unfair dismissal is *Hollister* v. *National Farmers' Union* (1979). H was employed as group secretary of the NFU in Cornwall. Most of his remuneration came about through commission on insurance effected through the Cornish Mutual Association. The NFU decided to reorganise its business and transfer insurance away from the Cornish Mutual Association. That meant changed terms and different working methods for H. H protested about the change and after fruitless negotiations and his refusal to accept the new terms, he was dismissed. The Court of Appeal reinstated the industrial tribunal decision that the dismissal was fair. The Master of the Rolls said that where it is essential as a result of a reorganisation that new contracts of employment be made, the only sensible way to deal with the situation is to terminate existing contracts and offer reasonable new ones. Consultation, or the lack of it, will be a factor for the tribunal to take into account in deciding whether the employer acted reasonably. But the issue of fairness was a matter for the industrial tribunal and the Employment Appeal Tribunal was wrong to interfere with its finding.

In *Chubb Fire Security Ltd* v. *Harper* (1983) the EAT approved the *Hollister* approach. The tribunal should consider the advantages to the employer of the proposed reorganisation and whether it was reasonable for him to implement them by terminating existing contracts and offering new ones. The cases stress management prerogative in determining on reorganisation but, to increase the chances of a finding of fair dismissal, employers should demonstrate the need for the reorganisation proposed and show attempts at negotiation and consultation. Also, the new terms offered should be reasonable in the circumstances. For example, in *Evans* v. *Elemeta Holdings Ltd* (1982) the EAT reversed a finding of fair dismissal where the new terms obliged the employee to work unlimited overtime during the week and up to four hours on Saturdays. That obligation was objectionable and oppressive and the tribunal had misdirected itself in finding the dismissal reasonable within section 57(3) EP(C)A 1978.

Several cases stress the relevance to fairness of the availability of alternative employment. If the employer reorganises so that the nature of the employee's job is very different, in order to defend a claim of unfair dismissal, he should consider the suitability of that employee for the new position. If he is not suitable, he should consider whether there is any alternative job available to which he could be moved. In *Oakley* v. *The Labour Party* (1988) the Court of Appeal reinstated a tribunal conclusion of unfair dismissal where the employee's department was reorganised and she was not offered a new post for which she applied. However, there was evidence that the reorganisation was a pretext to get rid of the employee and there was no real consideration of the employee for the new post.

6.06   Variation of contract terms and redundancy

Not every variation of contract terms will result in the original job being redundant. The issue is whether the employer's requirements for employees to carry out work of a particular kind have ceased or diminished.

So in *Nottinghamshire Combined Police Authority* v. *Johnson & Dutton* (1974) a change in the pattern of working hours did not result in the employees being redundant. And in *Chapman* v. *Goonvean & Rostowrack* (1973) the withdrawal of a transport service from home to work did not mean the employees affected were entitled to redundancy compensation. In both cases the employers' variation entitled the employees to claim constructive dismissal but dismissal was not by reason of redundancy. The employers continued to need employees to carry out the work previously done. (Circumstances like these would probably now lead to claims of unfair dismissal rather than redundancy. For a discussion of how to implement change and protect against unfair dismissal claims see above.)

There is a redundancy where the employer's requirements for employees to do work of a particular kind have ceased or diminished. That issue should not be confused with whether or not the work remains to be done. Though it will often be the case that the former follows from the latter it may be that the work level remains the same but the employer's reorganisation means that he needs fewer employees to do it. That will still be a redundancy situation. So in *McCrea* v. *Cullen & Davison Ltd* (1988) the applicant manager's work was absorbed by the company managing director when the former had to go into hospital. It became apparent that the arrangement was both practical and financially beneficial. An industrial tribunal held that the applicant was not redundant because the amount of management work had not diminished. The tribunal found he had been dismissed for 'some other substantial reason' and dismissal was unfair. The Northern Ireland Court of Appeal allowed the company's appeal. The applicant was redundant because the company's requirements for managerial employees had diminished. Lord Gibson also said that there was a redundancy where there was no reduction in the volume of work but the requirement for workers was reduced because of improved mechanisation, automation or other technical advance. Likewise there is a redundancy where a re-allocation of duties discloses a position of overmanning.

In such a case an employer would have to pay redundancy compensation but will not be liable in unfair dismissal provided that he acts reasonably in dismissing for redundancy. He will have to comply with any agreed or customary redundancy procedure, his selection criteria should be fair and objectively applied and he should enter into as early and extensive consultation as is practicable and reasonable in the circumstances. He should also consider the availability of alternative employment for employees who are redundant.

6.07   Redundancy compensation

The amount of redundancy compensation payable depends on the employee's age, length of service and earnings level and is:

- Half a week's pay for each year of service in which the employee was below age 22;
- One week's pay for each year of service in which the employee was below age 41;
- One and a half week's pay for each year of service in which the employee was below retirement age (but the redundancy entitlement is reduced during the final year of service before retirement).

A maximum of 20 years' service can be taken into account and the maximum earnings taken into account are £164 weekly (from 1 April 1988) so the greatest statutory redundancy compensation payable is:

$$1\frac{1}{2} \times 20 \times 164 = £4,920$$

The Wages Act 1986 abolished the entitlement to a redundancy rebate for any employer who employs ten or more employees.

6.08   Alternative employment

If the business reorganisation results in a different job being available, the employer should consider the redundant employee for that job. If he refuses it but it is a suitable alternative job he will forfeit his redundancy entitlement unless his refusal is reasonable. The cases show that the tribunals compare the old and new jobs in considering suitability but take into account the employee's personal circumstances (e.g. location of home, travelling time, domestic arrangements, age, etc.) in considering reasonableness of the refusal.

Where the redundant employee accepts different terms he is entitled to try out the new job for up to four weeks or such longer period as is agreed in writing. He may then leave during the trial period without forfeiting his redundancy compensation entitlement. In *Benton* v. *Sanderson Kayser Ltd* (1988) the EAT held that a break of 11 days during which the employers' premises were closed for Christmas were not included in the four week trial period. The EAT held that a literal calendar view should not be taken and the trial period had to be a trial period at work. Presumably, it follows that any annual or other holiday period is excluded from the four weeks and logically the reasoning would apply to require any period of sickness or other absence to be deducted.

Some cases suggest that where the employer does not actually terminate the old contract but moves the redundant employee to a different job he has longer than the statutory four-week period to make up his mind whether or not to accept the new terms. For example, in *Air Canada* v. *Lee* (1978) a telephonist who worked in a third floor room in plenty of natural daylight was moved to basement premises when the employer's lease on the original premises expired. She was never dismissed but worked at the new site for two months before claiming unfair dismissal compensation. The EAT found she was dismissed by reason of redundancy but that she was entitled to compensation in spite of having worked well in excess of the four weeks' trial period. The EAT held that where there is no redundancy notice but matters are dealt with on an informal basis the employee has a reasonable period within which to decide whether or not to treat the original contract as terminated. Then the statutory trial period begins from the end of that reasonable period. A similar decision was reached in *Turvey* v. *C.W. Cheyney & Sons Ltd* (1979).

If, therefore, an employee is told, without being dismissed, that his job is coming to an end but an alternative job on different terms is available, he has a reasonable time under the normal principles of the law of contract within which to decide whether or not to accept the variation. *Then* he has the further statutory four weeks within which to decide whether to continue on the new terms. If he decides not to do so he can claim dismissal by reason of the original redundancy. If the employer actually dismisses from the original contract, it is only the statutory trial period which is available. If the employee works beyond the four weeks and then leaves he will not be able to show constructive dismissal.

Where the redundant employee accepts the different job and remains in employment his continuity of employment runs without any break.

6.09 Transfers, mergers and take-overs – effect on contracts of employment

A worker's employment is presumed to have been continuous under para 1 Schedule 13 EP(C)A 1978. But that rule only applies to employment by the one employer; if there is a change of employer, normally that change will break the contract of employment and put an end to the employment relationship. (For discussion and other exceptions see Chapter 8.) However, where a trade or business is transferred, the employment contracts of the workers in that trade or business are subject to:

(a) section 94 EP(C)A which treats certain acts of the new owner of the business as the acts of the previous owner; and
(b) para 17 Schedule 13 EP(C)A which preserves the continuity of employment of workers transferred along with the business; and
(c) the Transfer of Undertakings (Protection of Employment) Regulations 1981 which normally provide for the continuation of the employment contracts of the workers employed immediately before the transfer.

Each of these provisions requires a transfer or change in the ownership of the business. A transfer of business assets is not enough to bring them into operation; the business or a part of the business must be transferred as a going concern.

The difference between a transfer of assets and a transfer of a business is illustrated by *Woodhouse* v. *Peter Brotherhood Ltd* (1972). In that case two employees had worked for four years at a particular factory with the same company. In 1965 the factory premises and fixtures were sold to the defendants who took on the two employees to work in the factory for the purposes of their new business. In 1971 when the two men were made redundant by the defendants the issue was whether the defendants were liable to compensate by reference to the total period of employment or only for the last six years. The Court of Appeal held that the defendants did not carry on the same business as successor to the former employers. All that had been transferred were certain business assets but the defendants then began their own business activity. Continuity of employment did not run in those circumstances.

A transfer of part of a business also triggers operation of the provision. According to the House of Lords in *Hector Powe Ltd* v. *Melon* (1981), whether there is a transfer of part of a business as a going concern is a matter of fact for the industrial tribunal. Lord Fraser said in that case of the operation of section 94 EP(C)A 'A change in ownership of part of a business will seldom occur except where that part is to some extent separate and severable from the rest of the business, either geographically or by reference to the products or in some other way'.

6.10   Change in ownership – Section 94 EP(C)A 1978

Where there is a change in the ownership of a business and

immediately before the change the transferor terminates the employee's contract of employment, any re-engagement or offer of re-engagement by the transferee has the same effect on redundancy entitlement as though it were made by the transferor. That means that workers taken on by the new owner on the same terms are not entitled to claim redundancy compensation from the old owner. Further, if the new owner makes one or more of the workers offers of suitable alternative employment which they unreasonably refuse they cannot claim redundancy compensation from the old owner. Also, if the new owner offers employment on different terms, any employee has the statutory four week period within which to try out the new job. If he leaves within that period he can still claim redundancy compensation from the old owner and will be entitled to it provided that he acted reasonably in leaving.

The section specifically applies to mergers as well as take-overs and transfers.

Para 17 Schedule 13 EP(C)A 1978

This provision applies where the new owner's offer of employment to the workers is accepted and they continue in their original jobs or in suitable alternative jobs. Their continuity of service runs: i.e. their service with the old employer is treated as service with the new employer.

6.11 The Transfer of Undertakings (Protection of Employment) Regulations 1981

Under the Regulations a transfer of an undertaking does not operate so as to terminate the contract of employment of any person employed immediately before the transfer. Such a person is treated as transferring automatically to the new owner. It can be seen that the Regulations have a much wider impact than the two previous provisions. Those provisions only apply where the new owner chooses to re-engage the workers. The Regulations, however, give the new owner no choice: workers employed 'immediately before' the transfer will become his employees by operation of law. Further, any employee who is dismissed because of the transfer, whether before the transfer by the old owner or after the transfer by the new owner, is treated as unfairly dismissed. The only exception is where an 'economic technical or organisational reason' entails changes in the workforce. Then the reason for the dismissal is treated as 'some other substantial reason' within section 57(1)(b) EP(C)A 1978 and the employer will not be liable in unfair dismissal provided he acted reasonably in dismissing in all the circumstances of the case.

It can be seen that it is crucial to determine which employees, if any, are employed 'immediately before' the transfer. There is, in effect, a statutory novation of the employment contracts. The transferee employer will take on all the transferor's rights, powers, duties and contractual liabilities in respect of such workers. The only provisions which do not pass to the transferee employer are those concerned with occupational pension schemes. Also, the meaning of the phrase determines which employer is answerable for any dismissal effected in connection with the transfer.

An early case established that the meaning of the phrase 'immediately before' was a matter for the industrial tribunal since it depended on the particular circumstances of the case. The tribunal was held entitled to conclude that employees dismissed on the Friday preceding a Monday transfer were employed 'immediately before' that transfer. That decision led to the common practice of the transferee employer insisting on dismissal of the workforce at least four weeks before the transfer was effective. However, in *Secretary of State for Employment* v. *Spence* (1986) the Court of Appeal held that obligations passed to the transferee employer only in respect of contracts subsisting at the moment of transfer. The court upheld a decision that workers dismissed three hours before the transfer were not employed 'immediately before' that transfer. The court justified that conclusion by referring to a decision of the European Court interpreting a European Directive which the Regulations were intended to implement. That decision required employment contracts to be in existence at the *time* of transfer in order to be affected by the Directive. The Court of Appeal held therefore that the earlier case was wrong in treating employment two days before a transfer as being sufficiently proximate to it to fall within the phrase 'immediately before' the transfer. Only contracts of employment subsisting at the moment of transfer will be binding on the transferee employers. And in accordance with usual conveyancing principles the 'transfer' will be effective when it is completed, i.e. there will often be a contract for sale followed by a conveyance of title some days or weeks later. The transfer is complete on the conveyance, not the contract. Since there might be some debate about the moment of transfer on any particular day, a purchaser of a business may be well advised to require the dismissal of the workforce the day before the transfer or, to be on the safe side, a few days before the transfer. The alternative strategy is to require some indemnity agreement from the vendor of the business or to reflect in the purchase price the transferee's liability for employment contracts which continue after transfer.

6.12   The Regulations and unfair dismissal

The other main effect of the Regulations is to treat a dismissal connected with any transfer as an unfair dismissal subject to the exception for an economic, technical or organisational reason. So if the purchaser does insist on the dismissal of the workforce before the transfer (perhaps intending to re-engage the valued, efficient workers afterwards) it is the vendor who is answerable. If the employment contracts run, either because the workers are employed 'immediately before' the transfer or because the purchaser has specifically agreed to take them, any dismissal by the purchaser for a reason connected with the transfer will have to be defended by him. In either case the employer will have to show 'an economic, technical or organisational reason entailing changes in the workforce' and that he acted reasonably in dismissing on that ground. It will not be a sufficient defence for the employer to claim that the dismissed workers are 'redundant'. He will have to show the reasons for the claimed redundancy (e.g. that the work is now to be performed by self-employed contractors) *and* that he acted reasonably in dismissing in those circumstances.

In *Anderson & McAlonie* v. *Dalkeith Engineering Ltd* (1984) it was the vendor of a business who was defending unfair dismissal actions. He had dismissed the workforce at the purchaser's insistence and claimed that that in itself amounted to an economic, technical or organisational reason for dismissal. The EAT upheld the tribunal decision that in those circumstances the dismissals were not unfair. The decision has been much criticised since unless the merits of the claimed economic reason are investigated the Regulations are useless. There the purchaser was not a party to the proceedings so it was said to be not practicable to allow the case to turn on his motives but the insistence of a third party is not a conclusive defence for a normal, unfair dismissal claim and it is not easy to see why it should be so here. In a more recent case the EAT chose not to follow the *Anderson* decision. In *Gateway Hotels Ltd* v. *Stewart* (1988) the dismissal of the workforce by the vendor was a pre-condition of sale insisted upon by the purchaser of the business. The EAT refused to accept that that insistence was an 'economic' reason within the meaning of the regulations and therefore the dismissals were all unfair. It remains to be seen which view will be preferred by the higher courts.

The Court of Appeal has held that the claimed economic, technical or organisational reason must entail 'changes in the workforce'. The employer cannot establish a fair dismissal if his changes are not related to the number of employees engaged but to the terms and conditions on which they are employed. In *Berriman* v. *Delabole Slate Ltd* (1985) the applicant was a quarryman in an undertaking transferred to the respondents. They continued to employ him but with changed pay and bonus arrangements so as to bring him into line with their other, existing employees. The applicant refused to accept the changes and claimed constructive unfair dismissal. The Court of Appeal held that the respondents had failed to bring their case within the exception allowed by the Regulations. No change in the workforce was brought about, merely a change in the terms on which the applicant was employed. The court took the view that the imposition of changed conditions of employment on workers caught up in a transfer was exactly what the Regulations were intended to prevent.

6.13   *The Regulations and trade unions*

As well as affecting individual contracts of employment in the two ways noted above, the Regulations also oblige the transferee employer to continue with any collective agreements affecting any employee whose contract is preserved and, so far as the undertaking transferred maintains an identity distinct from the rest of the transferee's undertaking, he is obliged to continue with any trade union recognition agreement. The Regulations also oblige both transferor and transferee employer to inform and consult with trade union representatives over the transfer. In the *Institution of Professional Civil Servants* v. *Secretary of State for Defence* (1987) where the union alleged breach of the duty to inform and consult over the transfer of dockyards to private contractors, the court held that there had been no breach since the Secretary of State held no detailed plans of manpower levels and redundancies envisaged. And the transferees would not have that information until they had experience in running the dockyards and sufficient time to formulate plans.

Where there is a failure to inform or consult, complaint lies to an industrial tribunal who can order payment of compensation to affected employees.

The Regulations only apply to commercial undertakings. There is no definition in the regulations but 'commercial' usually means 'with a view to profit' so it may be that non-profit-making public services are outside the Regulations. The privatisation of certain public services such as local authority refuse and cleansing services will produce litigation on the meaning of 'commercial venture'. In *Woodcock* v. *Committee of Friends' School, Wigton* (1987) the Court of Appeal held that a charitable school organised so as to break even was not a commercial venture and was not subject to the Regulations.

Chapter 7

The Contract of Employment and Discrimination

An employer is under a statutory duty not to discriminate against employees or potential employees on grounds of sex or race. Some aspects of this duty have been considered in relation to recruitment in Chapter 2. This chapter will consider equal pay entitlement, how to avoid infringement of the discrimination legislation and the effect of European law on employment practices.

7.01 Equal pay

Entitlement to equal pay is under the Equal Pay Act (EqPA) 1970 which became fully operative in December 1975. The title of the Act is misleading since it aims to achieve equal treatment not only in respect of pay but also in respect of other terms and conditions of the contract of employment. All terms and conditions of the contract are covered except those specifically excluded by section 6, i.e.:

(a) Protective, paternalistic terms regulating the employment of women, e.g. in relation to night or weekend work or length of consecutive hours to be worked by women. Note that the 1986 Sex Discrimination Act removes most of these statutory protective provisions. The prohibition on the employment of women below ground at mines and quarries continues but consultation is presently taking place with a view to its removal. The Act does not apply to service in the naval, military or air forces of the Crown.
(b) Terms providing special treatment to women in connection with pregnancy or childbirth.
(c) Terms providing for benefits under occupational pension schemes. But note that there should be equal *access* to such pension schemes. For a full discussion of the impact of European Law on pension benefits see later in this chapter.
(d) Terms related to death or retirement (see below).

The principle of equal treatment applies only in respect of employment *but* the definition in the EqPA is the wider definition which includes not only employees proper but also self-employed persons or independent contractors. The Act states that 'employed' means 'employed under a contract of service or of apprenticeship or a contract personally to execute any work or labour'. In *Quinnen* v. *Hovell* (1984) the EAT held that the definition included a self-employed salesman of fancy goods who demonstrated and sold goods from pitches in department stores.

The Act implies an equality clause into any contract where a woman is employed:

(a) on like work *or*
(b) on work which is rated as equivalent *or*
(c) on work which is of equal value to that of a man in the same employment.

The effect of the equality clause is that any less favourable term of the woman's contract is modified to be as beneficial as the comparable term of the man's contract and if any term is omitted from the woman's contract it is treated as being included. Or to state the effect shortly, the employer is obliged to employ the woman on the same terms as the man. This obligation is enforceable before the industrial tribunals.

7.02   *Like work*

The Act says that work is 'like' where it is the same or broadly similar and the differences (if any) are not of practical importance. In comparing work, regard should be given to the frequency with which any differences occur in practice as well as to the nature and extent of the differences. So, jobs do not have to be identical in order for the equal treatment clause to apply but they do have to be broadly similar. It is not possible for an employer to avoid the obligation of equal treatment by inserting 'empty' contractual terms in order to create an artificial distinction between the woman's job and the man's job. In *Hutchinson* v. *Electrolux Ltd* (1976) the EAT refused to accept that a contractual liability imposed on a man to transfer, or to work overtime amounted to a significant difference between his job and that of the applicant. Whether work is like depends on the work actually done, not work which could be called upon under the contract. Also, although there may be differences, if those differences occur very infrequently, a tribunal may still find that the work is 'like'. *Capper Pass Ltd* v. *Lawton* (1977) shows that there may be numerous differences between jobs and still a tribunal may hold them to be 'broadly similar'. The appeal tribunal will not interfere with the decision unless it is perverse or so unreasonable as to suggest an error of law.

A starting test for determining whether work is 'like' was advocated in *Dorman* v. *Hadrian Plastics Ltd* (1976), i.e. if the man with whom the female applicant is claiming comparison were replaced by the applicant, could the comparator's job be carried on substantially as before? Are the applicant and the comparator interchangeable? If not, their work is not like work.

If differences are so significant as to prevent a finding of like work, there is no requirement that the variation in pay should reflect the objective value of the differences.

Usually the time at which work is done is irrelevant to the nature of the work done. So it is possible for a woman engaged on a day shift to claim the same basic hourly rate, less any unsocial hours supplement, as that enjoyed by a man doing the same job at night (see *Dugdale* v. *Kraft Foods Ltd* (1977)). However, if the job is significantly different if performed at night it may not be possible to claim 'like work' or the employer may have a defence that the variation in pay is due to a genuine material non-sex difference (see below). For example, in one case a male controller/telephonist engaged at night was paid more than a female controller/telephonist who worked during the day at premises in a 'less salubrious' part of Manchester. The variation in pay was held to be partly a night shift allowance and partly a 'danger-money' payment to which the applicant was not entitled. And in *Thomas & Barker* v. *NCB* (1987) the EAT confirmed that additional responsibility entailed in working permanently at night alone and without supervision entitled a tribunal to find that that work was not 'like' with day-time work.

Differences in responsibility may prevent jobs being seen as 'like' even where they are performed at the same time (see *Eaton Ltd* v. *Nuttall* (1977)).

It was established in *Macarthys Ltd* v. *Smith* (1980) that comparison can be claimed with a previous occupant of the applicant's employment. In that case the applicant stockroom manageress was paid £400 per annum less than her male predecessor. After a reference to the European Court of Justice on the issue of whether our national legislation was an effective implementation of European law, the Court of Appeal held that contemporaneity of employment was not a prerequisite to comparision. In principle, then, a female employee could claim equal treatment with a male predecessor, or successor. However, it is still open for an employer to dispute the contention of like work or to argue a general material non-sex difference. The greater the gap between the employments compared, the more likely it is that any variation in pay will be explicable on grounds other than sex discrimination. So in *Albion Shipping Agency* v. *Arnold* (1981) the EAT held that an office reorganisation and diminution in the volume of work could justify a variation in pay between that of the applicant and her male predecessor.

7.03   Work rated equivalent

A woman has a claim for equal treatment with men under this head where her work and theirs have been rated equivalent in a job evaluation study. The study may rate value under numerous headings (for instance effort, skill, decision-making requirements) and the right to equal treatment will be enjoyed where the overall ratings are comparable or would have been so if the study itself were not sexually discriminatory, i.e. if the study set unjustified different requirements for men and women under any heading. In *Rummler* v. *Dato-Druck GmbH* (1987) a job-grading scheme used by a German printing company was alleged to be discriminatory. Jobs were classified under the scheme according to knowledge and concentration required, effort, exertion and responsibility demands. The female applicant claimed her job should have been given a higher classification under the exertion heading since she had to pack parcels weighing in excess of 20 kg. She argued that, for a woman, that was heavy physical work. Reference was made to the European Court on whether a job-grading system was discriminatory if physical effort was measured irrespective of the sex of the worker, or whether to be non-discriminatory the average female ability should be the yardstick. The European Court held that a grading system is not discriminatory solely because one of its criteria is based on characteristics more commonly found in men *but* if it is to be non-discriminatory overall it must also take into account other criteria for which female workers show particular aptitude. So a job classification system should not set different yardsticks of physical effort for men and women but should be so formulated that headings under which women score highly (e.g. manual dexterity) should be included. The nature of the work dictates what those appropriate headings should be.

Where a job evaluation study has been carried out it can form the basis of a claim under the Act even if it has not been implemented by the employer (see *O'Brien* v. *Sim-Chem Ltd* (1980)). But the study must have been completed and it is not complete unless and until the parties to it have accepted its validity (see *Arnold* v. *Beecham Group Ltd* (1982)).

If an employer does not carry out a job evaluation study there can, of course be no claim under this head. Until the EqPA was amended in 1983, there was no alternative claim to give equal entitlement as between the sexes where the work was not the same but was alleged to be of the same value. The adequacy of the original version of the EqPA was successfully challenged before the European Court of Justice in *The Commission of the European Communities* v. *UK* (1982). The court held that the United Kingdom had failed to meet its obligations under European law to provide a remedy where the principle of equal pay for work of equal value was not being adhered to and there was no system of job evaluation or grading in operation. That case resulted in the passing of the Equal Pay (Amendment) Regulations 1983 which created a very complicated (and some claim unnecessarily prolonged and technical) procedure for equal value claims.

7.04　*Work of equal value*

If an employee claims equal treatment with a man who is not doing like work or work rated equivalent but who is claimed to be engaged in work of equal value to hers a tribunal can throw out the case if it considers that there are no reasonable grounds for the claim.

Where the jobs have already been rated differently under a non-discriminatory study the Regulations state that there are no reasonable grounds for the claim and so it has to be dismissed. For an illustration see *Bromley* v. *H. & J. Quick Ltd* (1987) where an equal value claim was dismissed as showing no reasonable grounds even where the job evaluation scheme relied on to defeat it was 'non-analytic' and based on a 'whole job' comparison. The dissenting member of the EAT in that case thought that only a headings-based or analytical job evaluation study could defeat an equal value claim. The Court of Appeal agreed with the dissenting member when it was referred to them in 1988. An equal value claim can be dismissed only where the job evaluation study already carried out is an analytical study giving values under various headings. Only that sort of study satisfies the Act's requirements.

It does not seem easy for an employer to defeat an equal value claim by instituting his own job evaluation study after the equal value claim has been presented and thereby putting the claim into the no-hope category. In *Langley* v. *Beecham Proprietaries* (1985) a tribunal rejected the employers' voluntary job evaluation scheme since it was based entirely on management values and there had been no consultation with the equal value applicants. The issue was referred to an independent expert.

Unless it considers that there are no reasonable grounds for determining that the work compared is of equal value, the tribunal must refer the matter to an independent expert who prepares his own job evaluation comparison. The expert is obliged to consider representations from both sides and to send the parties written summaries of the information he relies on before drawing up his report. The report is available as evidence in the subsequent tribunal hearing and the tribunal may require the attendance of the expert who is then subject to cross-examination. The rules also allow either party to commission his own expert report and such experts are also subject to cross-examination!

7.05 The equal value procedure in operation

Just how cumbersome and drawn out the equal value procedure can be is illustrated in the *Hayward* v. *Cammell Laird Shipbuilders Ltd* (1988) case. The applicant, a cook in the works cafeteria at the respondents' Birkenhead shipyard claimed equal pay to that enjoyed by male painters, joiners and thermal insulation engineers on the basis that her work and theirs was of equal value. The claim was made early in 1984, soon after the commencement of the equal value regulations. In October 1984, an industrial tribunal accepted the independent expert's report that the applicant's job was of equal value to those of the male comparators. The expert compared the jobs under five factors – physical demands, environmental demands, planning and decision-making demands and responsibility demands – and rated each job under each heading as low, moderate or high. Although the respondents criticised the evaluation method used by the expert, they did not call their own expert and the tribunal accepted the report. However, the tribunal then left it to negotiation between the two sides as to how the equal pay claim should be settled. One year later, after it proved impossible for the parties to agree, the issue was referred back to the tribunal. The tribunal then looked at the details of the terms of employment: the applicant was paid £103 per week, her comparators were paid £126 per week; she had paid meal breaks, the craftsmen did not – those were worth £11.66 per week; she had a meal allowance, they did not – that was valued at £5 per week; the applicant had a better sick pay scheme which entitled her to full salary for up to 26 weeks – the men were entitled only to £35 weekly for up to 26 weeks. It was argued that half the difference in value of the sick pay schemes should be taken into account since it was reasonable to expect half the entitlement to be used in any one year! Half the difference in value between the sick pay entitlement was £884 per annum or £17 weekly. The employers claimed, therefore, that the applicant actually was better off than her male comparators! All the contract terms had to be considered as a whole and so viewed, the applicant's terms were not less favourable. It was argued for the applicant that the EqPA allowed comparison with particular terms and not the overall package. If any term was less favourable, it had to be amended. This issue eventually went to the Court of Appeal in March 1987, three years after the applicant's claim. The court found for the employer: an employer does not have to pay a woman employed on work of equal value the same basic wage as male comparators if, considered as a whole, her remuneration is not less favourable. (That principle, it is submitted, must also apply to like work and work rated equivalent claims.)

Whilst that principle appears logical and consistent with the aim of the Act to achieve overall equality, it seems odd that *contingent* benefits rather than actual benefits in kind or cash are included. However, the Court of Appeal thought that *all* contract terms should be valued and that tribunals, with their industrial expertise should have no insuperable difficulty in putting a fair value on such benefits. Whilst that may be an acceptable stance, it is still remarkable that the value of a contingent benefit like sick pay entitlement should be based on the assumption that an employee would take half a 26 weeks' entitlement in any one year. Not many employers would continue to employ a person who had that sort of absence rate! In May 1988 the House of Lords allowed the applicant's appeal. Their Lordships' held that a woman *can* point to any term of her contract which is less favourable than the corresponding term of a comparable man's contract and claim equal treatment in respect of that term irrespective of the value of the whole package of contract terms. That result was consistent with the statutory words.

The decision of the House of Lords has been much publicised and it has been seen both as a valuable landmark in the advancement of sexual equality at work and as a dangerous case which damages the cause of equality and licenses leap-frogging pay claims. In fact, the real merits of the argument were not thoroughly tested in the case because the employers failed to argue the genuine material non-sex difference defence (see below) at the tribunal stage.

Nevertheless the case is crucial and establishes the principle of the right to equal treatment in respect of any contract term. So if a man and woman are engaged on like work but the woman is paid £1000 per annum less she is entitled to the same salary, whether or not she also enjoys better fringe benefits. However, if the employer can show a non-sex reason for the variation in basic pay he has a defence under section 1(3). Also, if the variation in pay is because the employer operates a package benefits scheme which the employee chooses (e.g. £20,000 per annum *or* £17,500 per annum plus a company car worth up to £2,500 *or* £17,000 per annum plus a company car up to £2,500 per annum plus private sickness cover worth £500 per annum) the remuneration will be contained in a single term. In those circumstances a woman choosing the reduced basic salary could not, it is argued, subsequently claim entitlement to the greater sum.

Another Court of Appeal held in *Pickstone* v. *Freemans plc* (1987) that a female employee can present an equal value claim even where she is employed on not less favourable terms than a man engaged on like work. That claim would be prevented under our national legislation but the Court of Appeal has held that such a claim can proceed before our national tribunals and courts under European law. That decision has been upheld by the House of Lords (1988) apparently because it was felt that otherwise it would be too easy to defeat an equal value claim by employing a token male on the same terms as a grade largely occupied by women. So the decision is that a woman employed on work of equal value to that of a man is not debarred from seeking equal treatment by reason of the fact that she is already enjoying equal treatment with a man engaged on like work.

The *Pickstone* decision is unfortunate since the Act and the equivalent European rules are aimed at preventing sex discrimination. The case is not an example of sex discrimination and may well lead to leap-frog pay claims. Where for instance there are genuine uni-sex pay grades, any female in one grade could claim comparison on the basis of equal value to any man in a higher grade. It is true that where an employer can justify the difference he will have a genuine material non-sex difference defence (see below) but the EqPA was not intended to justify inquiry into the employer's pay structure except where it was sexually discriminatory. A better approach would be amendment of the EqPA to allow an equal value claim even where the applicant is engaged in the like work with a man but only where that man's presence in the pay grade is exceptional or designed to defeat the equal pay entitlement. If the 'like work' pay grade is genuinely non-sexually discriminatory, there is no justification for allowing an equal value claim as well.

7.06   *The genuine material non-sex difference defence*

The employer is not obliged to confer equal treatment where the variation between the applicant's terms and those of her comparator is genuinely due to a material factor which is not a difference of sex. Where, for example, the comparator's terms are superior because he has been demoted on grounds of ill-health but his pay and benefit terms have been protected this defence will be available (see *Methven & Musiolik* v. *Cow Industrial Polymers Ltd* (1980)). Alternatively, if a regrading exercise results in the downgrading of a particular job, good industrial relations practice will require that pay rates of employees in that grade will be protected but subsequent pay increases will not be made so that eventually comparably graded jobs will carry the same rate. In the interim, while higher rates continue, there will be no equal treatment claim since the defence will be available (see *Bedwell* v. *Hellerman Deutsch Ltd* (1976)). The defence will only succeed in these circumstances provided the employer makes no appointment subsequent to the regrading scheme at the protected rate: *United Biscuits Ltd* v. *Young* (1978). Also, the employer should phase out the protected rate as soon as practicable to ensure the availability of the defence: *Outlook Supplies Ltd* v. *Parry* (1978).

7.07   *Market forces*

Whether economic or market forces can constitute a genuine material non-sex difference defence has been a major issue of contention in the interpretation of the EqPA. The Court of Appeal in *Fletcher* v. *Clay Cross (Quarry Services) Ltd* (1978) held that economic factors were not relevant. In that case the employers advertised for a sales clerk at £x per week. The most suitable applicant was Mr T who was already being paid £x + y in his existing employment. The employers agreed to match his existing wage and employed Mr T at £x + y. The applicant, a female sales clerk who was being paid £x, claimed equal pay with Mr T. The employers argued that there was a genuine material non-sex difference between Mr Y's case and that of the applicant. They had to pay Mr T more because of market or economic forces; he was already earning more than the offered rate. They also argued the variation could not be sex-based since they would have matched the higher existing wage of a female applicant, had a female been the most suitable. The EAT allowed the employers' defence, accepting their contention that there was no intention to discriminate on grounds of sex. The Court of Appeal disagreed and said it did not depend on the employer's motivation or intention. Whether or not there was a genuine material non-sex difference depended on the personal equation of the applicant and the comparator; the circumstances in which they came to be employed, market pressures or factors extrinsic to their jobs or their personal skills were not relevant.

The Court of Appeal decision was taken to be definitive as ruling out an economic forces defence for some years although the European Court decision in *Jenkins* v. *Kingsgate (Clothing Productions) Ltd* (1981) did suggest that, at least under equivalent European rules, economic factors might be relevant. The House of Lords has now ruled that the *Fletcher* principle is unduly restricted and unjustified. In *Rainey* v. *Greater Glasgow Health Board* (1987) a female prosthetist who earned £7295 per annum claimed equal pay with a male prosthetist employed at the same hospital who was paid £10,085 per annum. The employers alleged that there was a genuine material non-sex difference between the two since the man was recruited from the private sector where salary levels were higher. Since it was not possible to staff the service from public sector-trained personnel the Health Board had decided to recruit from the private sector and to match private sector rates. The tribunal at first instance, the EAT and the Court of Session (the Scottish equivalent to the Court of Appeal) all thought the employers defence should succeed though they had difficulty in distinguishing the *Fletcher* case. In the Court of Session, Lord Cameron said that the distinction between intrinsic factors (which could be taken into account) and extrinsic factors (which according to *Fletcher* could not) could only be made on the facts of a particular case. There the tribunal had found that there were strong equitable considerations personal to the comparator which were wholly unconcerned with sex and warranted the continuance of his higher pay rate. But Lord Grieve dissented. He was unable to distinguish *Fletcher* since here there was no evidence that the comparator had better experience or greater skill or qualifications than the applicant. All that could explain the difference in pay was the circumstances under which they came to be employed. Though those circumstances were special, they were not personal and the case was, according to him, exactly the sort of case at which the EqPA was aimed. However, the House of Lords unanimously held that the employer's defence succeeded. The genuine material non-sex difference defence can include factors beyond a personal comparison of experience and skill to extend to objectively justified economic factors such as administrative efficiency. The NHS prosthetic service could not have been provided effectively without recruitment from the private sector. That was a good and objectively justified ground for offering the higher, private sector scale of remuneration. The fact that the prosthetist recruited from the private sector was male was fortuitous. The variation in pay was not sex-based.

It is not immediately clear how the *Rainey* decision affects cases like *Fletcher*. If, for example, a male employee is offered another job at a higher salary, does an employer who matches that offer in order to retain the employee risk an equal pay claim by women doing like work, or work rated equivalent? Or is the genuine material non-sex difference defence available? If the employer can show objectively justified grounds for the variation, he should be able to rely on this as a defence, i.e. if he can justify the variation on grounds other than sex he is protected. Borrowing from the principle relied on by the House of Lords, the employer would have to show the variation in treatment was appropriate and necessary to achieve his business objective. Provided the employer can show that business or administrative efficiency necessitates the variation the defence should be available. An employer is more likely to be believed if his evidence shows that a valued female employee has been or would be treated in the same way.

The EAT has recently held in *Reed Packaging Ltd* v. *Boozer & Everhurst* (1988) that separate pay structures resulting from the necessity to negotiate with two different trade unions can amount to a genuine material non-sex difference. The EAT held that the tribunal rejection of the defence was perverse.

7.08   Same employment

For any equal pay claim, the applicant must show she is in the same employment as her male comparator. According to the Act, men and women are in the same employment if they are employed by the same or an associated employer at the same establishment or at different establishments in Great Britain but which observe common terms and conditions of employment. So, if Miss X is employed at the same work place by the same employer as Mr Y, they are in the same employment. If Mr Y is employed at a different place by the same or an associated employer but, apart from pay rates, Miss X and Mr Y's terms are similar, e.g. in respect of holidays, pension schemes, sick-pay and union representation, Miss X could claim equal pay with Mr Y. Employers are associated if they are in the relationship of holding and subsidiary companies or one has control of the other or if a third party has control of both.

Where the employer argues that different pay rates are determined by location he will have to show the genuine material non-sex difference defence.

7.09 Sex discrimination

The EqPA 1970 obliges an employer to treat men and women equally in relation to any term or condition of the contract. The Sex Discrimination Act (SDA) 1975 applies to prevent discrimination in employment matters which are not governed by a term or condition of a contract. The Act applies to recruitment and offers of employment (see Chapter 2) and also to access to training, benefits facilities or services, promotion and dismissal or any other detriment.

An employer acts unlawfully if he discriminates directly, i.e. by treating a female employee less favourably (for example, by adopting a policy of not promoting females) or indirectly, i.e. by applying a condition or requirement which appears to be non-discriminatory but which adversely affects women and is not justifiable irrespective of sex (e.g. by only promoting people who have no domestic or child-care commitments).

7.10 Genuine occupational qualification

Obviously, there are certain jobs which require an employee of a particular sex. The SDA recognises nine such instances. In any of these nine cases, sex is a genuine occupational qualification for employment and an employer does not act unlawfully should he insist on employing a man (or a woman) if:

(i) the essential nature of the job calls for a man for reasons of physiology or authenticity (e.g. male role in a dramatic production or male model for male clothes);

(ii) the job needs to be held by a man to preserve decency or privacy (e.g. male assistant in men's outfitters, male attendant in men's toilets);

(iii) the job is to be performed in a private home and the degree of physical or social contact with the occupant or the knowledge of intimate details of the occupant's life is such that the job needs to be held by a man (e.g. male care assistant visiting or living with elderly male whose duties include bathing the householder). (Note that there used to be a general exception from the SDA where employment was for the purposes of a private household. That exception was removed by the SDA 1986 after it was successfully challenged before the European Court as being too wide. This present head of genuine occupational qualification was added by the SDA 1986 as limiting the previous exception to justifiable discrimination in relation to employment within private households.)

(iv)   the work is to be performed in a hospital, prison or other establishment for persons requiring special care and those persons are all men and it is reasonable having regard to the essential character of the establishment that the job should be held by a man (e.g. male prison warder in male prison);

(v)   the holder of the job has to live in communal premises provided by the employer which are not equipped with separate sleeping or sanitary facilities for women and it is not reasonable to expect the employer to provide those separate facilities or separate premises for women (e.g. male workers on oil rigs in the North Sea);

(vi)   the holder of the job provides individuals with personal services promoting their welfare or education or similar personal services and those services can most effectively be provided by a man (e.g. tutor in single sex residence at a college);

(vii)   the job needs to be held by a man because of restrictions imposed by the laws regulating the employment of women (e.g. employment below ground in a mine or quarry or employment with heavy, dangerous machinery – but note that many of the protective, paternalistic provisions were repealed in SDA 1986);

(viii)   the job needs to be held by a man because it is likely to involve the performance of duties outside the UK in a country whose laws or customs are such that the duties could not effectively be performed by a woman (e.g. sales engineer dealing with export contracts with the Middle East);

(ix)   the job is one of two to be held by a married couple (e.g. husband and wife living in, in connection with employment at social club).

Note that an employer can only rely on one of these nine exceptions where he does not already have a sufficient number of male employees who could reasonably perform those duties which bring the job into the exceptional area. For example, if the vacancy is for a sales assistant in a men's outfitters so as to bring the employment within exception (ii) above, the employer will only be able to insist on appointing a male if he shows that there are not already sufficient male sales assistants at the relevant premises to perform those duties which require to be done by a male to preserve decency or privacy, e.g. taking male customers' measurements!

7.11 Indirect discrimination – justification

Even where none of the exceptions applies, an employer does not act unlawfully if the alleged less favourable treatment is explicable on grounds other than sex discrimination or, if the allegation is of indirect discrimination, the requirement is justifiable irrespective of the sex of the employee.

Where, for example, an allegation is made that an employer did not promote the applicant because, being tied to her husband's location of employment, she was not sufficiently flexible such action is not necessarily in breach of the SDA. The employer would have to justify the requirement of mobility. If an employer fails to send a female employee on a training course because he believes she will not justify the expense since she is likely to leave his employment in the short term, he will have to justify that belief. He cannot merely rely on stereotyped assumptions that 'women follow their husbands' jobs' or 'women only work for a few years before leaving to start families'. But if the particular complainant has made it clear that she does intend to follow her husband whose career necessitates frequent transfers, or if her employment pattern to date bears out that belief, an employer does not breach the Act if he refuses her access to expensive training opportunities.

Similarly an employer is guilty of unlawful sex discrimination if he dismisses a woman with young children on the assumption that 'women who have young children at home are unreliable employees' (see *Hurley* v. *Mustoe* (1981)). But if the employer shows that the particular woman is indeed unreliable and frequently takes time off because of domestic difficulties, dismissal may not be in breach of the SDA and may not be held unfair.

Neither is it true that an employer acts unlawfully if he asks a female job applicant who has children about her domestic arrangements for caring for the children during working hours. Provided he would make the same enquiry of any applicant who was likely to have obligations inconsistent with reasonable commitment to the job, he is not discriminating on grounds of sex.

7.12 Sexual harassment

Though the phrase 'sexual harassment' does not appear in the SDA, the sort of behaviour which might be understood by that phrase has prompted a considerable number of complaints under the Act. The phrase suggests unwelcome sexual advances or discourteous or even abusive treatment of female employees because they are female. Such behaviour is 'less favourable treatment' within the meaning of the Act and is actionable if the employee suffers any 'detriment'. Employers should note that they may be vicariously liable if any of their employees are behaving in this way in the course of employment, i.e. the employer is liable for acts of his subordinates (for a consideration of the meaning of 'in the course of employment' see the discussion under Race Discrimination in [7.23]). It is a defence for the employer to show that he took such steps as were reasonably practicable to prevent the subordinate from sexually harassing the complainant.

A leading case in which an allegation of sexual harassment succeeded is *Porcelli* v. *Strathclyde Regional Council* (1986). The female applicant was employed as a science laboratory technician at a school within the respondent's area. Two male laboratory technicians were alleged to have sexually harassed the woman as part of a campaign to get her to transfer to another school. According to the appeal tribunal, the men pursued a policy of deliberate and vindictive unpleasantness of a sexual nature against the applicant. They made offensive comments about her physical appearance and suggestive remarks: they continually brushed against her and behaved in an intimidating manner. The applicant did in fact transfer to another school. At first instance the industrial tribunal held that though the men's behaviour was unpleasant and vindictive, it was not behaviour amounting to sex discrimination; the men would have treated a male colleague whom they disliked in as unpleasant a manner. The EAT and the Court of Session found otherwise. The nature of the behaviour complained of was based on the sex of the victim; they would have adopted a different method of intimidation against a male. The Court of Session disapproved of the phrase 'sexual harassment', however, preferring 'less favourable treatment' which is the statutory wording. The court did say that such conduct is only actionable if the applicant suffers a detriment, i.e. demotion, dismissal, denial of opportunity or benefit or transfer. It is not actionable *per se*. However, in *De Sousa* v. *Automobile Association* (1986), in a case concerning racial harassment, the Court of Appeal suggested that the offensive conduct might itself be the detriment referred to in the Act. If the conduct complained of so affects the working conditions or environment that a reasonable employee could justifiably complain, it is actionable without any further disadvantage to the applicant.

In a recent case, the EAT suggested that some women would suffer little or no detriment from sexual harassment which others might reasonably object to. The Act requires a disadvantage to be incurred by the complainant. In *Snowball* v. *Gardner Merchant Ltd* (1987) the applicant alleged that she had been sexually harassed by a district manager in that he had made suggestive remarks to her, had sent her sex magazines and erotic underwear and had pestered her with telephone calls. The manager denied the allegations but anyway the company sought to adduce evidence that even if the conduct complained of had taken place, the applicant would not have suffered any disadvantage. The company wished to call evidence that the applicant had talked to other employees about her black satin sheets and had referred to her bed as 'a play-pen'. The tribunal and the EAT both ruled the evidence admissible. They held that there needs to be an assessment of the injury to the woman's feelings, which must be looked at both objectively with reference to what an ordinary reasonable female employee would feel and subjectively with reference to the applicant as an individual. The case has been very much criticised as obliging female employees to tolerate unwelcome sexual advances or otherwise risk public scrutiny of their sexual attitudes. It cannot be right that women employees should be questioned about their private affairs which have no bearing on the matter. On the other hand if the evidence suggests that the applicant may have invited the conduct complained of, that evidence must be relevant. It must be left to the good sense of the tribunal members, in exercising their discretion over admissibility, to determine what constitutes relevant evidence after hearing the outline of the case and having seen and heard the relevant parties.

Attitudes to sexual harassment at work do appear to be changing and more complaints are being made through grievance and disciplinary procedures and through the courts. Enlightened employers are including in their disciplinary rules a clause stating that sexual harassment is destructive and intolerable and a disciplinary offence which may lead to dismissal. It is desirable to give some general description of the sort of conduct which might be included in the phrase – for example, 'behaviour of a sexual nature which is unwanted, unwelcome and unreciprocated and which creates a stressful or intimidating working environment. The behaviour can range from suggestive remarks and lewd jokes to physical contact and sexual assault'. Provided an employer has such a disciplinary clause and reacts reasonably to complaints of sexual harassment, his defence to vicarious liability should be accepted by a tribunal. However, it is better for employers to create such a working environment as to discourage such practices than leave employees to seek legal redress. That can be done through education of the workforce, publicity and firm reaction to justified complaints. Several cases have established that dismissal of the harasser is not unfair, provided an appropriate investigation is held, especially where the conduct is persistent or gross.

7.13   *Part-time employees and discrimination*

More women than men work part-time. Is an employment practice which acts to the disadvantage of part-time workers unlawful sex discrimination? Is an employer obliged to pay the same basic hourly rate to part-time employees as that paid to full-time employees doing the same or similar work? Early cases brought under the EqPA 1970 established that an employer has a genuine material non-sex differ-ence defence to claims for equal pay brought by part-time workers (see, for example, *Handley* v. *Mono* (1978)). In *Jenkins* v. *Kingsgate (Clothing Productions) Ltd* (1981) a part-time worker challenged the legality of a lower part-time rate under European law. The European Court of Justice ruled that a difference in pay rates between part-time work and full-time work does not amount to discrimination contrary to European law unless it is in reality merely an indirect way of reducing the pay of part-time workers on the ground that that group is exclusively or predominantly women. So it is unlawful to pay part-timers inferior rates merely because those part-timers are all, or nearly all, women but if the difference can be justified on economic, objective grounds the differential pay rates are lawful. Where the employer can show an objective benefit of full-time employment as where the proficiency or skill of performance is greater or where maximum utilisation of machinery is achieved by encouraging full-time employ-ment, a lower part-time rate is justified. According to *Bilka Kaufhaus GmbH* v. *Weber von Hartz* (1986) the employer would have to show a real need to encourage full-time employment and that the higher full-time rate was appropriate and necessary to achieve that need. That case concerned the denial to part-timers of access to the company occupational pension scheme. Since far more women than men work part-time it was alleged that the eligibility requirement to work full-time was sexually discriminatory. The company claimed there were objectively justified economic grounds for excluding part-timers from the pension scheme – the employment of full-timers was encouraged since ancillary costs were lower and full-time staff were available throughout the company store's opening hours. It was claimed that part-timers were reluctant to work late afternoons and Saturdays.

The European Court accepted in principle that an employer *could* justify an apparently discriminatory employment practice on grounds of economics and business necessity but remitted the issue to the national court to determine whether the employer's evidence amounted to such justification. It is interesting to note that the European Court uses the words 'appropriate' and 'necessary' in its test of justification. It is not a sufficient defence for an employer to state that he had no intention to discriminate or merely the wish to encourage full-time employment. He has to show the effect on his business and whether the employment practice complained about is appropriate and necessary to meet his reasons for preferring full-time employment. A court might hold that weighted hourly rates for late afternoon and Saturday working or modified pension benefits for part-timers were more appropriate to meet the objectives of the employer in a case like *Bilka Kaufhaus GmbH* rather than total exclusion of part-timers from the company pension scheme.

Higher administrative and national insurance costs of part-time employment are often relied on to justify a lower part-time rate of pay. It is claimed that those higher costs amount to objective, economic grounds which excuse an apparently discriminatory employment practice. However, the higher costs would have to be proved and anyway in *Norwich Union Insurance Group* v. *ASTMS* (1987) the Central Arbitration Committee (CAC) was not impressed by the cost argument and declared that a collectively agreed mortgage subsidy scheme which excluded part-time workers was sexually discriminatory and should be amended. The CAC said that denial of the mortgage allowance to part-time workers did constitute unlawful sex discrimination in the absence of justification. The evidence presented by the company did not come within sight of justification. The company argued that the cost of extension of the scheme to part-timers was prohibitive and it would have to be clawed back elsewhere within the remuneration package to the detriment of all employees. (Note that the procedure under which an allegedly discriminatory collective agreement could be referred to the CAC was repealed by the SDA 1986. The remedy now is an individual claim by the employee under the EqPA in respect of any term incorporated expressly or impliedly into the contract of employment.)

Cases brought under the SDA suggest that employment practices which disadvantage part-timers might amount to unlawful sex discrimination. In *Clarke & Powell* v. *Eley (IMI) Kynoch Ltd* (1982) the EAT endorsed a tribunal finding that the selection of part-timers before full-timers for redundancy dismissal was unlawful discrimination in the absence of justification on non-sexual grounds. The EAT also refused to interfere with the tribunal's finding that the employers had not justified the practice. The employers had claimed that the selection of part-timers before full-timers for redundancy was a long estab-lished practice and that, after a mass meeting of employees had supported that criterion, the relevant union had endorsed it. The EAT took the view that justification was a matter for the tribunal and it had noted that the union was prepared to vary the selection procedure if the practice of dismissing part-timers first was held to be discriminatory. The fact that an employment practice is based on long-standing attitudes does not give it hallowed status if those attitudes are outmoded and sexually discriminatory. Employers cannot acquire a prescriptive right to discriminate.

7.14   *Pensions, retirement and sex discrimination*

It is in the area of retirement and pensions that European law has had a marked effect on the development of our national anti-discrimination provisions. Both the EqPA 1970 and the SDA 1975 excluded from the requirement of equality of treatment between the sexes any provision of the employment contract relating to death or retirement. Several cases were fought on the basis that our national law was inadequate as being narrower than European law which contained no such general restriction. It was argued successfully that to the extent that protection was greater under European law, those provisions should take precedence over national provisions and individual employees could rely on the European law rules in courts and tribunals within the UK.

7.15   *Retirement ages*

The success of the action in *Marshall* v. *Southampton and S.W. Hampshire Health Authority* (1986) led to amendment of our national law removing the imposition of discriminatory retirement ages. Miss M was a senior dietician who was compulsorily retired at age 62 although men employed by the Health Authority were not compulsorily retired until age 65. Miss M had no chance of successful litigation under national law because of the exception in the SDA of provisions relating to death or retirement. She argued that that exception was in conflict with European law under which she was entitled to equal treatment with men. Particularly she argued that European Directive 76/207 obliged member states to ensure equal treatment in respect of all terms and conditions of employment, including terms related to dismissal. She succeeded before the European Court who held that any individual employee could rely on the terms of the Directive against a member state authority acting in its capacity as employer. European Law Directives could only bind member states and their agencies. That meant that female employees engaged by the 'State' were entitled to remain in employment up to the age of 65 (where that was the normal retirement age for men) but female employees in the private sector of employment had no such entitlement. Other cases followed which explored the distinction between 'State' and private employment. See, for example *Foster* v. *British Gas plc* (1987) and *Rolls Royce plc* v. *Doughty* (1987). However, that distinction was rendered redundant by the amendment contained in the SDA 1986.

From November 1987 all discriminatory retirement ages are unlawful under our national law. Individual employees no longer have to rely on European law. Employers must now have the same compulsory retirement age for men and women employees. Further, any employment practice in respect of promotion, transfer or training which is related to retirement age must be the same for men and women, i.e. if an employer has a policy of not sending for training or not promoting someone who is within x years of retirement, that policy must be applied to men and women in the same way.

7.16 Pensions

Pensions are made up of a flat-rate retirement pension paid by the State and financed through national insurance contributions and earnings-related payments which are made either by the State under the State Earnings-Related Pension Scheme (SERPS) or by the employer under a private, occupational pension scheme which is contracted-out of SERPS. The terms of access to the flat-rate and the earnings-related State schemes are not sexually discriminatory; contributions depend on levels of earnings.

The EqPA 1970 always required equal terms of access to private pension schemes which were contracted-out of SERPS. There has been no national initiative challenging the legality under European law of terms of access which appear equal as between the sexes but which in fact operate less favourably on women, e.g. a qualifying period of full-time employment as a condition of eligibility for membership. But in *Bilka Kaufhaus GmbH* v. *Weber von Hartz* (1986) a German national argued that a condition of eligibility of full-time employment was sexually discriminatory and contrary to European law. The European Court of Justice held that the occupational pension scheme was subject to the requirement of equal treatment and that the exclusion of part-time workers was apparently discriminatory. It remitted to the national court the issue of whether the employer could justify the practice on objective, economic grounds.

There has never been any entitlement to equality of treatment in respect of pension *benefits*. Indeed, the State scheme sets the pattern for discrimination by providing different pensionable ages for men and women. Private pension schemes frequently do discriminate against women members, for example by making payments to the estate of a female employee only on proof of the existence of dependants even though payments to the estate of a male employee are automatic (dependancy of any surviving wife being conclusively presumed). Litigation before the European Court has, so far, had very little effect on discriminatory pension benefits. This is because of the reluctance of the European Court to interfere with national social security legislation affecting pensions and pensionable ages. Indeed, the relevant Directive contains exceptions from the principle of equal treatment in respect of pensionable ages and pension benefits in private schemes where there is a corresponding statutory scheme which does not confer equal treatment. However, there are suggestions in some of the cases that to the extent that a private pension scheme confers benefits additional to the parallel State scheme, there may be an obligation to confer those benefits equally on men and women.

The distinction between pension benefits required by national social security legislation and those provided by private contract between employer and employee was made in *Defrenne* v. *Sabena* (1971) and followed up in *Worringham* v. *Lloyds Bank Ltd* (1981). But it is *Bilka Kaufhaus* v. *Weber von Hartz* which concludes that a contractual scheme which is financed entirely by the employer and which supplements minimum benefits required by national legislation is within the scope of Article 119 of the Treaty of Rome and subject to the requirement of equal treatment. The effect on UK occupational pension schemes is that only private contracted-out schemes which confer benefits additional to SERPS may be subject to the equal treatment requirement and then only to the extent of those additional benefits. Subject to that limited European legal obligation employers can continue to operate pension schemes which confer discriminatory benefits as between men and women.

7.17   Non-pension retirement benefits

After a reference to the European Court in *Garland* v. *British Rail Engineering Ltd* (1982) it was established that non-pension benefits enjoyed in retirement are subject to equal treatment requirements. That case concerned concessionary rail travel which was enjoyed by male and female employees and their families during employment but the concession was withdrawn from female employees and their families after retirement. The European Court held the practice to be in breach of European law and the House of Lords subsequently interpreted the SDA in such a way that only pension benefits are subject to the exclusion from equal treatment.

It follows that any benefit enjoyed in retirement must be available to male and female employees alike. Where, for example, a right to buy company products at a discounted rate continues in retirement the right must continue for females as well as males. It is only if the benefit is 'part and parcel' of the employer's system of catering for retirement that it is excepted under the SDA as a pension benefit.

7.18 Early retirement/voluntary redundancy opportunities

Cases like *Roberts* v. *Tate & Lyle Food & Distribution Ltd* (1986) and *Burton* v. *British Rail* (1982) established that it was not breach of European law to discriminate between the sexes by providing early retirement or voluntary redundancy opportunities linked to different retirement ages. So it was not unlawful to offer such opportunities to women over 55 and men over 60, i.e. both within five years of the normal retirement age. However, now that retirement ages have to be the same this discriminatory practice will no longer operate.

7.19 Redundancy payments

Redundancy compensation under the EP(C)A 1978 is reduced where the redundant employee is in his last working year before the normal age of retirement. For the purposes of this rule the last working year is from the age of 59 to 60 for a woman, and from the age of 64 to 65 for a man. It follows that a woman who is 59 years and six months old at the time she is made redundant will lose half her redundancy compensation. A man who is 59 years and six months old at the time of redundancy will enjoy his full entitlement. No reduction is made against a man's entitlement until he is in his 65th year.

This rule remains unchanged despite the SDA 1986 amendment which prevents compulsory discriminatory retirement ages. But it was successfully challenged as being contrary to European law in *Hammersmith & Queen Charlottes Special Health Authority* v. *Cato* (1987). It was accepted in that case that the employers were a state authority but since the EAT held that the redundancy payment was within Article 119 of the Treaty it would bind private employers within member states in any event. Indications are that our national law is to be changed to remove this discrimination.

7.20   Race discrimination

The Race Relations Act (RRA) 1976 follows the same structure as the
SDA 1975. It prohibits racial discrimination against job applicants and
employees. Racial discrimination can be direct (i.e. less favourable
treatment on racial grounds) or indirect (i.e. the application of a
requirement which appears non-discriminatory but which in fact has
a disproportionate impact on members of a racial group and which is
not justifiable irrespective of colour, race or nationality). According to
the Act a racial group is a group defined by reference to colour, race,
nationality or ethnic or national origins. In *Mandla* v. *Lee* (1983) the
House of Lords held that Sikhs were a racial group within that
definition. A religious group will not be a racial group merely because
of a common creed but if there are ethnic, historical and cultural links
as well and a common geographical origin or descent or a common
language and literature the group will constitute a racial group. Sikhs
are members of a racial group against that test and so are Jews. The
Act declares that segregation on racial grounds is less favourable
treatment.

It is unlawful for an employer to discriminate on racial grounds
against job applicants in the arrangements for offering employment, in
relation to the terms on which employment is offered or by refusing
to offer employment.

An example of direct racial discrimination against a job applicant is
Johnson v. *Timber Tailors (Midlands) Ltd* (1978) in which a black Jamaican
was given such a cursorary and superficial interview as to raise an
inference of racial discrimination.

Note the surprising decision of the Court of Appeal in *Simon* v.
Brimham Associates (1987) that a firm of employment consultants did not
discriminate against a Jewish applicant in connection with employment by Arab employers when the applicant was asked his religion and
told that if he were Jewish, it might preclude his selection for the job.
The Court of Appeal endorsed the tribunal and EAT decision that any
applicant would have been asked the same question and given the
same explanation. Correctly analysed, the effect of the question and
explanation was to discourage Jews from continuing with their
application, as it discouraged the particular applicant. It is argued that
that in itself was enough to amount to less favourable treatment.

An example of indirect racial discrimination is *Hussein* v. *Saints
Complete House Furnishers* (1979) in which a firm stipulated that job
applicants should not be resident in the 'Liverpool 8' district. That
district had a high immigrant population.

7.21 Indirect discrimination and justification

It is possible for an employer to justify an apparently discriminatory employment practice as in *Panesar* v. *Nestlé Co. Ltd* (1980). The employers refused to consider an orthodox Sikh applicant for a job as maintenance engineer at their factory which produced chocolate and coffee. They insisted that the person appointed should be clean-shaven. That requirement had a disproportionate impact on Sikhs (who were held by the House of Lords in *Mandla* v. *Lee* (1983) to be a racial group). However the tribunal and EAT both held that the requirement was justifiable in the interests of proper standards of hygiene in food manufacture.

The test of justifiability was held at first to be business necessity. That test was tempered in *Ojutiku* v. *Manpower Services Commission* (1981). In that case members of the Court of Appeal said that an employment practice was justifiably discriminatory if the employer produced reasons which would be acceptable to right-thinking people as sound and tolerable reasons. That the practice was convenient for the employer did not make it justifiable but the burden was not so strict that he had to show it was necessary. Note that, in the sex discrimination cases, a test of justification which has evolved is 'administrative efficiency' (see *Greater Glasgow Health Board* v. *Carey* (1987)).

7.22 Race as a genuine occupational qualification

Just as there are jobs which require members of a particular sex, so there are jobs which require members of a particular race. The RRA lists four situations in which it is not unlawful to discriminate on racial grounds because membership of a particular racial group is a genuine occupational qualification for the job:

(i)   authenticity requires a member of a particular racial group because the job is part of a drama or other entertainment (e.g. an employer can insist that a black actor be engaged to play a black character);

(ii) authenticity requires a member of a particular racial group because the worker is to be a photographic or artist's model;

(iii) the job involves working in a place where food or drink is provided to the public in a particular racial setting (e.g. Italian waiter in Italian restaurant);

(iv) the job holder provides persons of that racial group with personal services promoting their welfare and those services can most effectively be provided by a person of that racial group (e.g. a local authority recruiting an adviser or community liaison worker to help integrate Asian immigrants could insist on an Asian employee).

There is no small firms exception to the obligation not to discriminate on racial grounds but the obligation does not apply to employment for the purposes of a private household. There is no exception equivalent to that in the Sex Discrimination Act 1975 for jobs involving the performances of duties outside the UK in a country whose laws or customs are such that the duties could not effectively be performed by a member of a particular racial group. Thus a company which wants a salesman to service its contracts in Arab States acts unlawfully if it directly discriminates against Jews. If the discrimination is indirect the company would have to satisfy the tribunal that its practice is justifiable.

It is also unlawful for an employer to discriminate either directly or indirectly against employees in relation to promotion, training or other benefits or dismissal or any other detriment. See, for example, *Haroun* v. *Johnson (Troy Auto Spares)* (1979) where the applicant, who had insufficient service to claim unfair dismissal, succeeded instead under the RRA. The tribunal found there was racial antipathy between the applicant and his manager; racist graffiti had appeared in the toilets which could only have been directed against the applicant and the manager had taken no notice of his complaints. The tribunal found that the applicant had been dismissed by reason of racial discrimination.

7.23   Race discrimination and vicarious liability

Employers are vicariously liable for acts of racial discrimination committed by their employees in the course of employment, whether or not those acts are done with the employer's knowledge or approval. Whether the employee was acting in the course of his employment when he committed the act of racial discrimination was the issue in *Irving* v. *The Post Office* (1987). A postman employed by the respondents lived next door to the plaintiffs, who were black Jamaicans. While sorting mail, the postman saw an envelope addressed to the applicants and wrote on the back 'Go back to Jamaica, Sambo'. When it was discovered who was responsible the postman was disciplined but the plaintiffs also sought damages from the Post Office. The issue was whether the Post Office was vicariously liable. The County Court and the Court of Appeal both found the employers not liable since the postman was not acting in the course of his employment when he wrote the offensive words. The postman was allowed to write on mail only for the purposes of ensuring its effective delivery. In writing an offensive message out of personal malevolence he could not be regarded as performing an authorised act even in an unauthorised manner. The act was entirely outside the sphere of his employment. It is not enough to justify a finding that an employee acts in the course of his employment that the employment gives him the opportunity to commit the wrongful act or that it was committed during the period of the employment.

It is a defence to vicarious liability for the employer to show that he took such steps as were reasonably practicable to prevent the employee doing the acts complained of. This vicarious liability will apply to overt acts of race discrimination but, less obviously, will also apply to acts of racial harassment. *De Sousa* v. *Automobile Association* (1986) establishes that racial harassment can constitute a detriment of which the employee can complain short of any other disadvantage such as demotion, transfer or dismissal. To avoid vicarious liability for racial harassment the employer should make it clear that he will not tolerate such conduct as racist language, racist jibes or baiting of fellow employees on racist grounds. He should have an equal opportunities policy and should react strongly to complaints of racial discrimination so as to eliminate such behaviour.

7.24   *Proof of race/sex discrimination*

In seeking to establish a claim of sex or racial discrimination an applicant may issue pro formas seeking answers to questions set by statutory regulations (see the Sex Discrimination (Questions and Replies) Order 1975 No. 2048 and the Race Relations (Questions and Replies) Order 1977 No. 842). The forms are admissible as evidence in subsequent court or tribunal proceedings.

It is also possible for an applicant to seek discovery of documents within the employer's possession in order to establish his claim. Where, for example, an applicant claims that he was racially discriminated against in not being offered a job he may seek discovery of documents giving information about the other candidates and the successful applicant. Or an existing employee who alleges sex discrimination in that she was not promoted may seek discovery of documents appertaining to the successful employee. The difficulty which the reasonable employer has is in balancing disclosure necessary to show the applicant has no case with the need to protect confidentiality in relation to other employees or other applicants. In *Nasse* v. *Science Research Council* and *Vyas* v. *Leyland Cars* (1979) which were heard together by the House of Lords, it was held that orders for disclosure of confidential documents should be made rarely and only where disclosure was necessary for the fair disposal of the case. Where information contained in confidential documents had to be disclosed under that rule, all practicable steps should be taken to preserve confidence. For example, names of successful candidates could be blacked out, leaving other information visible, or disclosure could be made to the parties and their representatives but not publicly in open court. Employers might resist an application for disclosure of confidential documents by making them available to the tribunal chairman only to enable him to see that disclosure is not necessary for the fair disposal of the case.

For a successful application for disclosure of documents in discrimination cases see *Perera* v. *Civil Service Commission* (1980): the fact that assembly of the documentation would be difficult and expensive did not relieve the employer from the disclosure obligation. The tribunal will not order discovery of documents containing information relevant only to the credibility of the employer (see *Jalota* v. *Imperial Metal Industry (Kynoch) Ltd* (1979)) – i.e. no order would be made for discovery of any document to challenge the employer over his truthfulness about a matter unconnected with the allegation of racial discrimination.

7.25   Codes of Practice

The Commission for Racial Equality issued a Code of Practice for the elimination of racial discrimination in 1983. The Code gives practical guidance to help employers implement the provisions of the Act. Its provisions are not legally binding but are admissible in evidence in proceedings and are often taken as establishing reasonable employment standards. Similarly the Equal Opportunities Commission issued a Code of Practice for the elimination of sex discrimination in employment in 1985.

Chapter 8

Continuity of Employment, Normal Working Hours and a Week's Pay

8.01 Continuity of employment

'Continuity of employment' means the length of service which an employee has built up with his employer. Continuity may be a crucial factor in determining entitlement to statutory employment rights or compensation (the qualifying periods are given in Appendix D) and may determine eligibility and benefits under particular contractual schemes. For example, occupational sick pay schemes often provide for full benefits only after a specified period has been served.

Continuity of employment is made up of qualifying weeks but it is counted in months and years, i.e. if X begins work on 1 March 1982 and ends on 3 April 1986, he has four years' service. It is not necessary to count the total weeks and then divide by 52. Normally, if a week does not count towards continuity, it breaks it and service begins afresh. If, for example, X has six years' service then one week which does not count, his six years' continuity is lost and he must begin again. There are exceptions (see below) but that is the basic rule.

8.02 The statutory rules on continuity

Continuity is worked out in accordance with the rules contained in Schedule 13 EP(C)A 1978 as follows:

(1) An employee's service with the same employer is presumed to have been continuous, i.e. it is for the employer to show that there was some interruption in an apparently continuous period of the employment relationship. Continuity runs throughout variation of employment terms, e.g. change of duties, promotions, transfers, increases of wages/salary. See, for example, *Wood v. York City Council* (1978) where the employee had a number of different jobs without interruption with the council. When he was made redundant the council contested the length of his service and argued that his employment lasted only

123

for the duration of his final contract. The Court of Appeal held that in the absence of evidence to the contrary the employee's service with the council continued throughout all his contracts and he was entitled to compensation based on the whole period.

(2) Any week during which the employee actually works for 16 or more hours counts towards continuity. If an employee is contractually bound to work only 12 hours, but works overtime of five hours in any week, that week counts for continuity purposes. However, any week during which the employee reverts to the standard 12 hours will not count and will break continuity.

(3) Any week during which there is a contract subsisting between the parties normally involving employment for 16 or more hours counts towards continuity. This is the normal basis on which continuity accrues and the emphasis is on the contract, rather than the hours worked. Under this rule holiday periods and sickness absences will count since the contract goes on. Note that hours of preparation or stand-by do not usually count towards the 16 hours required (see *Suffolk County Council* v. *Secretary of State for the Environment* (1985)). The House of Lords held that a retained fireman who was permanently 'on-call' was not working under a contract for 16 or more hours weekly. He operated his own shop during normal shop hours and was free to pursue his own activities during evenings and weekends except that he had to be in close enough proximity to answer an emergency call. The House of Lords held that the stand-by hours were not hours of employment. 'Employment involves work or some other activity carried out for the purposes and at the behest of the employer' (Lord Fraser).

Meal breaks will not count towards the 16 hours if the employee is free to leave the premises or pursue his own activities during them. Also, time spent travelling to and from work is usually outside normal working hours.

A recent House of Lords decision prevents the aggregation of hours worked under separate but concurrent contracts with the same employer. In *Lewis* v. *Surrey County Council* (1987) a part-time teacher who worked on different courses under three separate contracts could not aggregate the hours so as to clear the 16 hours hurdle and establish continuity. The House of Lords held that the reference to 'contract' in Schedule 13 could not be read as including 'contracts' since the whole emphasis was on the particular contract of employment and the Schedule contained nothing suggesting that aggregation of hours worked under separate contracts was permissible. However, it was suggested that if an employer fragmented hours and duties into separate contracts with the intention of preventing continuity accruing, an industrial tribunal could treat the fragmentation as a sham and ignore it. There was no suggestion in the particular case that the contracts were not genuine, independent contracts.

Where an employer does take on a person in two or more separate capacities no one of which entails work for 16 hours he would be best advised to issue separate documention and separate pay statements to prevent any argument that there is a single contract so that aggregation is permissible.

(4) If the employee has normal contractual hours of 16 or more but those hours are temporarily reduced to between 8 and 16, those weeks of reduced hours count. However, not more than 26 such weeks count. A temporary shortfall of contractual hours does not stop continuity running.

(5) Once an employee qualifies for any statutory right he remains qualified unless or until his normal contractual hours are reduced to below 8 *and* he actually works less than 16 hours in any week. For example, if an employee has six years' service as a full-time employee and then his normal hours are reduced to 12 weekly he remains entitled to all the statutory protection of a full-time employee.

(6) Even though there is no subsisting contract of employment a week still counts if the employee is:

(i) incapable of work because of sickness or injury. (Note that normally any period of sick leave will count under (3) above because the contract will continue, with or without sick pay. It seems, however, that even if the contract ends and a new contract begins on the employee's recovery, continuity will run through the intervening period under this rule.) Not more than 26 weeks count under this head.

(ii) absent because of a temporary cessation of work.

(iii) absent from work in circumstances where by arrangement or custom employment is regarded as continuous.

Usually, continuity ends with the contract of employment and even if the employee is subsequently re-engaged his service under the previous contract is lost. However, continuity will run through immediately consecutive contracts and successive fixed term contracts (see *BBC* v. *Ioannou* (1975)). In order to break continuity there must be at least one week's gap between the end of one and the beginning of the next contract. Even then, continuity will run if the interval is regarded as a 'temporary cessation of work'. In *Ford* v. *Warwickshire County Council* (1983) the House of Lords held that a teacher employed under a series of fixed term contracts for each academic year, September to July, did have continuity in spite of the gaps of the summer vacations during which no contracts existed. The House of Lords treated each summer vacation as a period of absence on account of temporary cessation of work. Lord Diplock said that 'temporary' means 'transient', i.e. lasting only a short time in comparison to the duration of the contracts either side of the cessation of work.

In *Flack* v. *Kodak Ltd* (1985) the Court of Appeal, interpreting Lord Diplock's reference to temporary as transient, held that a tribunal should not take a strict mathematical approach in expressing the cessation as a percentage of employment periods before and after the gap. Where an employee works intermittently over a period of years in an irregular pattern, whether the gaps count towards or break continuity depends on the whole employment period. For example, if an employee works for 20 years, then has a three-month break, followed by 18 months' work, an industrial tribunal might reasonably conclude that the three-month break was a temporary cessation. Similarly, an employee who works 20 years then has two-week gap followed by one week's work, then a six-week gap followed by one week's work, then a two-week gap followed by 18 months' work still might be regarded as continuously employed throughout. But a purely mathematical approach would mean that the six-week gap would not be a temporary cessation since it is 300 per cent of the periods of employment immediately before and after. The court said that it would offend common sense if employment was not regarded as continuous in the second example where, in the first example, a longer break would count as temporary. The whole period of employment has to be taken into account in determining whether any interval(s) is(are) temporary cessation(s) of work. It is then a question of fact for the industrial tribunal.

If the employee leaves to go to work for another employer but returns after a short period continuity will not run under the temporary cessation rule since that requires a lack of available work with the original employer. Continuity may run, however, if there is 'an arrangement or custom' whereby employment is regarded as continuous. See, for example, *Wishart* v. *National Coal Board* (1974) where the employee continued to be treated as an employed member of the pension scheme during a period of employment with another employer.

The arrangement or custom rule was applied in *Lloyds Bank Ltd* v. *Secretary of State for Employment* (1979). The EAT held that a woman who worked 35 hours in alternate weeks did have continuity. The 'off-duty' weeks counted since there was an arrangement between the parties that the employment continued.

The decision has been very much criticised on the grounds that since there was a continuing contract, albeit one which did not require any work in alternate weeks, the arrangement or custom provision was not applicable. That provision should only apply where there is no subsisting contract. The case looks even more odd when compared with the decision in *Opie* v. *John Gubbins (Insurance Brokers) Ltd* (1978). There the employee worked alternating three-day and two-day weeks. In the three-day weeks she worked 20 hours (so those weeks counted) but in the two-day weeks she worked only 13 hours. The EAT held that each two-day week broke continuity. Those weeks clearly could not count under the present provision since the contract continued and anyway the employee was not absent from work. There is no justification in the Schedule for averaging irregular, but predetermined, hours.

(7) If a woman exercises her statutory right to return to work after maternity leave, the period of maternity leave counts as a period of continuous employment.

(8) Normally, a week which does not count breaks continuity and the benefit of previous service is lost. However, any week during which the employee is on strike or locked-out by the employer does not count but does not break continuity. The commencement of service is postponed by the number of days lost through the strike or lock-out.

(9) Normally, employment is continuous only if it is with the same employer; a change of employer breaks continuity. But there are the following exceptions to this rule:

(i)   If a trade or business is transferred, employees taken on by the transferee can count their previous service with the transferor and, under the Transfer of Undertakings (Protection of Employment) Regulations 1981 workers who are still employed by the transferor at the time of transfer are treated as employees of the transferee (see Chapter 6 above).

(ii) Continuous employment with associated employers is treated as employment by the same employer. The definition of associated employers is contained in section 153(4) EP(C)A 1978, i.e. 'any two employers are to be treated as associated if one is a company of which the other (directly or indirectly) has control, or if both are companies of which a third person (directly or indirectly) has control. That will include companies in the relationship of holding and subsidiary companies and companies which are both subsidiaries of a third company or under the control of a third person. Note that 'control' means voting control (see *Secretary of State for Employment* v. *Newbold* (1981)).

Neither local authorities nor health authorities are 'associated employers' so continuity does not run in favour of, for example, a doctor moving from one health authority to another or a teacher moving between education authorities. However, a special provision treats schools within the same local education authority as associated for the purposes of continuity.

(iii) If on the employer's death the personal representatives of the employer take on any employee, employment is treated as continuous.

(iv) Any change in the identity of partners, trustees or personal representatives is ignored for the purposes of continuity of employment of their employees.

(10) Where an unfairly dismissed employee is taken back into employment following a tribunal recommendation for reinstatement or re-engagement, continuity of employment is preserved. Likewise, continuity runs if the re-engagement or reinstatement is in consequence of ACAS conciliation.

Note that the parties cannot agree to vary these statutory rules. Any attempt to do so will be ineffective for the purposes of computation of continuity. However, the agreement between the parties may be actionable between themselves. See, for example *Secretary of State for Employment* v. *Globe Elastic Thread Co. Ltd* (1979) where an employee agreed to work for his original employer's brother in reliance on a representation that employment would be treated as continuous. Since the brothers were not associated employers, continuity did not run and the transferee employer could not claim the statutory redundancy rebate. If the transferee had refused to calculate the redundancy entitlement based on both periods of service the employee would have had to sue on the representation in the ordinary courts.

8.03   Normal working hours

The discussion of continuity above makes it clear that the build-up of service with an employer and the accrual of statutory employment protection usually hinges on 'normal working hours' exceeding 16 weekly. The calculation of a week's pay for the purposes of redundancy compensation, the unfair dismissal basic award and guarantee payment also depends on whether or not the employee has 'normal working hours'.

There is no definitive statutory provision on what are 'normal working hours' but usually they are the minimum hours weekly which the employee is obliged to work. The written statement of contract terms which an employer is obliged to issue (see Chapter 2 above) should contain details of the normal working hours and this will usually be taken as the best evidence of what was agreed between the parties. That is what happened in *Gascol Conversions Ltd* v. *Mercer* (1974). The employee claimed that his normal working hours were 54 weekly and his redundancy compensation should be calculated on that basis. The employer claimed normal working hours were 40, as stated in the written contract. The Court of Appeal regarded the written statement as determining the issue. However, if the written statement does not reflect the practice or the original agreement has been varied by subsequent practice and evidence is available to show the variation, a court or tribunal might find that the written statement is not conclusive (see the discussion in Chapter 2).

8.04 Implied agreement as to normal working hours

If the written statement does not contain details of what are the normal working hours or if, as is more likely, there is no written statement at all, the tribunal will have to try to work out what the parties agreed and infer a term. In *Dean* v. *Eastbourne Fishermen's and Boatmen's Protection Society and Club Ltd* (1977) there was no written statement and only an informal arrangement between the parties that the employee, a barman, would work normal club session hours and extra hours if required by the club manager. The EAT said that in such circumstances normal working hours depended on the hours actually worked during the relevant qualifying period. The employee was claiming redundancy compensation. The qualifying period was two years so that determination of normal working hours depended on hours actually worked in the two years before dismissal. In over 80 per cent of the weeks in that two-year period the employee had actually worked more than 21 hours (21 hours weekly was at that time the qualifying threshold: it is now 16 hours weekly). The EAT concluded that the barman's normal weekly hours exceeded 21 and he was entitled to redundancy compensation.

8.05 Overtime

Normal weekly hours do not usually include overtime hours. This point also is made by the Court of Appeal in *Gascol Conversions Ltd* v. *Mercer* (1974). Overtime hours are included *only* if they are contractually obligatory on both employer and employee, i.e. not only must the employee be bound to work a fixed number of hours overtime but the employer must be bound to supply work or pay for those overtime hours. Usually, if there is a reference in the contract or written statement to overtime hours it fixes pay rates in the event of overtime being worked. Sometimes a contractual obligation is imposed on the employee to work reasonable overtime, or even a fixed number of overtime hours, but it is very uncommon for an employer to be bound to provide overtime work.

One case in which a tribunal did find an implied contractual guarantee of overtime was where employees were told when they started work that their hours were 7.00 AM to 6.00 PM on weekdays. The employers operated a continuous process and two-shift system and could only have operated on the basis of mutually obligatory overtime. The tribunal held that normal working hours included overtime hours in excess of the 40 claimed by the employers.

Where the contract or written statement does not specify normal working hours but provides that overtime rates shall be payable after a fixed number of hours, the fixed number are the normal working hours. For example, in one case an agricultural worker claimed redundancy compensation on the basis of a normal working week of between 50 and 60 hours. There was no formal agreement between the parties about normal working hours but an Agricultural Wages Order provided that hours worked in excess of 40 should be paid at overtime rates. That Order was incorporated into the worker's contract with the result that his normal working hours were taken to be 40 and his redundancy compensation was calculated accordingly, excluding overtime.

However, where a fixed number of hours, including some at overtime rates, is obligatory it is the fixed number which are the normal working hours. If, for example, the contract states that normal working hours shall be 42 hours weekly but that hours in excess of 38 shall be payable at time and a half, the normal working hours are 42. This rule is contained in Schedule 14 EP(C)A 1978 and is consistent with the discussion above – overtime hours are now obligatory on both sides.

8.06   A week's pay

The rules for calculating a week's pay for any employee are contained in Schedule 14 EP(C)A 1978 and are as follows:

(1) Where there are normal working hours and the pay does not vary

with the amount of work done, a week's pay is the contractual remuneration for the normal working hours. If, therefore, normal working hours are 40 weekly and the employee is paid on a time basis at £3.50 per hour, a week's pay will be 40 × £3.50 = £140. Note that if shift supplements are included in the time rate then the week's pay includes those supplements.

(2) If there are normal working hours but the pay does vary according to the amount of work done (e.g. piece rates are payable) a week's pay is calculated by averaging the hourly rate over the 12 weeks preceding the calculation date. If, therefore, the employee normally works 40 hours weekly and received amounts varying between £150 and £170 in each of the preceding 12 weeks, an average hourly rate would be calculated by adding the sums received in each of the 12 weeks, then dividing by 12 and then dividing by 40. A week's pay is then the resultant figure multiplied by 40. This rule applies to determine the week's pay if only part of the contractual remuneration depends on work done, i.e. commission or bonus rates are payable in addition to a basic rate. For example, a basic hourly rate is £1.50 and then piece rates apply for work done over a fixed standard.

(3) If there are normal working hours but they are performed at different times in different weeks and at different rates a week's pay is determined by averaging over the 12 weeks preceding the calculation date. For example, an employee normally works 40 hours weekly but alternates eight hours on Saturday (at time and a half) in one week with eight hours on Sunday (at double time) in the next week. The remaining 32 hours are at standard hourly rates. The week's pay would therefore average out to give him 32 hours at basic rate plus eight hours at time and three-quarters.

Note that, for the purposes of rules 2 and 3, where the employee actually worked more than the normal working hours in the 12 weeks over which averaging occurs, those extra hours must be taken into account in determining the average hourly rate but ignoring any overtime supplement, e.g. the employee is paid piece rates and has normal working hours of 40 weekly. Piece rates rise by 50 per cent in respect of hours worked over 40 in any week. In each of the 12 weeks preceding the calculation the employee worked two hours overtime. In calculating his week's pay the 50 per cent supplement to piece rates would be ignored but the extra two hours weekly would be taken into account, thus reducing the average hourly rate. In *British Coal Corporation* v. *Cheesbrough* (1988) the Court of Appeal confirmed that such was the statutory rule in spite of the effect that a redundant employee who had worked a great deal of overtime would have a lower week's pay and so a smaller redundancy payment than one who had confined his effort to normal working hours.

Note also that the 12-week period must consist of weeks during which the employee actually worked and the pay he actually received during those weeks. If he did not work in any week (e.g. because of sickness) the next preceding week must be included to make up the twelve. If workloads are running down preceding a partial or total closedown, and hence redundancies, this rule means that average hourly rates will be depressed since an employee is likely to earn less in the 12 weeks preceding such a closedown. As long as the employee earns *something* in any week in the 12-week period, that week will be included in the calculation.

(4) If there are no normal working hours a week's pay is the average weekly remuneration over the 12-week period preceding the calculation date.

8.07　*Remuneration included in a week's pay*

The remuneration included in the calculation of a week's pay is the contractual monetary payment made by the employer for work done. That will include any contractual bonus or allowance but, normally, not overtime payments. Expenses are not included if they are paid by way of reimbursement of expenditure incurred by the employee. If there is a profit element, expenses would be included but if that method of payment appears to be a way of avoiding income tax a tribunal might conclude that the contract is illegal and refuse to enforce it. Benefits in kind are usually not included in determining the amount of a 'week's pay' under the statutory formula. So provision of a company car or free accommodation is left out of account. (Note that such benefits *are* taken into account where compensation does not depend on the statutory definition of a week's pay, e.g. the compensatory award in unfair dismissal or damages in wrongful dismissal.)

Tips and gratuities paid at the discretion of a third party are not part of a week's pay. If minimum wage levels are fixed by a Wages Council or Agricultural Wages Board it will be that minimum which is the week's pay where the contractual wage is less.

8.08　*Statutory ceiling on a week's pay*

There is a maximum limit on the amount of a week's pay (£164 with effect from 1st April 1988) which applies to the following awards:

(i) the basic award for unfair dismissal;

(ii) redundancy compensation;

(iii) the additional unfair dismissal award where the employer fails to comply with a reinstatement/re-engagement order;

(iv) debts payable by the Department of Employment on the employer's insolvency, i.e. arrears of pay (up to eight weeks), statutory notice pay, holiday pay (up to six weeks) and a basic award for unfair dismissal.

Chapter 9

Termination of the Contract of Employment

9.01 Forms of termination

The contract of employment can terminate *either* by act of the parties (e.g. resignation or dismissal) *or* by operation of law (e.g. where the common law doctrine of frustration applies because performance is no longer possible or is radically different to that contemplated by the parties or where the law regards the contract as discharged by performance).

9.02 Termination by act of parties

Notice

The contract of employment or the written statement of contract terms should refer to the period of notice to which the employee is entitled and also the period of notice which he is obliged to give on resignation. Where the contract contained no express notice provision there used to be a resumption of a yearly hiring but that gradually gave way to an implied term that the employer would give reasonable notice. So, in *Richardson* v. *Koefod* (1969), Lord Denning in the Court of Appeal referred to the presumption of a yearly hiring as a consequence of an agriculturally based society which had ceased to be valid in modern industrial circumstances. Cases in the 1930s had doubted the validity of the presumption and Lord Denning felt able to state explicitly that there was no longer any such presumption. He said, 'in the absence of express stipulation, the rule is that every contract of service is determinable by reasonable notice'.

In fact, statute has displaced the reasonable notice implication and section 49 EP(C)A 1978 provides for minimum notice entitlement which is linked to continuity of employment (see Appendix D where the minimum periods are set out). The section also obliges an employee with at least one month's continuity to give at least one week's notice of resignation.

The contract can, and frequently does, provide for longer periods of notice but the parties cannot contract out of the minimum entitlement. Section 49 says that there is nothing to prevent either party from waiving his right to notice on any occasion but the waiver cannot be general but must be linked to the particular termination. However, there is no right to notice of termination where a party has acted in gross breach of contract (e.g. serious or gross misconduct on the part of the employee) and where there is no such gross breach the employee can always accept wages in lieu of notice. It is generally the case that an employer can *insist* on paying wages in lieu of notice since there is usually no obligation to provide work as well as pay wages (see [3.13]).

Section 50 EP(C)A 1978 protects the employee's payment rights during the notice period. These provisions will be of no practical application where the employee works the notice period under normal working conditions but will apply where work levels have declined or the employee is away sick or on holiday during the notice period. Under these provisions the employee is entitled to the average hourly rate of remuneration for normal working hours. Any payments made by the employer in respect of sick pay, holiday pay or otherwise can be deducted.

If the employer fails to give the statutory minimum notice or due contract notice if that is longer, the remedy of the employee is a breach of contract action in the normal courts. The employee is similarly liable for breach of contract if he leaves with short or no notice but it is unlikely to be worthwhile for the employer to sue. Normally an employee will not be compelled by any court to remain at work during the notice period and the employer will have some difficulty in establishing the level of damages suffered through loss of the employee's services.

9.03   Dismissal

Wrongful dismissal

Dismissal may be without notice (summary dismissal) i.e. with short notice or no notice at all. The action in wrongful dismissal was all that used to be available to an employee at common law and that only applied where dismissal was without due contractual notice and he himself had not acted in gross breach of contract. The employee had no complaint at law if he was dismissed, however unreasonably, with full notice or wages in lieu of notice. Neither could he complain if he had acted in serious breach of contract since the law regarded the employer as entitled to 'accept' his repudiation of the contract by dismissing. Further, even if an employee was dismissed with no or inadequate notice in circumstances which did not justify summary dismissal complaint had to be made through the ordinary courts and damages were usually limited to the wages which the employee would have received if he had been given due contract notice.

Conduct which would justify summary dismissal depends on the circumstances of the particular case but the following examples illustrate the courts' approach.

Jupiter General Insurance Co. Ltd v. *Shroff* (1937)
The manager of the employing insurance company's Life Department agreed to grant a policy to X knowing that the managing governor had already refused him a policy. The court upheld his summary dismissal on the grounds of his intolerable behaviour and misconduct.

Clouston & Co. Ltd v. *Corry* (1906)
The summary dismissal of a manager of a grain and produce department for persistent drunkenness and the use of foul language was held justified.

Savage v. *British India Navigation Co.* (1930)
The gross negligence of a ship's master in failing to notice that a sea valve was open causing flooding to the hold was held to justify summary dismissal.

Sinclair v. *Neighbour* (1967)
Summary dismissal was justified where an employee 'borrowed' money from the till and put in an IOU.

Pepper v. *Webb* (1969)
The summary dismissal of a gardener for refusing to obey instructions and insolence to his employer was upheld. The Court of Appeal held that his attitude showed a pattern of non-co-operation and careless performance.

From 1972 onwards the action in unfair dismissal before industrial tribunals has been available. It continues to be possible to complain of wrongful dismissal before the normal courts but for most employees the tribunal action will be preferable as being cheaper, quicker, less formal and more accessible. However, there has been a marked recent tendency for employees in the public sector to revert to breach of contract actions or to seek judicial review of the dismissal (see [10.16] – [10.18] below).

Most instances of conduct which would justify summary dismissal at common law would result in a finding of fair dismissal before the industrial tribunals.

9.04 Unfair dismissal

The right not to be unfairly dismissed was introduced by the Industrial Relations Act 1971, preserved by the 1974 Trade Union and Labour Relations Act which repealed nearly all other of the 1971 provisions and is now contained in the EP(C)A 1978. The right is enforceable by any employee (though not an independent contractor) provided he has two years' service down to the effective date of termination and provided he is under the normal retirement age. In calculating the two years' service statutory minimum periods of notice are added if the employer purported to dismiss summarily. The two year service requirement does not apply if the reason for dismissal was because the employee was a member of an independent trade union or participated in the activities of an independent trade union.

9.05 Procedure of unfair dismissal

To complain of unfair dismissal the employee must present his 'originating application' (form IT1) to the Central Office of Industrial Tribunals (or a Regional Office) within three months following the effective date of termination. A tribunal can allow a late application where it finds that it was 'not reasonably practicable' for the employee to present in time. The originating application is forwarded to the appropriate Regional Office of Industrial Tribunals and all further communication with the parties is through that office. A copy of the originating application is sent to the employer and he has 14 days within which to file his response – his 'notice of appearance' (form IT3). The employer should take care in completing the notice of appearance since, though he will not necessarily be limited at the hearing to giving evidence only about the matters entered on the form, substantial change at the hearing is undesirable since it might adversely affect credibility or occasion an adjournment application from the other side and result in greater costs.

If the originating application does not give sufficient information to enable an adequate defence to be prepared the employer can seek further and better particulars of the complaint from the employee, through the Regional Office. Orders for discovery of documents and attendance of witnesses can also be made through the Regional Office.

Where the originating application appears to show no hope of success the employer can seek a pre-hearing assessment. Normally, cases where the employee's service qualification is inadequate or other cases in which the tribunal clearly has no jurisdiction are weeded out at an earlier stage by the Regional Office. The pre-hearing assessment is designed to stop wholly meritless claims from proceeding. The procedure also applies to wholly meritless defences but it is almost always the employer who applies for any pre-hearing assessment.

Copies of the originating application and the notice of appearance are sent to ACAS (the Advisory Conciliation and Arbitration Service) and an ACAS officer attempts conciliation and settlement of the claim without the matter going forward to a tribunal hearing. Statistics show that almost three-quarters of unfair dismissal applications are settled or withdrawn without a hearing. A large number of settlements are reached under the auspices of ACAS since such settlements are binding and the complaint cannot be resurrected. Regional Offices are usually susceptible to applications for extension of time where the parties are negotiating and a settlement is possible.

If no settlement is reached and the application is not withdrawn the matter is listed for hearing after at least 14 days' notice to each party. The notice of hearing includes information and guidance about the hearing, the bringing of documents and witnesses and representation. Either side can be represented by any person: representation before industrial tribunals is not limited to qualified lawyers. Legal aid is not available to the employee to meet the cost of legal representation at the hearing. Employees' representatives are commonly lay persons or trade union officials. It is more common for employers to be legally represented though often a personnel or other manager presents the employer's case. Tribunals have wide discretion over the conduct of proceedings at the hearing and a good deal of help and latitude is given to unrepresented parties.

9.06   The tribunal hearing

The tribunal hearing takes place in public unless the tribunal grants a request for a private hearing which can be made only on very limited grounds. The proceedings should be free from undue formality (there are no gowns or wigs, bars or witness boxes) and the tribunals do not adhere rigidly to the rules of evidence which apply in normal court proceedings.

Where dismissal is admitted by the employer the normal procedure at the hearing is as follows:

(1) The employer (or representative) makes an opening statement which outlines the case and draws attention to the main issues (e.g. dismissal was for persistent absenteeism, the job was redundant, the applicant persistently refused to obey instructions reasonably and legitimately given, etc.). The opening statement usually identifies the principal witnesses and their evidence and identifies any documentation.

(2) The employer calls his witnesses in turn to give evidence.

(3) Each witness is cross-examined by the applicant (or his representative).

(4) The chairman and lay-members ask questions of each witness after cross-examination.

(5) The employer has the opportunity to re-examine on any of the matters arising on cross-examination or from the tribunal's questions.

(6) The applicant puts his case giving evidence himself and then calling his witnesses.

(7) Cross-examination, tribunal questions and the re-examination of the applicant and his witnesses in turn follow.

(8) The applicant makes a summary of his case identifying areas of conflict, referring to authorities and inviting tribunal conclusions.

(9) The employer makes his final address.

(10) The tribunal retires to consider its decision.

(11) The tribunal announces its decision and, if the claim succeeds, makes inquiry of the applicant as to the remedy sought.

(12) The tribunal may take evidence from the applicant about loss of wages, his efforts to find alternative work, etc. Employer may cross-examine.

(13) The tribunal retires to assess the remedy.

(14) The tribunal returns to announce the remedy.

9.07 Proof of dismissal

If dismissal is disputed, the employee goes first and presents his evidence to justify his claim of dismissal. He has the burden of proving dismissal. If he cannot show dismissal the claim is lost at that stage.

'Dismissal' is defined in section 55(2) EP(C)A 1978 and is:

- termination by the employer with or without notice (note this major difference from the common law action in wrongful dismissal which only applies where dismissal is without due notice);
- expiry of a fixed term contract without renewal (but a waiver clause avoiding unfair dismissal protection can be inserted in a written contract for one year or more and is effective if the employee signs his agreement to waiver);
- resignation by the employee with or without notice prompted by the employer's repudiatory breach of contract.

Employers do sometimes dispute dismissal and claim that instead the contract terminated by operation of law, e.g. frustration or discharge by performance (see below). Alternatively, the employer may argue that the contract was terminated by mutual agreement or that the applicant dismissed himself because of his conduct. Judicial decisions suggest that these arguments are not easily accepted and, even if the employee has acted in breach of contract the employer still has to 'accept' the breach in order to terminate the contract and that acceptance is the dismissal. See, for example, *London Transport Executive* v. *Clark* (1981) where the Court of Appeal held by majority that the removal of the employee's name from the company books because of extended unauthorised absence was still a dismissal in spite of the repudiatory breach by the employee. Two of the three judges regarded the contract of employment as subject to the normal contractual rule that a repudiatory breach is ineffective until the innocent party accepts it and terminates the contract. Lord Denning, in the minority, thought that certain fundamental breaches (including extended unauthorised absence) would terminate the contract of employment automatically without the need for acceptance. In such a case there would be no effective dismissal and so a claim for unfair dismissal could not proceed. But it seems that the majority view prevails and it was affirmed by another Court of Appeal decision in *Igbo* v. *Johnson Matthey Chemicals Ltd* (1986) which held in addition that any document by which the employee purports to consent to the automatic termination view is invalid and unenforceable.

Termination by mutual consent is not a dismissal but a finding of mutual termination is rare and will not usually be made where the employer has dismissed with notice but then allows the employee to leave before expiry of the notice. It is still the employer's act which is the cause of termination and that will constitute a dismissal. See *McAlwene* v. *Boughton Estates Ltd* (1973) in which Sir John Donaldson said:

'... it would be a very rare case indeed in which it could properly be found that the employer and the employee had got together and, notwithstanding that there was a current notice of termination of employment, agreed mutually to terminate the contract ...'

A similar result was reached by the Court of Appeal in *Lees* v. *Arthur Greaves (Lees) Ltd* (1974) where the employer 'persuaded' the employee to leave before the notice expired and then contested dismissal. Where a dismissal notice has been issued mutual termination will only be found if the employee agrees to a variation of the termination method with full knowledge of the implications.

Note that it remains a dismissal if it is the employee who gives counter-notice to terminate the contract earlier than the expiry date of the employer's notice (section 55(3) EP(C)A 1978).

An enforced resignation will be treated as a dismissal. See, for example, *Thames Television Ltd* v. *Wallis* (1979) where the employee was given no real choice. However, even where the employer instigates termination negotiations, if an arrangement is reached whereby severance terms are agreed and the employee then resigns a tribunal might well conclude that there is no dismissal. It depends on the circumstances and the respective bargaining strengths of the parties; a senior member of management might be regarded as better able to protect his interests than an inarticulate and unrepresented worker. In *Sheffield* v. *Oxford Controls Co. Ltd* (1979), for example, a director who signed a letter of resignation setting out severance terms which included a substantial payment was held not to have been dismissed. The tribunal concluded that the terms of severance had emerged and the threat of dismissal was no longer an operative factor in the employee's decision to resign. An employer in this position of reaching severance agreement is best advised to embody the agreement in an ACAS settlement form (COT 3) which precludes the possibility of the employee subsequently denying resignation or mutual termination and claiming unfair dismissal. In *Hennessey* v. *Craigmyle & Co. Ltd* (1985) the Court of Appeal refused to set aside such an ACAS settlement on the grounds of the economic duress of the employee. An oppressive, enforced settlement might be set aside on the grounds of economic duress but the evidence did not support that contention in the case.

9.08 Constructive dismissal

If the employee resigns because of the employer's conduct he is treated as dismissed for the purposes of unfair dismissal and redundancy.

There was some initial uncertainty over whether the employer's conduct had to be in repudiatory breach of contract, i.e. fundamental or gross breach or whether it was enough to justify resignation if the employer acted unreasonably. The Court of Appeal held in *Western Excavating Ltd* v. *Sharp* (1977) that repudiatory breach of contract by the employer was required. Lord Denning said that for constructive dismissal there had to be a significant breach going to the root of the contract by the employer or his conduct must show an intention no longer to be bound by the terms of the contract.

If the employer breaks a basic term, e.g. he does not pay the employee, the employee is entitled to resign and claim constructive unfair dismissal. The same is true if the employer breaks one of the terms implied by the common law. There have been several cases presented on the basis of breach of the implied term of mutual respect, trust and confidence (see [3.16] above).

Note that, even though the employer must have acted in repudiatory breach of contract in order for the employee to claim constructive dismissal, the dismissal is not necessarily unfair. Cases of constructive dismissal are subject to the same test of fairness embodied in section 57(3) EP(C)A 1978 as all other claims of unfair dismissal. See, for example, *Savoia* v. *Chiltern Herb Farms Ltd* (1982).

9.09   Reason for dismissal

If dismissal is established or it is admitted by the employer, the burden of showing the reason for it is on the employer. He must show that the reason falls within one of the following categories:

(i)   the capability or qualifications of the employee;
(ii)   the conduct of the employee;
(iii)   redundancy;
(iv)   the employee's continued employment would be in contravention of a statutory rule or restriction;
(v)   or some other substantial reason of a kind as to justify the dismissal.

The fairness or otherwise of the dismissal is then determined by the tribunal against the test of section 57(3) EP(C)A 1978 – whether in the circumstances, including the size and administrative resources of the employer's undertaking, the employer acted reasonably or unreasonably in treating the reason as sufficient for dismissing the employee: that question is determined in accordance with equity and the substantial merits of the case.

Note that under section 53 EP(C)A 1978 the dismissed employee is entitled to a written statement of the reasons for his dismissal to be provided within fourteen days of a request. That written statement is admissible as evidence in the subsequent unfair dismissal hearing. Again, the employer should be circumspect when compiling this written statement since a tribunal is likely to regard that statement as embodying the true reason for dismissal and may not be susceptible to subsequent claims that the written statement was not comprehensive and so allow the employer to introduce major additions to his allegations and complaints. If an employer unreasonably refuses to provide a written statement of reasons for dismissal or the particulars of reasons are inadequate or untrue the tribunal will award damages of two weeks' pay to the employee. The Court of appeal held in *Gilham* v. *Kent County Council* (1985) that it was not a failure to comply with section 53 where the employer referred the employee to an earlier letter setting out the reasons for dismissal. A claim for breach of the right to a written statement is unusual. That is partly because employees may not know of the right and so not make the request but also because in an unfair dismissal claim, the reasons for dismissal are set out in the employer's notice of appearance.

The following decisions illustrate the operation of the five categories of reasons for fair dismissal:

(1) Capability or qualifications of the employee

Alidair Ltd v. *Taylor* (1976)
Following an incident at Guernsey Airport the pilot of a passenger aircraft was dismissed. The EAT held that there are certain occupations in which the degree of skill required is so high and the consequences of departure from the high standard are so serious that one failure to perform in accordance with that standard is enough to justify dismissal.

Post Office v. *Mughal* (1977)
The EAT held that a probationary employee should be given guidance, training and appraisal throughout the probationary period in order to render dismissal for incapability a fair dismissal.

(2) Conduct of the employee

This head will include refusal to obey reasonable instructions, sleeping at work, misuse of safety equipment, fighting at work, absenteeism, lateness, clocking offences, dishonesty etc.

Examples include:

Ayub v. *Vauxhall Motors Ltd* (1978)
A production operator working on the night shift was dismissed for sleeping during working hours. That would normally be a fair dismissal provided a fair procedure were followed, but here the evidence was that the employee had finished his work quota and it was practice for workers on the night shift to sleep after the quota was attained. Management knew of the practice and had impliedly condoned it. Dismissal was held unfair.

Martin v. *Yorkshire Imperial Metals Ltd* (1978)
The employee was held not unfairly dismissed for deliberately rendering inoperative a safety device on his automatic lathe.

Parsons & Co. Ltd v. *McLoughlin* (1978)
An employee was held not unfairly dismissed for fighting at work. Though there was no express provision in the contract specifically forbidding fighting the EAT held that a specific rule was not necessary. It was obvious that fighting at work would be regarded very gravely by management.

Stewart v. *Western SMT Co. Ltd* (1978)
A public service vehicle driver was not unfairly dismissed for falsifying his clock card and absenting himself before the end of his shift.

Usually, the employer can rely only on conduct at work or during the course of employment to justify dismissal but where the employee's misconduct outside working hours or in his private life adversely prejudices his acceptability in his employment such misconduct may make dismissal fair. See, for example:

Nottingham County Council v. *Bowly* (1978)
A teacher of thirty years' standing was convicted of an offence of gross indecency in a public lavatory. He was responsible for young boys in the course of his employment and the EAT held that his dismissal was not unfair.

Spiller v. *F.J. Wallis Ltd* (1975)
A claim of unfair dismissal brought by a married female employee was rejected where the reason was her involvement in an adulterous relationship with another employee. The employers were able to show that the affair had caused disruption to the employment because of unseemly conduct. (The man had resigned before the hearing.)

Dishonesty dismissals create special difficulties for the employer especially where criminal proceedings are pending in respect of the incident. The fair dismissal requirements are those set out in *British Homes Stores* v. *Burchell* (1978):

- the employer must establish a belief in the employee's dishonesty;
- that belief must be held on reasonable grounds; and
- in forming the belief the employer must have carried out such investigation as was reasonable in the circumstances.

If the employee refuses to co-operate with the employer's investigation, for fear of self-incrimination, the employer does not act unfairly in dismissing even without hearing the employee's side of the story provided such investigation as was possible was conducted and pointed to guilt. It may be desirable to insert in the contract a provision or disciplinary procedure justifying suspension without pay pending any such investigation since there is no implied right of suspension without pay.

Note that even where criminal proceedings are pending it is not essential that the employer awaits the outcome before deciding whether or not to dismiss. It does not follow that subsequent acquittal will necessarily result in a tribunal's finding of unfair dismissal. The burden of proof is different in criminal cases where conviction requires proof beyond reasonable doubt. To justify a dismissal the employer has to clear the lower hurdle of section 57(3), i.e. that he acted reasonably in the circumstances according to equity and the substantial merits of the case.

Where one of two employees must have been guilty of dishonesty but the employer cannot, after reasonable investigation, determine which it was the Court of Appeal has held that an employer does not act unreasonably in dismissing both (*Monie* v. *Coral Racing Ltd* (1980)). Where the employer does so and both bring unfair dismissal claims the employer should ensure that the cases are joined and heard together because otherwise different tribunals might hold both dismissals unfair because the evidence at each tribunal implicates the other employee. That happened in *William Hill (Scotland) Ltd* v. *Learmont & Hood* (1987).

A recent decision of the EAT has applied this 'blanket dismissal' principle to the capability head. In *Whitbread & Co. plc* v. *Thomas* (1988) the EAT held it was not unfair to dismiss all three employees where one of them must have been incompetent in relation to stock control procedures. The decision has been much criticised and may be changed on appeal but it is consistent with the test of unfair dismissal as reasonableness of the employer's action, not whether the employee suffered an injustice. If the test were the latter, section 57(3) EP(C)A would be differently worded.

(3) Redundancy

For a discussion of the definition of redundancy and the employee's entitlement to redundancy compensation see below. This section deals with the interaction of redundancy and unfair dismissal, e.g. where the claim is of unfair selection for redundancy dismissal or the manner of redundancy dismissal is unfair.

Section 59 EP(C)A 1978 provides that a dismissal is unfair where the employee dismissed was selected because of trade union membership or participation in trade union affairs or in contravention of an agreed selection procedure such as 'last in, first out'. The cases suggest that a dismissal will be held unfair even where there is a redundancy if there is no warning and no consultation with workers or their representatives. Though an employer has no obligation to create a position for an otherwise redundant employee, he is obliged to consider redeployment especially where the undertaking is large or the employing concern is part of a vast consortium of companies. Selection criteria should be fairly and objectively agreed and applied. If an employer is trying to justify selection on the grounds of retention of the most able and committed employees, he should adduce and present evidence in support of his contention, e.g. where X is selected for redundancy because of a poor attendance and performance record but has longer service than Y and Z, the employer should produce the documentary evidence to show the superior claims of Y and Z.

Note that the selection of part-time workers for redundancy dismissal before full-time workers may be unlawful sex discrimination (see [7.13] above).

(4) Contravention of an enactment

There are very few reported illustrations of this reason for dismissal. In *Sutcliffe & Eaton Ltd* v. *Pinney* (1977) the EAT was prepared to accept the application of this reason where a trainee hearing aid dispenser failed to pass an examination within a period prescribed by statutory regulations but a complaint of unfair dismissal succeeded because an extension to the prescribed period on application was probable.

(5) Some other substantial reason

It is this reason for dismissal which is relied on where business is reorganised so that different terms and conditions of employment are required. If the employer changes the terms and conditions he acts in breach of contract (see Chapter 6) but even where an employee objects to the change and is dismissed or leaves but then claims unfair dismissal, tribunals tend to find dismissal not unfair. Again the issue is the reasonableness of the employer's action, not whether the employee has suffered an unfairness or injustice (see *Hollister* v. *The National Farmers' Union* (1979)). The Court of Appeal held that where there is a sound business reason for a reorganisation and an essential consequence is that new contracts of employment are necessary, the only sensible way to deal with the situation is to terminate existing contracts and offer new ones on reasonable terms. Such a termination will not be an unfair dismissal. That approach was followed in *Chubb Fire Security Ltd* v. *Harper* (1983) where a reorganisation changed the areas served by the sales team. One salesman refused to accept the change and his eventual dismissal was held not unfair. But note *Oakley* v. *The Labour Party* (1988) where it was held that the reorganisation or restructuring must not be a device to get rid of the employee and *Evans* v. *Elemeta Holdings Ltd* (1982) where it was held that the new terms must not be oppressive or unreasonable.

The 'some other substantial reason' head has also been used to justify dismissal and avoid compensation payment where there is a personality clash between employees, where a vital customer or other third party insists on the particular dismissal and where the absence of further funding prevents renewal of a fixed term contract. Provided the employer shows he acted reasonably within section 57(3) EP(C)A any claim of unfair dismissal will fail.

9.10 Several reasons given

A very important decision from the House of Lords requires that where an employer puts forward several reasons for the dismissal he must show evidence to support each one of them unless the circumstances show that any unsupported allegation was not in fact relied on when the dismissal decision was taken (see *Smith* v. *City of Glasgow District Council* (1987)). So, even where an employer could have reasonably dismissed for reason A, if he adds reason B but cannot support it on reasonable grounds, the dismissal will be unfair. An employer should resist the temptation to throw everything into the dismissal interview, the letter of dismissal and the notice of appearance and should instead include only allegations which can be made out fairly and objectively.

9.11   Fair manner of dismissal

The employer must adopt a fair dismissal procedure which means he should comply with the basic rules of natural justice, his own disciplinary procedure and the guidelines of the ACAS Code of Practice on Disciplinary Procedures. The rules of natural justice require that the employee is given notice of the complaints against him and has an opportunity to answer them. He has a right to an unbiased hearing and to knowledge of the evidence against him. He must also have the opportunity to challenge that evidence and the right to representation at the disciplinary hearing. The ACAS Code envisages a system of warnings for shortcomings other than gross misconduct which should give an opportunity for improvement, e.g. a first written warning, a second final warning followed by dismissal for the third breach. Some disciplinary procedures provide that warnings shall stay on the record for a specified time but shall lapse thereafter if there has been no repetition of any breach. Employers should be careful that warnings are indeed warnings, i.e. an exhortation to 'improve' or an assertion that some conduct is unsatisfactory is inadequate unless it is joined with a threat of discipline in the event of repetition or failure to improve.

There was a period of some years during which the law of unfair dismissal tied itself in knots over the effect of failure to adopt a fair procedure. The basic principle was that a fair procedure should be adopted and if it was not the dismissal was unfair (*Earl* v. *Slater & Wheeler (Airlyne) Ltd* (1973)). But then it was established in *British Labour Pump Co. Ltd* v. *Byrne* (1979) that if the adoption of a fair procedure would not have affected the dismissal anyway, dismissal in breach of a fair procedure could be fair. So if, for example, the evidence at the hearing showed that the employee did not have any explanation so could not have changed the dismissal decision even if he had been heard, the dismissal was not unfair. That position was not satisfactory since it conflicted with the principle that reasonableness of dismissal must be judged at the time of dismissal and led to speculative exercises as to what would or might have happened in different circumstances. The uncertainty was resolved by the House of Lords in *Polkey* v. *Dayton*

Services Ltd (1987). The House held that the *British Labour Pump Co. Ltd* v. *Bryrne* principle was wrong: the reasonableness of the employer's dismissal decision has to be judged by what he does, not what he might have done. In deciding reasonableness it is right to take into account failure to consult or warn. Failure to observe the consultation and warning requirements of the ACAS Code will not necessarily render a dismissal unfair. Whether it does or not is a matter for the tribunal to judge. If the employer could reasonably have concluded in the light of circumstances known to him at the time of dismissal that consultation or warning would be utterly useless he might well have acted reasonably even if he did not observe the provisions of the Code.

The judgment from the House of Lords has meant a tightening up of the application of disciplinary rules and procedures in practice. The House did acknowledge that there may be cases where the offence is so heinous that no explanation could make any difference but that will be a very rare case. The example approved by Lord Mackay, the Lord Chancellor, of a worker seen to stab another in the back with a knife will not exactly be a common occurrence! The remarks of Sir Robert Megarry in a 1969 case are to the point:

> 'The path of the law is strewn with examples of open and shut cases which somehow were not; of unanswerable charges which, in the event, were completely answered; of inexplicable conduct which was completely explained; of fixed and unalterable determination that, by discussion, suffered a change.'

However apparently damning to the employee the circumstances are, the employer should cover himself against any possibility of a tribunal finding he acted unreasonably by giving the chance to explain and otherwise complying with a fair procedure.

The procedural aspect of unfair dismissal now squares with the approach of the House of Lords in *Devis & Sons Ltd* v. *Atkins* (1977) – employers cannot rely at the hearing on evidence which evolves after the date of dismissal; reasonableness of the decision to dismiss must be judged according to the knowledge of the employer at the time the decision to dismiss was taken.

Taking all these factors into account the tribunal must decide whether the employer acted reasonably in accordance with section 57(3). The tribunal members must not substitute their own decision as to what they would have done in the circumstances. The issue is whether the employer acted within a band of reasonable responses; see *Iceland Frozen Foods* v. *Jones* (1982).

9.12　*Illness and fair dismissal*

The extended illness of an employee rendering him unfit for work will be a theoretically acceptable reason for dismissal as relating to his capability. But employers must adopt a fair manner of dismissal and, though warnings are inappropriate in these circumstances, fairness requires consultation with the employee and reference to his medical advisors (with his permission). Alternatively it may be reasonable to ask the employee to submit to examination by the company doctor or a doctor nominated by the employer. The employer must form a balanced view about the employee's health and make the dismissal decision taking into account the need for the work to be done and the likely length of the employee's continued absence. If recovery is not total so that the employee cannot return to his old job, a reasonable employer will consider whether there is a suitable available vacancy which entails lighter duties which the employee could perform.

A tribunal is likely to expect greater leniency from an employer where the illness or incapacity is induced by the duties of the job itself.

9.13　*Remedies*

If the tribunal concludes that dismissal was unreasonable it then goes on to consider remedies. The claimant will have indicated on his application form the remedy sought and usually that remedy is compensation. The tribunal has power to order reinstatement or re-engagement, as well as punitive damages if the employer unreasonably refuses to comply. However, reinstatement and re-engagement orders are not common, perhaps because relationships deteriorate, even after dismissal, because of the litigation. Damages awarded by the tribunal are split into the basic award and the compensatory award. A discussion of how damages for unfair dismissal are computed is contained in [10.05]. Tribunals do not usually award costs to the successful party in an unfair dismissal hearing but the rules of procedure provide that they may do so where the proceedings have been 'frivolous, vexatious or otherwise unreasonable'. The outcome of a pre-hearing assessment may have been a costs warning and there have been suggestions that a party who continues with proceedings in spite of such a warning should be required to deposit a sum of money as a condition of being allowed to continue. There is no such requirement at present.

9.14   Dismissal for redundancy

An employee who has at least two years' continuous service and is dismissed for redundancy is entitled to compensation under the EP(C)A 1978. Again, the employee has the burden of showing that he was dismissed and dismissal is defined in exactly the same way as for unfair dismissal, i.e.

- termination by the employer with or without notice;
- expiry of a fixed term contract without renewal (but a waiver clause can be inserted into a fixed term contract for two years or more);
- resignation by the employee with or without notice because of the employer's repudiatory breach of contract.

The discussion of proof of dismissal above in relation to the unfair dismissal claim is equally relevant to proof of dismissal for the purposes of a redundancy claim. One extra dimension in redundancy cases is the effect of the employee 'volunteering' for redundancy. It is not uncommon for employers facing the need to cut the workforce to ask first for volunteers or for employees who want to take early retirement. Are the volunteers who come forward still entitled to redundancy compensation or are they unable to show dismissal? In *Birch & Humber* v. *University of Liverpool* (1985) the Court of Appeal held that employees who were accepted for premature retirement and received severance payments could not also claim redundancy compensation since they had not been dismissed. Whether or not there is a dismissal is a matter for the tribunal but, on the whole, tribunals have been reluctant to deprive employees of statutory compensation by too readily inferring resignations. That reluctance has been the more marked where there has once been a dismissal and it is argued that subsequent events have converted the dismissal into a resignation or mutual termination. But recently in *Scott* v. *Coalite Fuels & Chemicals Ltd* (1988) the EAT refused to endorse that view holding that even where the applicants were under redundancy notice their subsequent acceptance of voluntary early retirement converted the dismissal into termination by themselves. The EAT claimed that the whole point of the industrial relations legislation is to allow discussion, negotiation and agreement and that where agreement is reached it should be of effect. That view may ignore the realities of industrial practice, however. An employee under notice of redundancy dismissal will be under some pressure to convert the stigma of redundancy into dignified early retirement. That does not mean he approves of or agrees with the termination of his contract and his acceptance of early retirement cannot realistically be regarded as the cause of termination.

The justification for the *Birch & Humber* decision is that there had been no dismissals in that case: the employees were truly volunteers and they caused the termination of the contract. The *Scott* case is not nearly the same. However, it stands for the time being.

9.15   *Presumption of redundancy*

If dismissal is established, there is a presumption that it is by reason of redundancy, i.e. the employer must show that there was some other reason if he is to defend the claim for redundancy compensation. It should be noted that between 1965 and 1972 a redundancy dismissal was the only likely basis for compensation. The claim in unfair dismissal did not begin until 1972. So, between those years an employer would have tried to resist a finding of redundancy and an employee would have tried to establish redundancy. In more recent years, and especially when employers could obtain a substantial refund on the redundancy compensation, there was an about-turn. Redundancy compensation cost less than the likely damages award in unfair dismissal and so it became common for employers to argue that redundancy was the reason for dismissal and for employees to argue that there was no redundancy, or, if there was, the selection for redundancy dismissal was unfair (see above for redundancy as a head of unfair dismissal). Note that the Wages Act 1986 abolished the right to any refund of redundancy compensation for all employers except those with less than ten employees. However, even given the loss of the refund it remains cheaper to compensate for loss of employment as a result of redundancy than for unfair dismissal.

9.16   *Meaning of 'redundancy'*

There is a redundancy where:

- the employer ceases business in the place where the employee is employed; or
- the employer's requirements for employees to carry out work of a particular kind in the place where the employee is employed cease or diminish.

The first situation is the most obvious. The employer closes down his business undertaking and all employees are redundant. However, the issue of *place of employment* introduces a complication. If the employer has three business premises at A, B and C and closes his undertaking at A, the employees at A are only redundant if, under their contracts of employment, their place of work is A. If they can be transferred to B or C and there is work available at B or C, the employees are not redundant and are not entitled to compensation if they refuse to transfer. Where there is a clear and unrestricted express clause in the contract which entitles the employer to transfer the employee, the tribunal will not imply a restriction limiting any transfer to reasonable daily travelling distance from the employee's home (see *Rank Xerox Ltd* v. *Churchill* (1988)).

It is advisable to include a reference to 'place of employment' in the written statement of contract terms. Otherwise the tribunal will hear evidence to decide what must be taken to have been the implied agreement on place of work. See, for example, *Stevens* v. *Stitcher & Sons Ltd* (1966) where the place of employment of a shop assistant was held to be the Chingford area of East London, not the particular shop in which she worked. When the particular shop closed for business she was offered work at another of the employer's shops in Chingford. A tribunal held she was not redundant. In *Courtaulds Northern Spinning Ltd* v. *Sibson* (1988) the Court of Appeal considered the basis for the implication of a term about place of work. The judges thought that a contract could not be silent about place and where a term had to be implied because there was no express agreement it should be on the basis that the term was that which the parties would probably have agreed if they were being reasonable. They thought that meant a power given to the employer to direct the employee to work at any place within reasonable daily reach of home. When exercising that power the employer had discretion; he did not have to show a transfer was for genuine operational reasons. So when the employers in the particular case asked the employee to transfer to avoid industrial action because the employee was not a union member they did not act in breach of contract entitling him to resign and claim constructive dismissal.

It may be that an employer could show mobility as an implied term on the basis of custom and practice (e.g. workers in the contruction industry) but it is better management practice to insert an express mobility clause into the contract. Even if that is done, an employer representation that it will not be relied upon will render it invalid – see *Wilson-Undy* v. *Instrument & Control Ltd* (1976). All employees were taken on on the basis that they could be transferred to any site operated by the employers anywhere in the UK. However, a particular employee was given an assurance that because of his family commitments he would be asked to work on sites only within daily travelling distance of his home. When work on the local sites finished, the employee was held to be redundant.

The second redundancy situation is rather more complicated; the business continues but the employer's needs for workers in the place of employment cease or diminish. Note that the volume of work can remain the same but if reorganisation or new technology means fewer workers are needed to do it any workers dismissed are redundant. See *McCrea* v. *Cullen & Davison Ltd* (1987) in which a manager's work was taken over by the employing company's managing director and the manager was dismissed as redundant. An industrial tribunal held there was no redundancy and dismissal was unfair. The Northern Ireland Court of Appeal allowed the employer's appeal. The manager was redundant because although there had been no diminution in work the employers no longer needed two managers to do it. There is a redundancy if the volume of work diminishes leading to diminution in requirements for workers but it is the diminution in requirements for workers which determines redundancy and that can occur without a diminution of work, e.g. because of improved mechanisation, automation or other technical advance or because of a reorganisation and a reallocation of duties.

What is the position if competition is such that the employer's product has to be available more cheaply so that he cannot continue to employ the workforce at the same pay rates? In *Chapman* v. *Goonvean & Rostowrace* (1973) Lord Denning in the Court of Appeal suggested that employees dismissed in these circumstances would probably be entitled to redundancy compensation. However, the facts of that case occurred before a claim of unfair dismissal was available and it is difficult to square the result with the statutory definition of redundancy since the employer still needs as many workers as before, but not on the same pay terms. In *Pillinger* v. *Manchester Area Health Authority* (1979) the dismissal of an experienced research biochemist was held not to be by reason of redundancy where the employer intended to replace him with a junior researcher on a lower pay grade. The EAT held that there was no change in the type of work to be performed and so no diminution in the needs of the employer to do work of the particular kind performed by the claimant. This case is one in which the employer was arguing redundancy as the reason for dismissal by way of defence to an action in unfair dismissal. If an employer is faced with financial difficulties and needs to keep his workforce but change the basis of pay rates, fringe benefits, etc. any consequent dismissals of employees who refuse to accept the change would be better defended under the 'some other substantial reason' head of dismissal rather than redundancy. Likewise, if an employer reorganised by way of dismissing workers so as to replace them with younger, cheaper workers, the dismissed workers would not be redundant and would be unfairly dismissed and entitled to damages for unfair dismissal unless the employer satisfied a tribunal that he acted reasonably in dismissing under the 'some other substantial reason' head.

Redundancy should be relied on only where there is a diminution in the employer's needs for workers, not a diminution in his needs for workers on the same terms and conditions of employment. See, for example, *Nottinghamshire Combined Police Authority* v. *Johnson & Dutton* (1974) where the employers changed the pattern of hours worked, the number of hours remaining the same. The employees who refused to accept the change were held not entitled to redundancy compensation. These days that would be a 'some other substantial reason' dismissal and the employer would have to negotiate, consult and demonstrate reasonable grounds for the change to defend any unfair dismissal claim.

9.17   Loss of redundancy compensation

Even if there is a redundancy situation, an employee has no entitlement to redundancy compensation if

(a) the real reason for dismissal is his gross misconduct; or
(b) he unreasonably refuses an offer of suitable alternative employment.

9.18   Redundancy and misconduct

If the employer uses the misconduct as the reason for selecting the employee for redundancy he is still entitled to redundancy compensation if he would not have been dismissed for the misconduct alone. An employer should make it clear when he is dismissing for misconduct rather than redundancy by dismissing summarily, by giving short notice or giving full contract notice plus a written statement that he could have dismissed summarily because of the employee's misconduct. An employee who is guilty of an act of misconduct during the running of redundancy notice should be treated in the same way. If the employer does nothing and allows the redundancy notice to expire the employee is entitled to redundancy compensation. Note that even where the employer does act as set out above to show that misconduct is the reason for dismissal, an industrial tribunal can award such part of the redundancy compensation as it considers just and equitable in the circumstances.

9.19   *Unreasonable refusal of suitable alternative employment*

The cases suggest that suitability of the alternative employment offered is judged objectively and reasonableness of the employee's refusal is judged subjectively, i.e. the jobs are compared in terms of status, pay, duties in determining suitability and the personal circumstances of the employee affect reasonableness of refusal. Some factors may be relevant to both issues. See, for example, *Spencer & Griffin* v. *Gloucester County Council* (1985) where school cleaners who were offered similar duties to be shared between fewer employees claimed that the lower standards to be achieved rendered the new jobs unsuitable and their refusal reasonable. The Court of Appeal upheld their claims for redundancy.

Note that if the employee begins to work under the new terms he has a trial period of four weeks during which to decide whether or not to stay. If he leaves or is dismissed during the trial period he is still treated as dismissal for redundancy and, in the former case he is entitled to redundancy compensation if he acted reasonably in leaving. The trial period of four weeks applies where the employee has been given notice of dismissal for redundancy. Employers should be aware that informal arrangements under which an employee tries out an alternative job instead of being dismissed for redundancy may mean an extended trial period at common law *plus* the statutory four week period (see also [6.08] above).

9.20   *Lay-off, short-time working and redundancy*

There is no implied right given to an employer to lay-off without pay or put workers onto short-time working which results in loss of pay. There must be an express power to do so in the contract, otherwise the employer acts in breach of contract. Even where there is an express power to lay-off or put on short-time the EP(C)A 1978 allows the affected employee to leave and claim redundancy compensation if the lay-off or short-time goes on for any extended period. Under the Act, lay-off means a workless week and short-time working means a diminution of work resulting in less than half a normal week's pay. If either go on for four or more consecutive weeks or six or more weeks in any period of thirteen weeks the employee can terminate the contract and present a written claim for redundancy compensation. The employer can contest the claim only if he does so in writing and promises full-time working for at least thirteen weeks to commence within four weeks of the employee's notice of claim. Some tribunals have bypassed this procedure and have held that employers laid-off or kept on short-time working for longer than a reasonable period are entitled to consider themselves constructively dismissed and can claim direct to an industrial tribunal. This approach was doubted by the EAT in *Kenneth MacRae & Co. Ltd* v. *Dawson* (1984) but in that case there was a contractual right to lay-off without pay indefinitely. The EAT said the employee's remedy was to use the procedure in the Act to challenge the duration of the lay-off.

9.21   Handling redundancies

The Employment Protection Act 1975 requires an employer to consult with the appropriate recognised trade union when he is proposing to declare redundancies. The consultation is supposed to begin at the earliest opportunity and at least 90 days before the first dismissal where 100 or more employees are to be redundant and at least 30 days if ten or more are to be made redundant. For the purposes of the consultation the employer should disclose in writing to trade union representatives:

- the reason for his redundancy proposals;
- the numbers and descriptions of employees to be dismissed;
- the proposed method of selection;
- the proposed method of carrying out the dismissals and the period over which they are to take effect.

The employer should consider any representations made by the trade union representatives, reply to them and give reasons for any rejected.

The employer need not fully comply with these consultation requirements where 'special circumstances render it not reasonably practicable' to do so but then he must take all such steps as are reasonably practicable. It was established by the Court of Appeal in *Clarks of Hove Ltd* v. *Bakers' Union* (1978) that the employer's insolvency is not necessarily a 'special circumstance' and only becomes so if it occurs in uncommon, exceptional or extraordinary circumstances such as a sudden disaster which makes it necessary to close the concern. A gradual run-down of the business which leads to insolvency is not a special circumstance rendering it not reasonably practicable for the employer to consult.

If the employer fails to comply with these consultation requirements the union can complain to an industrial tribunal which may make a just and equitable 'protective award' of wages to the redundant employees linked to the duration of the lost consultation period.

To avoid a claim by any individual employee based on an unfair manner of redundancy dismissal the employer should comply with the guidelines of *Williams* v. *Compair Maxam Ltd* (1982), i.e. give as much warning as possible to employees likely to be dismissed as redundant and have fair and objective selection criteria which are fairly and objectively applied. The employer should also consider redeployment and transfer possibilities as alternatives to redundancy. (Of course, an employer and employee can always agree generous voluntary severance terms and avoid a redundancy dismissal within the meaning of the law.)

Where an employee is under notice of redundancy dismissal he is entitled to reasonable time off with pay during the notice period to look for a new job or to make arrangements for training. The right accrues to any employee who has two years' continuous service down to the date of expiry of the notice. Complaint of infringement of that right lies to an industrial tribunal which can award compensation of up to two-fifths of the employee's normal week's pay.

9.22   *Termination by operation of law*

Frustration

At common law a contract is brought to an end automatically if, without the fault of either party, something happens to make performance no longer possible or performance, though possible, would be so radically different under the changed circumstances that it cannot be taken to be within the parties' agreement. A frustrating event relieves either side of further performance under the contract.

It was recognised at common law that the illness of an employee might lead to frustration of a contract of service if it was sufficiently serious as to go to the root of the contract. So in *Poussard* v. *Spiers* (1876) the illness of a professional singer engaged to sing a key solo part in an opera caused the contract to terminate automatically. Because of her illness she missed a month's rehearsals and the four opening performances. It was held that she could not insist on going on with the contract on her recovery; the contract was at an end. A similar result was reached in *Condor* v. *Barron Knights* (1966) in which a drummer with the defendant group suffered a nervous illness which prevented him going on tour for twice nightly performances, seven nights each week. It was not forseeable that he would recover sufficiently to resume the expected level of performance and the contract was held to be frustrated.

If the contract is frustrated, it terminates automatically. It follows that the employee cannot establish dismissal for the purposes of an unfair dismissal or redundancy claim. Employers were quick to see that it was possible to stop a claim in unfair dismissal (or redundancy) by arguing that there was no dismissal but that the contract was frustrated by the illness or imprisonment of the employee. The higher in the employer's management hierarchy and the more crucial the employee's services, the easier it was to show an extended sickness absence frustrated the contract. Of course, the period of illness had to exceed the period during which the employee was entitled to sick pay under an occupational sick pay scheme. If the employer had anticipated payment for, for example, three or six months' sickness, he could hardly argue that three or six months' sickness absence caused performance to be radically different from that contemplated. Also, the longer the continuity of service the longer the period of sickness absence an employer might be expected to accept. However, several cases in the 1970s illustrated the success of the frustration argument. That trend was brought to a halt by an EAT decision in 1980. In *Harman v. Flexible Lamps Ltd* the EAT expressed the view that the concept of frustration is not appropriate to a permanent contract of employment which is determinable by notice. That leads to too easy an avoidance of the protective provisions of the EP(C)A 1978. Where a contract is determinable by notice the employer should rely on the notice clause to end the relationship, not on the doctrine of frustration. But in *Notcutt v. Universal Equipment Co. (London) Ltd* 1986 the Court of Appeal said it could not agree with a view which went further than warning any court or tribunal to look carefully at a submission of frustration. The Court of Appeal held that there was no reason in principle why a contract determinable by notice should not in appropriate circumstances be held to have terminated by reason of frustration.

It seems then that the frustration argument can be deployed in cases of extended sickness absence of personnel. Any employer relying on that ground of termination should take care to avoid language of dismissal when bringing the termination to the employee's notice. He should 'acknowledge termination of the contract' by reason of the absence and not refer to 'dismissal' or 'notice'. It is not a defence that should be too readily relied on since it does suggest sharp practice and good managers will be willing to have their actions in dismissing for illness subjected to the reasonableness test of section 57(3) EP(C)A 1978. For a discussion of how it might apply to an illness dismissal see [9.12] above.

9.23   *Frustration and fault*

Although the classic formulation of the doctrine of frustration is that the frustrating event must occur without fault on either side, the Court of Appeal held in *F.C. Shepherd & Co. Ltd* v. *Jerrom* (1986) that the imprisonment of an employee is capable of frustrating a contract of employment in spite of the fact that it arises as a result of fault on the employee's part. In that case an apprentice plumber was sentenced to a period of Borstal training of between six months and two years as a result of his involvement in a motor cycle gang fight. The employee claimed he had been dismissed and that the contract was not frustrated. The Court of Appeal held that the no-fault requirement meant that the party asserting frustration must show the absence of fault on his side. But the party against whom frustration is asserted cannot rely on his own misconduct by way of answer. To allow him to do so would be an 'affront to common sense' and an infringment of the principle that a man cannot take advantage of his own wrong.

One factor in determining whether the employee's imprisonment has frustrated the contract is the duration of the sentence compared to the employee's continuity of service. In *Hare* v. *Murphy Bros Ltd* (1973) a sentence of twelve months for unlawful wounding imposed on an employee with 25 years' service was held to frustrate the contract. In *Waudby* v. *HFM (Transport) Co. Ltd* (1976) 28 days' imprisonment for failure to pay a maintenance order was enough to frustrate the contract of a lorry driver with eight months' service.

9.24   *Discharge of the contract by performance – fixed term contract*

The expiry of a fixed term contract without renewal is treated as a dismissal for the purposes of the law of unfair dismissal and redundancy. However, a contract under which an employee is engaged to perform a particular task is discharged by performance when the task is completed and the contract comes to an end automatically by operation of law. There is no dismissal in the latter case. Sometimes it is difficult to distinguish between the two. Normally a fixed term contract will have a definite beginning and a definite end but where the contract is to terminate on the occurrence of a specified event is it one for a fixed term or not?

In *Ryan* v. *Shipboard Maintenance Ltd* (1980) the employee worked for a company of ship repairers on a job-by-job basis. He claimed he had been dismissed for redundancy after his last job was completed. The

EAT held there had been no dismissal: at the end of each job there was a discharge of the contract by performance. A contract for the duration of a job cannot be a fixed term contract because it is indeterminate in duration. The EAT refused to hold that Parliament intended the phrase 'fixed term contract' to include one terminable by an event which is identifiable in character but which cannot be identified with a precise date in the future.

The Court of Appeal considered the matter in *Wiltshire County Council v. National Association of Teachers in Further and Higher Education & Guy* (1980) and approved the principle in *Ryan* although reaching a different decision on the facts. The employee was taken on as a part-time teacher at one of the council's colleges at the beginning of each academic session. The hours and days worked were agreed and she finished working whenever her courses finished. The finishing dates varied and she did not work right up to the end of any session. Her appointment was not renewed for a particular session and she claimed unfair dismissal. The Court of Appeal held she was working under a fixed term contract and not a contract to perform specified work which, when the courses ended, was discharged by performance. If the correct construction of the agreement between the parties had produced the latter result she would not have been employed under a fixed term contract. However, the reality here was that the employee was engaged for the session, a term of definite duration, to teach such courses during it as were required of her. She could claim that she was dismissed, therefore, when her fixed term contract expired without being renewed.

Another case involving a temporary college teacher produced the opposite finding in *Brown* v. *Knowsley Borough Council* (1986). This employee had been employed under a series of fixed term contracts for academic sessions but the final contract stipulated that the appointment would last only as long as sufficient funds were provided by the Manpower Services Commission. (MSC). Towards the end of the session the employee was informed that the MSC had not sponsored any more courses at the college and her appointment would terminate at the end of the session. An industrial tribunal and the EAT held that the employee could not establish dismissal because she was not employed under a fixed term contract; the contract terminated automatically when the MSC funding ended.

Both tribunals purported to follow the *Wiltshire County Council* decision but it is not easy to see how the result reached is justifiable. The withdrawal of MSC funds did not cut short the contract term; it ran its full course. It certainly was a fixed term contract in retrospect and Mr Justice Popplewell in the EAT said he did not find it easy to regard the contract as one for a particular purpose. He preferred to regard the contract as one terminable on the happening or non-happening of a future event. However, that is not what occurred in fact, and furthermore, the decision leaves open the possibility that the continuance of any contract of employment could be made subject to the receipt of revenues from particular sources or commercial contracts. If those revenues stop, are the contracts discharged by performance? It is argued that the concept of discharge by performance should not be relevant here since the engagement was not for a particular task. Either the contract was one for a fixed term or, if not, the contract was terminated by the employer's reliance on the occurrence of a condition which had been written into the contract. That reliance in invoking the condition to terminate the contract should have amounted to a dismissal in law.

9.25   *Death of the employer or dissolution of the employing undertaking*

At common law, the death of either party to a contract of employment brings the contract to an end automatically. Statute qualifies the position so that under section 93 EP(C)A 1978 the death of an employer is treated as a termination by him which allows employees affected to claim redundancy payments from his estate. If the deceased employer's personal representatives carry on the business and renew any contract of employment, then employees cannot claim redundancy dismissal. The same is true if the employee unreasonably refuses an offer of renewal from the personal representatives.

Schedule 12 EP(C)A 1978 preserves litigation rights under the Act to the estate of either a deceased employer or employee and provides that an employee may proceed or continue to proceed before an industrial tribunal against a deceased employer's estate. If the employee dies whilst under notice of dismissal he is treated for the purposes of unfair dismissal and redundancy as if the dismissal were effective.

Dissolution of a partnership ends contracts of employment with the partnership at common law and again section 93 EP(C)A treats this event as a dismissal in order to preserve employee's redundancy rights. Where the partnership is reconstituted and the employee goes on working for a new partnership his continuity is preserved.

Where there is no reconstitution but the business previously carried on by the partnership is transferred to a new owner the employment contracts in existence immediately before the transfer are continued with the substitution of the new owner as the employer.

Any employee who is dismissed by the partnership on dissolution and before the business transfer will forfeit his right to redundancy compensation if he unreasonably refuses an offer of suitable alternative employment by the new owner. If any dismissed employee is not offered work by the new owner he has an action in unfair dismissal unless an economic, technical or organisational reason can be shown (see Chapter 6).

In the case of a company, a compulsory winding up order of a court operates as a dismissal of the company's employees. A voluntary winding up has the same effect if the business is not to be carried on. Short of liquidation, the appointment of a receiver may or may not terminate the employment contracts depending on whether he acts as agent of the creditors or the company. There is no provision in the EP(C)A to preserve dismissal and redundancy rights on the winding up of a company or the appointment of a receiver but in *Deaway Trading Ltd* v. *Calverley* (1973) the niceties of company law were glossed over and continuity was held to bridge a voluntary liquidation and a transfer to new owners. However, it is unsatisfactory that employment rights should be uncertain in these circumstances and desirable that the statutory rule applying to death of the employer or dissolution of a partnership should also apply to company dissolutions.

Chapter 10

Remedies

10.01 *Remedies available in actions before industrial tribunals*

The remedies which industrial tribunals can award are considered under the following heads:

(i) redundancy;
(ii) unfair dismissal;
(iii) equal pay, sex and race discrimination.

10.02 *Redundancy*

The amount of compensation which a tribunal can award to an employee dismissed by reason of redundancy is linked to his normal week's pay, his period of continuous service and his age at the relevant date.

The basic entitlement is:

* half a week's pay for each complete year of service between the ages of 18 and 21 inclusive;
* one week's pay for each complete year of service between the ages of 22 and 40 inclusive;
* one and a half week's pay for each complete year of service between the ages of 41 and normal retirement age (but there are tapering provisions applying to redundancy dismissal in the year before normal retirement age – see below).

Redundancy entitlement is calculated by working backwards from the termination date and a maximum of twenty years' service can be taken into account. With effect from April 1988 the maximum limit on a week's pay is £164 so the maximum redundancy compensation is $1\frac{1}{2} \times 20 \times 164 = £4920$.

Examples of redundancy calculations:

Example 10.1

X is dismissed for redundancy with effect from 30 September 1988 when he is 57 years old. His normal weekly earnings are £204 at the date of dismissal. He has 15 full years' service. His earnings are over the statutory maximum so it is that maximum which applies.

All 15 years which count in the computation were years when he was 41 or over so his redundancy entitlement is $15 \times 1\frac{1}{2} \times £164 = £3690$.

Example 10.2

Y is dismissed for redundancy on 31 July 1988 when he is 45 years old. His earnings are £155 weekly and he has 12 full years' service. Four of those years were years when he was 41 or over.

The redundancy entitlement is:

$(4 \times 1\frac{1}{2} \times 155) + (8 \times 1 \times 155) = 930 + 1240 = £2170$.

Example 10.3

Z is dismissed for redundancy with effect from 31 October 1988 when he is 23. He has six years' service and his earnings are £110 weekly. Only five years count because any period during which the employee is below 18 is excluded.

His redundancy entitlement is:

$(4 \times \frac{1}{2} \times 110) + (1 \times 110) = 220 + 110 = £330$.

At the moment there is an upper age limit for redundancy entitlement of 60 for women and 65 for men and tapering provisions that apply to redundancy dismissal after the 59th birthday of a woman and the 64th birthday of a man. This unequal treatment continues even after the Sex Discrimination Act 1986 equalised the compulsory retirement ages for men and women for the purposes of unfair dismissal claims.

However, in *Hammersmith & Queen Charlotte's Special Health Authority* v. *Cato* (1987) the EAT held that a contractual redundancy scheme which conferred benefits additional to the statutory scheme but which had the same retirement age difference and the same tapering relief provisions as the statute was in breach in EEC provisions requiring equality in terms of pay. The benefits under the redundancy scheme fell within the meaning of 'pay' in Article 119 of the Treaty of Rome. Since Article 119 is directly enforceable by individual employees in member states of the EEC it follows from the decision that any redundancy scheme which incorporated the statutory differences of treatment of men and women would be unlawful. Clearly, the statutory scheme itself is breach of the EEC provision since the exception in the social security Directive 79/7 in respect of the determination of pensionable age was held not to apply. The Government have announced an intention to change the law so as to comply with the *Cato* decision as soon as legislative time permits.

The tapering provisions which apply at present mean that redundancy compensation is reduced by one-twelfth for each month after the attainment of 59 for women, 64 for men. When the rules are changed to achieve equality the tapering provisions will still apply but from the same birthday for men and women.

10.03 *Unfair dismissal*

The remedies which an industrial tribunal can award to an unfairly dismissed employee are reinstatement, re-engagement and/or damages.

10.04 *Reinstatement/re-engagement*

Orders for reinstatement and re-engagement are rare and are at the tribunal's discretion. When exercising its discretion the tribunal takes into account the employee's wishes, the practicability of compliance with an order and whether the employee caused or contributed to his dismissal so that the justice of any such order is affected. The fact that the employer has engaged a replacement does not affect practicability of compliance unless the employer shows that he could not otherwise have arranged for the dismissed employee's work to be done or he waited a reasonable period before taking on the replacement without having heard from the dismissed employee that he was seeking reinstatement or re-engagement.

The difference between reinstatement and re-engagement is that reinstatement means the employee goes back to his old job on the same terms and conditions as though he had never been dismissed. If the employee is re-engaged he goes to a different, though comparable job or other suitable employment. His continuity is specifically preserved. If an order for reinstatement or re-engagement is made but the employer refuses to comply the tribunal can award damages additional to the normal computation of between 13 and 26 weeks' pay. An even higher additional award of between 26 and 52 weeks' pay can be made where the dismissal constituted unlawful discrimination under the Sex Discrimination Act 1975 or the Race Relations Act 1976.

10.05 *Damages in unfair dismissal – the basic award*

Damages for unfair dismissal are divided into a basic award and a compensatory award.

The *basic award* is calculated in exactly the same way as redundancy compensation and depends on age, continuity and normal weekly earnings at the date of dismissal. However, employment below the age of 18 does count for continuity purposes in determining the amount of the basic award and the upper age limit is 65 which applies to both men and women. There are also tapering reduction provisions for dismissal in the final year before reaching retirement age – the award is reduced by one-twelfth for each month after the 64th birthday of the employee.

The basic award entitlement is:

- half a week's pay for each complete year of service below the age of 22;
- one week's pay for each complete year of service between the ages of 22 and 40 inclusive;
- one and a half week's pay for each complete year of service between the ages of 41 and 65 inclusive.

A maximum of 20 years' service can be taken into account and the ceiling on a week's pay is £164 (from April 1988) so the maximum basic award is $1\frac{1}{2} \times 20 \times £164 = £4920$.

The tribunal can reduce the amount of the basic award which would otherwise be due only where:

- the employee has unreasonably refused an offer of reinstatement and it is just and equitable to reduce the award; or
- the employee's conduct before the dismissal makes a reduction just and equitable; or
- the employee has received a redundancy award in respect of the same dismissal.

The tribunal has no power to reduce the amount of the basic award where the dismissed employee has suffered no financial loss. The basic award compensates for loss of continuity; it is the compensatory award which takes account of financial loss.

10.06   *Damages in unfair dismissal – the compensatory award*

The *compensatory award* is of such amount as the tribunal considers just and equitable in all the circumstances having regard to the loss sustained by the applicant as a consequence of the dismissal. The loss is taken to include any expenses reasonably incurred and loss of any benefit which the applicant might reasonably be expected to have had but for the dismissal. The maximum amount of a compensatory award is £8,500. (Note that this sum is the maximum which can be awarded for compensatory loss by an industrial tribunal hearing an unfair dismissal claim. For damages before the County Court or High Court see [10.16] below.)

Tribunals usually calculate the compensatory award under the two heads of immediate loss and future loss.

Immediate loss is the loss suffered down to the date of the hearing and is usually loss of wages between dismissal and the hearing. Damages for loss of wages are computed on the basis of *net* wages, i.e. after deduction of income tax, national insurance contributions and pension contributions. It is now settled by the Court of Appeal in *Addison* v. *Babcock FATA Ltd* (1987) that a deduction is to be made against damages under this head for payment of wages in lieu of notice. Earnings from another employer in the notice period, however, are not deducted. According to the case law stemming from *Norton Tool Co. Ltd* v. *Tewson* (1973) the right to notice or wages in lieu of notice is an irreducible minimum required by good industrial relations practice. Although the failure to deduct earnings from new employment during the notice period appears to conflict with the statutory duty on the employee to mitigate his loss the principle that they are not deducted now seems to be firmly entrenched. One recent EAT decision referred to the principle as 'so embodied in the law that it is to be treated as a rule of law'. However, that same EAT refused to extend it to the unexpired term of a fixed term contract during which the unfairly dismissed employee had set up his own business and received earnings greatly in excess of what he would have received from the employer. In the course of his judgment, Mr Justice Popplewell suggested that the *Norton* principle might not be appropriate to employees entitled to years or months of notice or with a fixed term contract since the award is intended to be compensatory and not to provide a bonus for the claimant.

It is clear that earnings from another source outside the notice period are to be deducted from the loss of wages head of damages. If the unfairly dismissed employee has entered permanent employment with another employer the original employer's liability in damages ceases from the date of that entry.

10.07   *Examples showing calculation of loss of wages down to the date of hearing*

Example 10.4

X is unfairly dismissed without notice or pay in lieu of notice from a job paying him £110 weekly *net*. He remains out of work for six weeks. The tribunal hearing takes place eight weeks after dismissal. X's immediate loss of wages is 6 × 110 = £660.

Example 10.5

Y is unfairly dismissed without notice or pay in lieu from a job paying him £120 weekly net. He is entitled to four weeks' notice. He obtains temporary employment which pays £60 net from week two to six inclusive following his dismissal. The hearing is nine weeks after the dismissal. Y's immediate loss of wages is:

4 × £120 (without deduction, i.e. earnings in week 2 – 4) plus 2 × (£120 – 60) (he must bring into account earnings outside the notice period, i.e. weeks 5 – 6) plus 3 × £120 (for the final 3 weeks) = 480 + 120 + 360 = £960.

Example 10.6

The facts are as above but Y is paid wages in lieu of notice. His immediate loss of wages now are:
weeks 1 – 4: no loss and no set-off (i.e. of earnings in weeks 2 – 4)
weeks 5 – 6: loss is 2 × 120 less 2 × 60
weeks 7 – 9: loss is 3 × 120.
= 120 + 360 = £480.

Note that it is the salary or wage which the employee should have received which is the base for the calculation of loss of earnings. So if an order of a Wages Council fixes a higher amount than that actually paid it is the higher amount which is compensated and if an increment was due that increment is taken into account.

10.08   The 'prescribed element'

The head of damages for immediate loss of earnings can be reduced by
such amount as the tribunal considers just and equitable to reflect the
employee's contributory fault. The figure left is the 'prescribed
element' for the purposes of the rules for recoupment of unemploy-
ment benefit or other DHSS payment to the claimant. The 'prescribed
element' of damages is not immediately handed to the claimant by the
employer. The appropriate DHSS office is informed by the tribunal of
the amount of the damages referable to the period before the hearing,
i.e. the 'prescribed element' and the DHSS can recover from the
employer any payment made to the unfairly dismissed employee up to
the level of that 'prescribed element'. (Note that the recoupment rules
do not apply where the parties agree damages and the tribunal is not
required to make any award.)

10.09   Future loss

The future loss element of the compensatory award is much more
arbitrary and depends on the tribunal's discretion and its assessment
of how long a claimant who remains out of work at the date of the
hearing is likely to continue to be unemployed. If the employee would
have received an increase in pay if he had not been dismissed the
higher figure is used in the assessment of loss. It is common for
tribunals to award sums based on three to six months' future loss of
earnings but if the unfairly dismissed employee is nearing retirement
age, the tribunal may compensate for future loss right up to
retirement age, subject to the overall limit of £8,500.

It is clear that the claimant's personal circumstances have to be taken
into account. In *Fougere* v. *Phoenix Motor Co. Ltd* (1976) the claimant was
aged 58 and in poor health when he was unfairly dismissed. The EAT
said that the estimate of future loss should take into account his
difficulty in obtaining new employment because of his age and poor
health. On the other hand, the assessment of damages for future loss
should also take into account the possibility that he might have been
fairly dismissed for incapacity in the near future anyway.

If the claimant has a new job at wages as favourable as from the
original employer there will be no future loss of earnings. If, however,
at the date of the hearing the claimant has another job but on less
favourable terms the tribunal will have to estimate how long those less
favourable terms are likely to last and when he might be expected to
catch up to the wages of the old job.

10.10 Other heads of loss

The compensatory award will also include a sum for loss of *statutory rights* since the claimant will have to work another two years with a new employer before he qualifies for unfair dismissal and redundancy protection. £100 is the sum usually awarded under this head.

Loss of a *company car* also comes under the compensatory award. Computation of damages to reflect the loss depends on the basis on which any car is supplied but it is loss of private usage that is compensated. AA and RAC running costs figures may be relied on, or the Inland Revenue car benefit tables may be invoked but a conventional figure is £40–£50 weekly.

Compensation for loss of *pension benefits* is an increasingly important element of the computation of damages and also the most complex. The claimant must prove his loss and it may become apparent that the loss is clearly over £8,500 so no detailed computation is necessary. (The tribunal cannot award compensatory damages in excess of £8,500.) There are guidelines from the Government Actuary's Department suggesting methods of computation of pension loss which were published in 1980. One method, the contributions method, calculates the amount of contributions paid to date by the employee and the employer accumulated at a rate of interest broadly in line with the investment yield of the fund. If using this method of calculation a tribunal will commonly assess the employer's contribution as a percentage of salary as at dismissal. For example, X is paid £10,000 per annum and the employer's pension contribution is 10 per cent, the employee's 7 per cent of gross salary. X has 4 years' pensionable service at dismissal. Pension loss using the contribution method would be (4 × 10% × 10,000) + (4 × 7% × 10,000) = 4,000 + 2,800 = £6,800 *plus* compound interest at an appropriate rate per annum up to retirement age. Note that this example values loss of pension benefits to date but if the employee is still unemployed or in new employment which does not carry membership of an occupational pension scheme, the loss will be greater. Where the figure for past service is already above the statutory maximum, it is that figure which will represent the total compensatory award.

The 1980 guidelines suggest that the second method, the actuarial method, is to be preferred especially for long-serving employees. This requires accrued benefits from pensionable service to date to be calculated. Then a multiplier is applied according to the age and sex of the claimant to give the sum which would produce those benefits at retirement age. From that sum is deducted the value of the deferred pension which the employee will receive and then there is a further reduction to reflect the possibility that the claimant may have withdrawn from the scheme before retirement anyway.

Example 10.7

X is aged 38 with 16 years' pensionable service when he is unfairly dismissed. His salary at dismissal is £15,000 per annum and pension accrues at one-sixtieth of final pensionable salary for each year of pensionable service. Damages for loss of pension will be calculated as follows:

Accrued benefits are $16/60 \times 15,000 = 4,000$.
The multiplier according to the tables is 6.3. So the value of the loss to date is $4,000 \times 6.3 = £25,200$. The deferred pension of $4,000 \times 2.1 = 8,400$ is then deducted and the withdrawal factor applied to the resultant figure is 30 per cent, thus $(25,200 - 8,400) \times 30\% = £5040$. Damages due will be £16,800 (i.e. 25,200 - 8,400) less £5040 = £11,760. Since that is over the statutory maximum it is that statutory maximum which would be due.

Again, if the employee has entered a new job without a pension scheme at the date of the hearing, the tribunal will have to add on a sum to compensate for future loss of pension benefits but subject to the overall maximum of £8,500. Usually the tribunal will compensate for future loss of pension benefits using the employer's rate of contributions and an appropriate multiplier reflecting an estimate of the years before the employee enters pensionable employment, or his earnings rise to make good the loss of membership of a scheme or until retirement.

10.11   *Contributory fault*

The tribunal can reduce both the basic award and the compensatory award where it finds that the dismissal was to any extent caused or contributed to by the employee. The reduction is of such amount as the tribunal considers just and equitable to reflect its assessment of the employee's contributory fault. The award of damages can be totally eliminated under this provision. That may happen, especially after the 1987 *Polkey* decision, where the dismissal is held to be procedurally unfair but the evidence given to the tribunal shows that in fact dismissal was justified, e.g. the employee was not given a chance to explain but had no answer to the allegations. Alternatively, a nil award of damages may be made in circumstances similar to those in *W. Devis & Sons Ltd* v. *Atkins* (1977), i.e. evidence of the employee's gross fault was not known to the employer at the date of dismissal so the decision to dismiss was not reasonable at that time. In these circumstances a finding of unfair dismissal would be made by the tribunal. However, if post-dismissal evidence became available at the hearing and showed that the employee deserved to be dismissed, the award of damages would be reduced to nil and reflect the justice of the case.

Where the case is not so extreme the reduction on the grounds of contributory fault will be much less. Tribunals do seem to use the contributory fault reduction provision by way of compromise judgment and in *Hollier* v. *Plysu Ltd* (1983) the Court of Appeal held that the EAT was not entitled to interfere with a tribunal's assessment unless the tribunal goes wrong in law or makes a decision which is perverse. The tribunal in that case had reduced the damages by 75 per cent. The EAT had allowed the employee's appeal and substituted a reduction figure of 25 per cent. According to the Court of Appeal the tribunal's function in considering the matter of contributory fault is to take a broad, commonsense view of the situation. The apportionment of responsibility for dismissal is so obviously a matter of impression, opinion and discretion that there must be a plain error of law or something like perversity to entitle an appellate tribunal to interfere with the decision entrusted by Parliament to the industrial tribunal.

10.12 Duty to mitigate loss

The EP(C)A 1978 obliges the tribunal in assessing loss for the purposes of the compensatory award to apply the common law duty on a claimant to mitigate his loss. The practical effect of this duty to mitigate loss in unfair dismissal cases means that the employee must take all reasonable steps to seek new employment and reduce his loss of earnings. Employers defending claims of unfair dismissal should be prepared to present evidence or to question the employee about attempts to find other work since the cases show the employer has the burden of showing that the applicant has failed to mitigate his loss. Where, for example, it can be established that there are a number of suitable vacancies in the locality, an employee who remains unemployed should be challenged. Questions should be asked about the number of applications the employee has made, the number of interviews he has attended, etc.

According to the EAT decision in *Peara* v. *Enderlin Ltd* (1979) a tribunal should not make a percentage reduction when it concludes that the employee has failed to mitigate but should decide a date by which the employee could have begun new employment and assess compensation on the basis of that date.

10.13   *Equal pay, sex and race discrimination*

If an individual employee presents a complaint under the Equal Pay Act 1970, the industrial tribunal will decide whether or not the applicant's contract must be amended to give equal terms and conditions to those of the comparator. If the claim is successful the applicant's future treatment will be the same as that of the comparator, i.e. she must be paid the same rates from the date of the hearing. As well, the tribunal can award damages representing arrears of pay for up to two years before the date on which the proceedings were begun.

It is also possible for an employer to apply to an industrial tribunal for an order declaring the rights of the parties in a dispute over equal treatment. This step was taken by an employer in *Trico Folberth Ltd* v. *Groves & Aiston* (1976) after a long dispute and unsuccessful negotiations with a union over equal pay.

The remedies under the Sex Discrimination Act are more complicated. If a tribunal concludes that a complaint is well founded it can make such of the following as it considers just and equitable:

(a) an order declaring the rights of the parties;
(b) an order requiring the employer to pay compensation;
(c) a recommendation that the employer take practicable steps within a specified period to obviate or reduce the adverse effect on the complainant of the discriminatory act complained of.

The usual remedy is compensation. The maximum compensation which can be awarded is the same as the maximum compensatory award in unfair dismissal, i.e. £8,500. However, in June 1988 an industrial tribunal awarded the complainant in the leading case of *Marshall* v. *Southampton & S.W. Hampshire* a sum far in excess of the statutory maximum. The case succeeded under European Law provisions (see [7.15]) and the tribunal said that the national statutory maximum was contrary to European law and the right to an effective remedy.

Compensation awarded under the SDA 1975 is computed on the basis of damages recoverable in the County Court. This will usually be financial loss. In *Prestcold Ltd* v. *Irvine* (1981) damages awarded were the equivalent of the increased salary the applicant would have received if she had not been discriminated against and passed over for promotion.

The Act expressly states that damages may include compensation for injury to feelings. According to one judge in the Court of Appeal in order for damages to be awarded under this head the injury to feelings must result from the knowledge that the act was one of sex discrimination. Sums of £50 and £100 have been awarded under this head but in sexual harassment cases substantially greater sums have been awarded. In one case a figure of £3,000 was awarded to cover injury to feelings, emotional stress and strain and damage to health.

If the case is one of indirect discrimination no damages are awarded if the respondent shows that when applying the discriminatory requirement or condition he had no intention of discriminating on the grounds of sex.

Recommendations for action within a specified period must relate to action affecting the individual complainant. A general recommendation that the employers discontinue a discriminatory practice was set aside by the EAT in one case. However, in most cases the action necessary to obviate the discriminatory effect on a particular complainant will result in improved treatment of persons similarly affected. Having lost one case, it would be a foolish employer who did not remedy the particular discriminatory practice. Failure to comply with a recommendation without 'reasonable justification' can result in an award or an increased award of damages.

The remedies available under the Race Relations Act 1976 are exactly the same as under the SDA 1975. Again the maximum possible compensation is £8,500.

Where the Equal Opportunities Commission or the Commission for Racial Equality has issued a non-discrimination notice against an employer in relation to employment practices, appeal lies to the industrial tribunals. Any appeal must be lodged within six weeks of service of the non-discrimination notice. The tribunal can confirm, quash or amend the notice.

10.14 Remedies available in actions before civil courts

Actions founded on the contract of employment, rather than statutory employment rights, are still pursued through the normal civil courts, i.e. the High Court in the first instance (or the County Court if the claim is for less than £5,000) with appeal to the Court of Appeal. The usual remedy sought is damages but a party to a contract of employment may also seek a declaration as to the efficacy of a contract term. The traditional view has been that the contract of employment is not specifically enforceable by a court but notable developments of the 1980s have been the attempted use of the procedure for judicial review by public sector employees to challenge dismissal decisions and a more liberal judicial attitude to the availability of injunctions and declarations in private actions which have the effect of continuing the contract. This section will consider the available remedies under the following headings:

(1) damages for breach of contract;
(2) judicial review and public employment;
(3) declarations and injunctions.

10.15   *Damages for breach of contract*

The most common action for damages is that brought by an employee who alleges wrongful dismissal. There is no maximum on damages which the High Court is competent to award but because this action is for breach of contract the amount of damages awarded is usually the equivalent of wages which would have been earned if the employee had received the notice of termination which was due. (It will be recalled that it is no breach of contract to terminate, however unreasonably, with due contract notice and in such a case the only remedy available is unfair dismissal.) In *Addis* v. *Gramophone Co. Ltd* (1909) the House of Lords held that no damages for injury to feelings or for impairment to reputation were generally available in wrongful dismissal actions. Further, only contractual remuneration during the notice period was relevant; discretionary bonus payments could not be included in financial loss. However, in exceptional employment contracts where the contractual consideration is something more than the monetary remuneration, e.g. a reputation-enhancing public appearance, damages may reflect this further loss.

If the contract is for a fixed term which is not terminable by notice, wrongful termination will lead to an award of damages representing financial loss during the remainder of the term, subject to the duty of the employee to mitigate his loss by finding alternative work.

It has been suggested recently that damages in wrongful dismissal might be increased to reflect the loss of an unfair dismissal remedy where the employer dismisses without notice or by short notice so as to prevent the employee acquiring the necessary continuity of service to qualify for unfair dismissal.

The general rule is that damages for lost wages are computed net of tax to reflect the employee's actual financial loss (*British Transport Commission* v. *Gourley* (1956)). Since the first £30,000 compensation for loss of office is not taxed under the tax statutes but would have been taxed if received as normal remuneration under the contract, that sum must be reduced by the tax that would have been paid. Damages in excess of £30,000 will be taxed in the hands of the recipient so no reduction is made by the court.

The employee may also sue in breach of contract to recover wages wrongly withheld. That action was taken in *Burdett-Coutts* v. *Hertfordshire County Council* (1984) where school dinner ladies continued to work under protest over new terms which meant lower pay rates. The High Court awarded damages representing arrears of wages due under the original terms of the contract. The House of Lords reached a similar conclusion over unilaterally imposed changes resulting in lower pay rates in *Rigby* v. *Ferodo Ltd* (1987) (see Chapter 6 above).

10.16 The employer as plaintiff

It is unusual for the employer to be the plaintiff in a breach of contract action seeking damages as remedy. However, it is not unheard of and a leading illustration is the case of *National Coal Board* v. *Galley* (1958) in which the employer sued a pit deputy who took strike action in breach of contract. The defendant was held liable in damages for the cost of a substitute worker. The case is unusual and should not be relied on readily by an employer with a view to obtaining damages against a striker. The measure of damage recoverable is not at all clear (is it lost profits or the cost of the lost labour?) and it is arguable that the employer would be under a duty to mitigate his loss by engaging replacement labour. A more recent example of the employer suing the employee for damages for breach of contract is *Strathclyde Regional Council* v. *Neil* (1984). The employee was taken on as a trainee social worker and sent on a training course for which she was given paid leave of absence. She signed a document agreeing to remain in the council's service for at least two years following completion of the course and to refund a proportion of the council's expenses if she left voluntarily before that period. In fact, she left fifteen months after completing the course and the (Scottish) Sheriff Court held that loss recoverable by the employer was a proportionate part of her salary and the expenses of sending her on the course equal to that part of the two years' service uncompleted. Damages of £2336 were awarded. The court refused to accept that the service requirement was unenforceable as being an unreasonable restraint on the employee's freedom nor that it was unconscionable as a penalty clause. The repayment provision was a genuine pre-estimate of damage resulting from the employee's breach. The court refused to hold that *NCB* v. *Galley* limited damages recoverable to the cost of hiring a substitute worker. Where the employer can demonstrate financial loss suffered as a direct consequence of the breach that loss is compensatable.

Other circumstances in which an employer might seek damages against an employee are where there has been a mistaken overpayment of wages or salary. If payment systems are computerised, errors in input information might not come to light so readily as where cash payments are made up and handed over weekly. In practice, minor errors would be adjusted in subsequent pay periods but if the overpayment is substantial or is made to an employee who is absent on long-term sick leave, the employer might wish to sue to recover the sum involved. Provided the mistake was one of fact the employer would have the *prima facie* legal right to recover any overpayment. That was established as a matter of principle by the Court of Appeal in *Avon County Council* v. *Howlett* (1983). In that case an employee who was absent from work because of injury was overpaid by a computerised payment system by some £1,000 over a two year period. Incorrect information had been fed into the computer. Although, the employers had a *prima facie* right to recover the overpayment the court held that they were estopped from pursuing that right because they had represented to the employee that the payments were correctly made and he had relied on those representations and spent the money on ordinary living expenses. In those circumstances it was inequitable to require the employee to repay the money.

The law report does not make it clear what actions constituted sufficient representation to raise the estoppel apart from reference to 'conduct' and 'conversations'. Presumably, if an employee who suspects he has been overpaid makes inquiry of the employer and is told, after investigation by the appropriate agent, that the payment is correctly made that would be sufficient to raise the estoppel. The case shows that it behoves an employer to have careful and thorough checking procedures and to advise employees as to whom they should properly address payment inquiries. Of course, the estoppel principle is based on justice and fair-play and if the employee knows perfectly well that he is not entitled to the money he has received the employer is not likely to be barred from recovery. The larger the sum the greater the inquiry expected of the employee and the more difficult it will be for him to argue the estoppel.

10.17 *Judicial review and public employment*

The traditional view of the contract of employment is that since it is founded on mutual trust and confidence the only remedy for breach is damages. The contract is not specifically enforceable at the suit of either party against the wishes of the other. As well, it is regarded as inappropriate and smacking of serfdom to compel an employee to work for a particular employer. It follows that normally a court will not make any order requiring the contractual performance to continue (an order for specific performance) nor an order or declaration which has that effect (a declaration that dismissal is ineffective so that the employee must be regarded as still in the employer's service). It will be recalled that, consistently with the traditional common law view, an industrial tribunal has no power to compel an employer to take back an unfairly dismissed worker. A tribunal can make a reinstatement or re-engagement order but cannot force the employer to comply. All it can do is increase the award of damages.

In fact, such reinstatement and re-engagement orders are very rarely made and there has been a noticeable trend in the 1980s for employees to go back to the common law for an adequate remedy rather than rely on unfair dismissal damages. In particular, the use by employees of the procedure for judicial review of dismissal and disciplinary proceedings by employers in the public sector has been seen as an attempt at circumventing the unavailability of enforcement injunctions generally. Basically, 'judicial review' is the jurisdiction which the courts have over public agencies to ensure that their authority and duties are properly carried out. Public agencies subject to judicial review include government departments, health authorities, local government authorities and agencies set up by statute. Those bodies are large employers and it has been argued on behalf of certain of their employees that in failing to carry out disciplinary or dismissal procedures properly the public bodies have acted contrary to their public obligations. Therefore more advantageous public law remedies are available to ensure continuation of the contracts of employment. This argument was deployed in *R* v. *British Broadcasting Corporation ex parte Lavelle* (1982), *R* v. *East Berkshire Health Authority ex parte Walsh* (1984) and *R* v. *Secretary of State for the Home Department ex parte Benwell* (1985).

In *Lavelle* the employee used the judicial review procedure to challenge the validity of disciplinary proceedings which led to her dismissal. The disciplinary hearing had been arranged at one hour's notice and she claimed that such short notice in effect denied her the right of representation. She sought a public law order to quash the dismissal decision on the grounds that the public authority had improperly carried out its public powers. The High Court refused the application and held that the employee was relying on a purely private right derived solely from the contract of employment. In *Walsh* a senior nursing officer applied for an order to quash his dismissal on the grounds that the district nursing officer who purported to dismiss had no power to do so and that there had been a breach of the rules of natural justice in the dismissal procedure. Although the employee succeeded at first instant, the Court of Appeal allowed the appeal and again held that no public law right had been infringed and the employee was wrongly attempting to use a public law procedure to enforce a wholly private, contractual right.

In *Walsh*, Sir John Donaldson said that employment by a public authority does not of itself inject any element of public law. It is only where the employment is underpinned by statutory provision or some statutory restriction limits the public body in dealing with its employees that a public law remedy might be available. He said that where statute requires public employees to be engaged on certain terms any employee not engaged on those terms has a public law action. Where, however, the employee has a contract in accordance with the statutory requirements but the public employer acts in breach of that contract the employee's only remedy is a private action for breach of contract. The Court of Appeal judges were clearly not sorry to reach that result since otherwise all National Health Service employees (and indeed all employees of public agencies) could seek judicial review of their employers' decisions. Under the *Walsh* principle it will only be the rare case in which employment terms are not in accordance with the public body's statutory instructions that a public law action will lie in respect of an employment matter.

Alternatively, if there is no contract of employment between the parties but service is founded solely on statute, a public law action might lie. That was the position in *Benwell* where a High Court judge granted an order quashing the Home Secretary's dismissal of a prison officer. The essence of the employee's case was that the Home Secretary had taken into account matters with which the employee had never been charged and in respect of which he had been given no opportunity to explain. Those matters should never have been on the employee's file. In taking them into account the Home Secretary had acted contrary to the Code of Discipline covering prison officers which was derived from statutory authority. According to the judge, so far the facts of *Benwell* and *Walsh* were the same. But the big distinction was that in *Walsh* the statutory terms were incorporated into a contract of service which created private law rights and barred any public law action. In *Benwell* there was no separate contract of employment. A prison officer is appointed by the Home Secretary in accordance with standing orders and instructions issued by the Home Department. Such a person has *only* a public law remedy (and no unfair dismissal remedy). A similar result was reached in respect of police officers in a 1986 decision but in a 1987 decision civil servants, traditionally regarded as not serving under contracts of employment, were refused leave to use the judicial review procedure largely because of available remedies in unfair dismissal.

Despite the exceptional decision in *Benwell*, the principle in *Walsh* will prevent most public sector employees from challenging dismissal under judicial review. It is clear that private sector employees are outside the scope of judicial review actions. That leaves most employees with only the remedies available in private contract actions.

10.18 *Declarations and injunctions*

As explained above, the eagerness of public sector employees to invoke the procedure for judicial review was a consequence of the general unwillingness of the courts to grant orders or declarations which had the effect of enforcing contracts of employment. That traditional judicial unwillingness is supported by statute: section 16 of the Trade Union and Labour Relations Act 1974 provides that no court shall compel an employee to work and an unfairly dismissed employee cannot insist on reinstatement. However, the developments in judicial review have produced a side-effect in private law: where there has been a procedural irregularity in disciplinary hearings or a denial of natural justice, a judicial declaration might be available in a private law action which will have the effect of continuing the contract pending compliance with the correct procedure. It used to be argued that only 'office' holders had the implied right to natural justice before a dismissal could be effective. However, in the *Lavelle* case the judge said that times had changed and even an ordinary contract of service had many of the attributes of an 'office' in the sense that the power to dismiss is restricted by elaborate disciplinary rules and procedures. Where that was so, a declaration or injunction might be available even in a private action to restrain dismissal contrary to those rules and procedures.

In fact, most employees have the benefit of disciplinary procedures incorporated into their individual contracts. Indeed, the Employment Protection (Consolidation) Act 1978 requires reference to a disciplinary procedure in the written statement of contract terms and the ACAS Code gives guidance on appropriate rules and practice. It follows that the decision in *Lavelle* opens up the possibility of protection at common law for most employees in respect of procedural injustice.

It must always be remembered that the making of any equitable order is at the judge's discretion and, in fact, the judge in *Lavelle* declined to grant an injunction because he felt that the employee had suffered no inequity. However, in several recent cases injunctions have been granted to restrain implementation of a dismissal decision in breach of proper procedure. In *Irani* v. *Southampton & S.W. Hampshire Health Authority* (1985) an injunction was granted preventing the employers from dismissing a part-time ophthalmologist before carrying out a disputes procedure laid down in the employee's conditions of service. Mr Justice Warner made much of the fact that the employer still had confidence in the employee's ability to do his job (the cause of dismissal was that the employee had quarrelled with the consultant in charge). He also relied heavily on *Hill* v. *C.A. Parsons & Co. Ltd* (1971). That in itself shows a change of emphasis since *Hill* v. *Parsons* has always been regarded as an anomalous case in which an injunction was granted only because of very special facts: the employer dismissed the employee with one month's notice because of union pressure when the employee, a chartered engineer, refused to join the union in accordance with a new closed shop agreement. The employee was 63 years old with 35 years' service with the employer. Such an employee was entitled to much longer notice of termination and if proper notice had been given the employee's service would have lasted until the implementation of the unfair dismissal remedy. The Court of Appeal granted an injunction restraining the employer from treating his dismissal as effective under the one month's notice. The Court of Appeal took the view that damages would not be an effective remedy and since personal confidence still existed between the parties the principle objection to the availability of an injunction to continue the contract did not exist.

In the *Irani* case the judge echoed these principles: damages would not be an adequate remedy and if an injunction was granted to stop the dismissal from taking effect the employers would have to use the disciplinary procedures established under the Whitley Council rules. Pending proper disciplinary procedures, the employee could return to work since there had been no criticism of his performance. Indeed, the evidence was that the Authority would be willing to continue to employ the plaintiff if his employment and that of the consultant were compatible. In those circumstances an injunction was the appropriate remedy.

There have been several cases since *Irani* in which attempts have been made to restrain employers from effecting dismissals in breach of

contractual disciplinary procedures. The courts have shown a willing-
ness in principle to grant injunctions provided the evidence shows
trust and confidence still to exist and that damages would not be an
adequate remedy.

This change of attitude does not extend so far as to suggest that a
contract of employment can be subject to a perpetual injunction
requiring performance. The continuation orders are limited to the
period necessary for the employer to comply with proper disciplinary
procedures. Also, if the allegation against the employee adversely
affects the employer's trust in his performance it is likely that damages
only would be regarded as the appropriate remedy. Of course, any
employer is best advised to comply strictly with contractual disciplinary procedures to block the risk of expensive and time-consuming
litigation before the usual civil courts and ensure a successful defence
of any unfair dismissal claim before an industrial tribunal.

The more liberal judicial attitude towards the availability of
injunctions to enforce the contract of employment has not been
restricted to procedural irregularities over dismissal. Two recent cases
have resulted in interim injunctions being granted pending the hearing
of substantive breach of contract actions where the contractual
relationship was continuing. In *Powell* v. *London Borough of Brent* (1987),
the plaintiff employee, who worked as a Senior Benefits Officer,
applied for promotion to Principal Benefits Officer and after several
candidates had been interviewed she was told she had been successful.
She duly reported to her new place of employment. Some days later,
after another candidate submitted a grievance over the matter, the
plaintiff was told she could not be appointed and although she
continued to work at the new post the council decided to readvertise
the position almost two months later. The plaintiff sought an
injunction restraining the readvertisement and requiring the council
to treat her as Principal Benefits Officer pending full trial of the breach
of contract action. The Court of Appeal granted orders in those terms.
The evidence showed that full trust and confidence did continue to
exist since the plaintiff was actually working in the higher post to the
employers' satisfaction. Damages would not be an adequate remedy
and the Court of Appeal thought she had a real prospect of succeeding
in her claim for a permanent injunction at the full hearing since the
case was exceptional.

Powell has been regarded as a landmark case in the utilisation of
common law and equitable remedies to resolve employment issues. It
was followed in *Hughes* v. *London Borough of Southwark* (1988) in which a
court order was made to restrain employers from requiring compliance with an unreasonable instruction to do work which was not

part of the employees' contracts. The plaintiffs, social workers, had been instructed to move to another location within the council's area for three days each week. The court accepted that there was no breakdown of trust and confidence and that damages would not be adequate remedy and therefore granted the order.

These cases are important as illustrating a trend back towards reliance on the normal breach of contract action as an effective employment remedy. If courts are willing to grant interim injunctions and even permanent injunctions in exceptional cases it may be that employees will see more frequently the common law as providing greater employment protection than the mass of statutory provision. It is not only higher status employees who are turning back to the common law. Groups of workers affected by an employment practice imposed in breach of contract, especially where they are backed by union representation, may feel they are more likely to obtain an effective remedy from the High Court than an industrial tribunal. The management of change in employment matters has become a more delicate issue as a result of these recent cases.

10.19   The employer as plaintiff for an injunction

So far this section has discussed the availability of an injunction for specific performance of the contract directed against the employer at the instigation of the employee. The traditional judicial reluctance to order specific performance of an employment contract has been even stronger where the employer sought an injunction against the employee. The basic principle that an employer cannot compel an employee to work under a contract of service has been entrenched since 1852 and in 1891 the Court of Appeal held that whatever remedy in damages an employer might have for breach of an exclusive service clause, such a clause was not capable of specific enforcement. However, where the enforcement of a negative stipulation not to render service similar to that contracted to the employer to any other person would not compel specific performance, an injunction might be granted.

That happened in *Warner Brothers Pictures Incorporated* v. *Nelson* (1937). The employers sought an injunction restraining breach of an undertaking by the actress Bette Davis that she would not, during the currency of her contract with Warner Brothers, render any services in any motion picture or stage production for any person other than Warner Brothers. The judge held that an injunction should be granted since the effect of enforcement did not compel Bette Davis to perform her contract with Warner Brothers: she could employ herself elsewhere in some other sphere of activity apart from motion pictures or stage productions. Also, damages would not be an adequate remedy.

A recent case has developed that reasoning. In *Evening Standard Co. Ltd v. Henderson* (1987) the contract of the defendant newspaper production manager contained an exclusive service clause and a provision for the giving of one year's notice of termination on either side. The defendant purported to give short notice and intended to join the staff of a new rival London evening newspaper which would pose a serious threat to the plaintiffs' newspaper's circulation figures. The plaintiffs wanted to prevent the defendant working for the rival newspaper during the full year's notice period. The High Court refused to grant an injunction but before the Court of Appeal the plaintiffs argued that they were willing to pay the defendant throughout the notice period whether or not he returned to work for them. They wished to prevent him working for the rival newspaper during the contractual termination period. In those circumstances the Court of Appeal granted the injunction. The defendant could not be forced to work for a particular employer even if he had broken the contract by giving short notice. But the offer of payment without requiring him to work overcame the objection to the grant of an injunction. He could remain idle or he could find employment in a separate sphere: the injunction did not oblige him to work for the employer.

Obviously, it will not be the ordinary case in which an employer can succeed in a claim for an injunction or order for specific performance. Usually, damages will be an adequate remedy for the loss of the employee's service and realistically it will be only in respect of service of a key employee that the employer will consider any sort of breach of contract action.

10.20 *Declaration*

Either party to a contract of employment can seek a declaration of the court as to the validity of a contract term. Often the application for a declaration is combined with a request for an order restraining breach of the declared term but the declaration alone is sometimes sufficient remedy. That remedy was sought, though unsuccessfully, in *Cresswell v. Board of Inland Revenue* (1984) when the employees wanted clarification of whether or not the employers were entitled under their contracts to require them to operate computerised tax systems (see Chapter 6). An employer might seek a declaration as to the efficacy of a clause restricting competititon (see Chapter 4), or his right to modify working conditions (see Chapter 6).

Model Form of Written Statement of Contract Terms under the Employment Protection (Consolidation) Act 1978

Part I

This statement sets out particulars of the terms and conditions of your contract of employment and is issued in accordance with Section 1 of the Employment Protection (Consolidation) Act 1978.

Date:

Name of employer:
[*If headed notepaper is used and the employer party to the written statement is the same, the name need not be repeated.*]

Name of employee:

Date employment began:
[*This should be the actual date of commencement. Where the contract is for a fixed term the expiry date should also be given.*]

Continuous employment:
Either – No employment with a previous employer counts as part of your period of continuous employment.
or – Your employment with [*name of previous employer*] which began on [*date on which previous employment commenced*] forms part of your continuous employment.

Remuneration:
Your remuneration is £ .... per [*hour, week or month*] payable [*weekly or monthly*]
[*Note that where wage rates are fixed by collective agreement this clause should state that the employee will be paid in accordance with the agreement currently in force between the employer and the named trade union and that copies of the current agreement are available at a specified place.*]

Hours of work:
[*This clause should give details of the pattern of hours normally worked. If the employer wishes to reserve a right to vary normal working hours it is desirable expressly to reserve that right.*]

Examples: Your daily hours of work are 9.00 AM to 5.00 PM Monday to Friday. These hours include a paid daily lunch break from 1.00 PM to 2.00 PM.

or

Your normal hours of work will alternate from 8.00 AM to 3.30 PM Monday to Saturday one week, and 10.00 AM to 5.00 PM Monday to Friday the following week. These hours include daily paid meal breaks of $1\frac{1}{2}$ hours to be taken in agreement with your supervisor.

or

Your normal weekly hours will be 39 to be worked over any five days Monday to Saturday as the employer shall determine from time to time.

or

There are no normal working hours but the employee is required to work at such times and for such periods as the efficient and conscientious performance of his duties demands.

[*Note: If the employer anticipates that overtime working will be required there should be a clause to that effect.*]

Example: The employee will be expected to work such overtime as the employer reasonably requires. At least 24 hours' notice of the requirement to work overtime will be given. Overtime will be paid at the rate of $1\frac{1}{2}$ times the standard rate.

Holidays:

Example: You are entitled to paid holidays on each of the public holidays of 1 January, Good Friday, Easter Monday, the first and last Monday in May, the last Monday in August, 25 December and 26 December. In addition you are entitled to 18 working days holiday in each calendar year.

Holiday entitlement accrues at the rate of $1\frac{1}{2}$ days for each complete calendar month worked in the calendar year.

[*If there are restrictions on how many days holiday can be taken together or times of the year at which holidays may not be taken those restrictions should be mentioned.*]

Sickness and sick pay:

[*The employee may be entitled only to statutory sick pay or there may be an occupational sick pay scheme. If entitlement is limited to the former that fact should be stated. If there is an occupational sick pay scheme details of qualification, procedure and benefit rates should be given in the statement or reference should be made to another document containing those details. For a discussion of the statutory sick pay rules see Chapter 3.*]

Examples:

You are entitled to only statutory sick pay in the event of absence from work by reason of sickness.

or

Normal remuneration is payable during sickness absence or incapacity for work by reason of injury up to a maximum of (....) weeks in any twelve months *provided* the employer is notified of your absence as soon as reasonably practicable on the first day of absence and if the absence continues for a period of eight calendar days or more, a medical certificate is provided. If your absence lasts for less than five working days or seven calendar days you must complete a self-certification form on your return to work. This form is obtainable from .... The remuneration for any such period of absence will include any entitlement to statutory sick pay.

[*Note that it is common for occupational sick pay schemes to provide for full pay for a fixed period, then half-pay for an extended period. Such details should be specified. The employer's contractual scheme cannot confer lesser benefits than those enjoyed under the statutory scheme, i.e. 28 weeks at £49.20 where average earnings are £79.50 or more, or 28 weeks at £34.25 where average earnings are less than £79.50 but more than £41.00 weekly.*

These rates are those applicable for 1988–89.

It may be desirable to insert a clause under which the employee is examined by an employer-nominated medical practitioner after a specified period of sickness absence.]

Pension:

Either: There is no pension or pension scheme applicable to you.

or There is a contributory (or non-contributory) pension scheme applicable to you which you are required (or eligible) to join (after ... months service with the employer). Full details are set out in the accompanying schedule (or in a booklet obtainable from ...).

A contracting-out certificate under the Social Security Pensions Act 1975 is (or is not) in force in respect of your employment.

Job title:

[*The definition of 'job' in the EP(C)A 1978 refers to the nature of work, capacity and place of employment. The statement need not contain a full description of duties but there should be a job designation and reference to the location at which duties are to be performed. If the employer wishes to ensure mobility a clause to that effect should be included. See [2.07].*]

Example:

The title of your job is .... at .... (You may be required to transfer to any of the premises in the UK from which the employer's business is conducted.)

or

The employer carries on business at three branches in the .... City area. You will normally work at the .... Street branch but may be transferred to either of the other two branches at .... Street or .... Road from time to time.)

Notice:
[The minimum period of notice to which an employee is entitled cannot be less than the statutory periods contained in the EP(C)A (see [9.02] and Schedule.D). The employer can agree longer periods of notice.]
Either: After 4 weeks' employment you will be entitled to one week's notice of termination of your employment. After employment of between 2 and 12 years you will be entitled to one week for each year of service. After 12 years' employment you will be entitled to 12 weeks notice.
or
You are entitled to (three months) notice of termination of your employment (ending on ....).
You are required to give (.......... weeks/months') written notice of your intention to leave this employment.

Disciplinary rules:
[Where disciplinary rules are detailed it is usual to have them set out in a separate document. The written statement should refer to that document. For a suggested model of disciplinary rules see Appendix B.]
Disciplinary rules and procedure are contained in a document which is obtainable from ..../has been handed to you separately.

Grievances:
If you have any grievance relating to your employment you may apply in the first place to .... The application should set out the grievance complained of with as much detail as practicable. The steps consequent upon such application are ..../set out in a document obtainable from .... (A model grievance procedure is set out at Appendix C.)

Clause of acknowledgment:
I acknowledge receipt of this written statement setting out particulars of the terms and conditions of my employment in accordance with Section 1 of the Employment Protection (Consolidation) Act 1978.

Date ....

Signature of Employee ....

Part II

This section contains additional model clauses which deal with particular issues and can be adapted to fit the circumstances.

(1) Probationary service

This contract is subject to a period of probationary service of ......
months. The employee shall be advised at ...... monthly intervals by
.... [*supervisor/department head/personnel officer*] concerning the progress
of his probation and shall be informed at least ...... months before the
expiry of the probationary period whether or not his service is
satisfactory and whether or not his appointment is to be confirmed as
permanent.

[*Any training programme or supervisory scheme for probationers should be referred to
and if payment rates for probationers are not the full normal adult rate that fact should
be stated. Probationary periods are commonly six to twelve months but should certainly
be less than two years to avoid unfair dismissal rights accruing.*]

(2) Exclusivity of service

The appointment under this contract is a full time appointment and
the employee shall devote his full commitment, energy and attention
to the employer's business. He shall not at any time during the
continuance of this contract whether for reward or otherwise engage
as principal, partner or as employee, agent, director or otherwise on
behalf of any person, firm or company in any trade, business or
profession without the written consent of [*the employer*].

(3) Non-solicitation clause

The employee shall not at any time during the [*six/nine/twelve*] months
following the termination of this contract whether on his own behalf
or on behalf of any other person, partnership or company solicit
custom from, deal with or supply any person, partnership or company
with whom he dealt on behalf of the employer at any time during his
employment. Neither shall he for the same period solicit custom from,
deal with or supply any person, partnership or company carrying on
business within a [*ten*] mile radius of [*the employer's premises*] who or which
was a customer of the employer's at any time during his employment.

(4) Trade secrets/confidentiality

The employee undertakes, without prejudice to any general duty of
confidentiality, not to disclose during the continuance of this contract
or afterwards any of the trade secrets of the employer. Trade secrets
shall include the following which shall not be regarded as exhaustive
...... [*appropriate matters should be specified, e.g. technical information concerning*

manufacturing processes/unpublished data from research and development/price sensitive information, etc.]

The employee further undertakes immediately on the termination of his employment to deliver up to the employer all documentation in his possession belonging to the employer including documents made by him in the course of his employment. Any copy, abstract, summary or precis of any document belonging to the employer made by the employee or any other person shall itself belong to the employer.

Disciplinary Procedure

(Note that any disciplinary procedure should take into account the 1977 ACAS Code of Practice entitled *Disciplinary Practice and Procedures in Employment*. The following model disciplinary procedures are taken from the 1987 ACAS advisory handbook entitled *Discipline at Work*.)

Model A (any organisation)

(1) Purpose and scope

This procedure is designed to help and encourage all employees to achieve and maintain standards of conduct, attendance and job performance. The company rules (a copy of which is displayed in the office) and this procedure apply to all employees. The aim is to ensure consistent and fair treatment for all.

(2) Principles

(a) No disciplinary action will be taken against an employee until the case has been fully investigated.

(b) At every stage in the procedure the employee will be advised of the nature of the complaint against him or her and will be given the opportunity to state his or her case before any decision is made.

(c) At all stages the employee will have the right to be accompanied by a shop steward, employee representative or work colleague during the disciplinary interview.

(d) No employee will be dismissed for a first breach of discipline except in the case of gross misconduct when the penalty will be dismissal without notice or payment in lieu of notice.

(e) An employee will have the right to appeal against any disciplinary penalty imposed.

(f) The procedure may be implemented at any stage if the employee's alleged misconduct warrants such action.

(3) The procedure

Minor faults will be dealt with informally but where the matter is more serious the following procedure will be used:

Stage 1 – Oral warning
If conduct or performance does not meet acceptable standards the employee will normally be given a formal *oral warning*. He or she will be advised of the reason for the warning, that it is the first stage of the disciplinary procedure and of his or her right of appeal. A brief note of the oral warning will be kept but it will be spent after ... months, subject to satisfactory conduct and performance.

Stage 2 – Written warning
If the offence is a serious one, or if a further offence occurs, a *written warning* will be given to the employee by the supervisor. This will give details of the complaint, the improvement required and the timescale. It will warn that action under Stage 3 will be considered if there is no satisfactory improvement and will advise of the right of appeal. A copy of this written warning will be kept by the supervisor but it will be disregarded for disciplinary purposes after .... months subject to satisfactory conduct and performance.

Stage 3 – Final written warning or disciplinary suspension
If there is still a failure to improve and conduct or performance is still unsatisfactory, or if the misconduct is sufficiently serious to warrant only one written warning but insufficiently serious to justify dismissal (in effect both first and final written warning), a *final written warning* will normally be given to the employee. This will give details of the complaint, will warn that dismissal will result if there is no satisfactory improvement and will advise of the right of appeal. A copy of this final written warning will be kept by the supervisor but it will be spent after .... months (in exceptional cases the period may be longer) subject to satisfactory conduct and performance.

Alternatively, consideration will be given to imposing a penalty of a disciplinary suspension without pay for up to a maximum of five working days.

Stage 4 – Dismissal
If conduct or performance is still unsatisfactory and the employee still fails to reach the prescribed standards, *dismissal* will normally result. Only the appropriate Senior Manager can take the decision to dismiss. The employee will be provided, as soon as reasonably practicable, with

written reasons for dismissal, the date on which employment will terminate and the right of appeal.

(4) Gross misconduct

The following list provides examples of offences which are normally regarded as gross misconduct:

- theft, fraud, deliberate falsification of records;
- fighting, assault on another person;
- deliberate damage to company property;
- serious incapability through alcohol or being under the influence of illegal drugs;
- serious negligence which causes unacceptable loss, damage or injury;
- serious act of insubordination.

If you are accused of an act of gross misconduct, you may be suspended from work on full pay, normally for no more than five working days, while the company investigates the alleged offence. If, on completion of the investigation and the full disciplinary procedure, the company is satisfied that gross misconduct has occurred, the result will normally be summary dismissal without notice or payment in lieu of notice.

(5) Appeals

An employee who wishes to appeal against a disciplinary decision should inform .... within two working days. The Senior Manager will hear all appeals and his/her decision is final. At the appeal any disciplinary penalty imposed will be reviewed but it cannot be increased.

Model B (small firms)

(1) Purpose and scope

The Company's aim is to encourage improvement in individual conduct. This procedure sets out the action which will be taken when disciplinary rules are breached.

(2) Principles

(a) The procedure is designed to establish the facts quickly and to deal

consistently with disciplinary issues. No disciplinary action will be taken until the matter has been fully investigated.
(b) At every stage employees will have the opportunity to state their case and be represented, if they wish, at the hearings by a shop steward if appropriate, or by a fellow employee.
(c) An employee has the right to appeal against any disciplinary penalty.

(3) The procedure

Stage 1 – Oral warning
If conduct or performance is unsatisfactory, the employee will be given a formal *oral warning*, which will be recorded. The warning will be disregarded after ..... months satisfactory service.

Stage 2 – Written warning
If the offence is serious, if there is no improvement in standards, or if a further offence occurs, a *written warning* will be given which will include the reason for the warning and a note that, if there is no improvement after ..... months, a *final written warning* will be given.

Stage 3 – Final written warning
If conduct or performance is still unsatisfactory, a *final written warning* will be given making it clear that any recurrence of the offence or other serious misconduct within a period of ..... months will result in dismissal.

Stage 4 – Dismissal
If there is no satisfactory improvement or if further serious misconduct occurs, the employee will be *dismissed*.

(4) Gross misconduct

If, after investigation, it is confirmed that an employee has committed an offence of the following nature (the list is not exhaustive), the normal consequence will be dismissal:

theft; damage to company property; fraud; incapacity to work due to being under the influence of alcohol or illegal drugs; physical assault; and gross insubordination.

While the alleged gross misconduct is being investigated the employee may be suspended, during which time he or she will be paid the normal hourly rate. Any decision to dismiss will be taken by the employer only.

(5) Appeals

An employee who wishes to appeal against any disciplinary decision must do so to the employer within two working days. The employer will hear the appeal and decide the case as impartially as possible.

Grievance Procedure

1. An employee with a grievance relating to his terms and conditions of service should discuss the matter with his immediate superior in the first instance.

2. If the grievance is not resolved to the employee's satisfaction at that stage he should raise the matter with ... (section head, department head, manager, etc.) The employee may be accompanied at this or any subsequent stage in the grievance procedure by another employee who may be a trade union representative.

3. If the employee is still not satisfied in respect of the grievance he may apply in writing to ... (personnel officer, director, etc.). The ... (personnel officer, director or other designated person) will hear the employee's grievance within ... working days of receipt of the written application. His decision shall be communicated to the employee in writing and shall be final.

[*Note: larger firms may have another stage in the grievance procedure of reference to the managing director or adjudication by a panel established for the purpose which includes worker representatives. Small firms may have a truncated managerial structure and therefore a foreshortened grievance procedure. Wherever possible at least a two-stage procedure should be established and the employee should always be allowed a proper opportunity to air any grievance and representation if he chooses.*]

Continuity

(1) *Continuity of employment required for entitlement to statutory rights*

Unfair dismissal:
Two years (unless dismissal is for trade union reason in which case no qualifying period is required or medical suspension in which case period is one month).

Redundancy payment:
Two years.

Right to return to work after maternity leave/maternity pay:
Two years.

Written reasons for dismissal:
Six months.

Written statement of contract terms:
Thirteen weeks.

Guarantee payment:
One month.

Minimum notice periods:
One week if employed more than one month but less than two years;
One week for each year between two years' and twelve years' employment;
Twelve weeks if employed for twelve years or more.

(2) *Statutory rights which do not require qualifying continuity of employment but which are only available to employees working 16 hours+ weekly*

Time off for trade union duties.
Time off for trade union activities.
Itemised pay statement.

Note that all the rights listed under 1 and 2 above are conferred after *five years* on employees working between 8 and 16 hours weekly.

(3) *Statutory rights which do not require any continuity of employment*

Rights under the Equal Pay Act 1970, the Sex Discrimination Act 1975 and the Race Relations Act 1976.
Unfair dismissal for trade union reasons.
Rights on the employer's insolvency.
Time off for ante-natal care.
Time off for safety representatives (but the ACAS Code of Practice *advises* that employees should have two years' service before appointment as safety representative).

(4) *Redundancy payments and unfair dismissal basic awards*

Compensation entitlement for a redundancy dismissal and the basic award of damages for a successful unfair dismissal action are linked to continuity of employment as follows:
Half a week's pay for every year of service between age 18 and 20;
one week's pay for every year of service between age 21 and 40;
one and a half week's pay for every year of service between 41 and retirement age.

Note that a maximum of 20 years' service is taken into account and there is a maximum limit on the amount of the week's pay taken into account which is £164 from 1st April 1988.

Table of Cases

Note

The following abbreviations are used:

AC	–	Law Reports, Appeal Cases
All ER	–	All England Law Reports
Ch	–	Law Reports Chancery Series
ER	–	English Reports
ECR	–	European Court Reports
ICR	–	Industrial Cases Reports
IDS	–	Income Data Services
IRLR	–	Industrial Relations Law Reports
ITR	–	Industrial Tribunal Reports
KB	–	Law Reports, King's Bench
QB	–	Law Reports, Queen's Bench
SLT	–	Scottish Law Times
TLR	–	Times Law Reports
WLR	–	Weekly Law Reports

References are to section numbers of the text.

Table of Statutes and Statutory Instruments

208

Index

References are to section numbers of the text.